SPIRITUAL JOURNEYS

HOW FAITH HAS INFLUENCED
TWELVE MUSIC ICONS

JOHNNY CASH P. DIDDY LAURYN HILL MOBY

AL GREEN WYCLEF JEAN SCOTT STAPP DESTINY'S CHILD

BOB DYLAN LENNY KRAVITZ T-BONE BURNETT

SPIRITUAL JOURNEYS

HOW FAITH HAS INFLUENCED TWELVE MUSIC ICONS

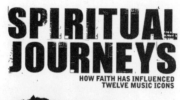

JOHNNY CASH   P. DIDDY   LAURYN HILL   MOBY

AL GREEN   WYCLEF JEAN   SCOTT STAPP   DESTINY'S CHILD

BOB DYLAN   LENNY KRAVITZ   T-BONE BURNETT

Published by Relevant Books
A division of Relevant Media Group, Inc.

www.relevantbooks.com
www.relevantmediagroup.com

© 2003 by Relevant Media Group

Design: Relevant Solutions
Danny Jones, Aaron Martin
www.relevant-solutions.com

Relevant Books is a registered trademark of Relevant Media Group, Inc., and is
registered in the U.S. Patent and Trademark Office.

For information:
RELEVANT MEDIA GROUP, INC.
POST OFFICE BOX 951127
LAKE MARY, FL 32795
407-333-7152

Library of Congress Control Number: 2003093114
International Standard Book Number: 0-9729276-0-3

03 04 05 06 9 8 7 6 5 4 3 2 1

Printed in the United States of America

CONTENTS

INTRODUCTION

In the early 1800s, a portraitist asked Ludwig van Beethoven to pose for him. Assenting, the great composer sat with the intention of maintaining a single position until the painter could arrive at an acceptable likeness. This lasted five minutes. Beethoven quickly grew bored and made his way to his piano. There he began noodling around, improvising across the keys. Following the master's lead, the artist took up a suitable spot nearby and went to work. He painted and painted until, satisfied with the portrait, he gathered up his materials and left the room. Beethoven, enthralled by his own music, never even noticed.

In 1913, Russian composer Igor Stravinsky premiered *Le Sacre du Printemps (The Rite of Spring)* on a warm May evening to a Parisian audience. The work was brassy and innovative, its wild rhythms intense and disturbing. Accompanied by a primitive, sensual ballet, the performance so unsettled the men and women in the audience that they rioted. Yes, rioted. According to legend, the orchestra's conductor so feared for his life he had to slip out a back door.

In 1988, at a school dance, I experienced my first kiss. The song playing at the time was "The Flame" by Cheap Trick. If you ask, I'll sing it to you.

Music matters. It enraptures us. It polarizes us. It bookmarks our memories, giving context to the important moments of our lives. It engages us physically, urging us to move, as anyone who ever let himself go during Nirvana's "Smells Like Teen Spirit" can attest. It touches us emotionally, forcing us to feel: witness the tear-welling power of Samuel Barber's "Adagio for Strings." It offers spiritual uplift, from the stately melodies of Protestant hymns to the rich tradition of Negro spirituals. Music is much more than a collection of notes and lyrics, of vibrations, and frequencies. It's a medium of consequence.

Case in point: In 10th grade, I spent an entire year in chemistry class learning the elements of the Periodic Table. Today, I can still recall maybe five percent of it—including hydrogen and oxygen, which are pretty much givens. The same year, I purchased a three-dollar cassette single of the lyrically complex "I Go to Work," by old school rapper Kool Moe Dee. More than a decade later, I can still recite the entire song.

Music matters.

Religion, on the other hand, increasingly does not, especially to those of us who, as members of a younger generation, are the primary audience for popular music. Any number of studies over the last ten years have indicated that people in their late teens and 20s are less inclined to attend church and, more than any other age group, are suspicious of official religious institutions. We're alienated from traditional faith. And though we aren't attuned to religion, we recognize the value of spirituality. Each of us is seeking some sort of religious experience. And irreverent though it may seem, we've found a bulk of that experience in pop culture. Truth be told, the culture is our church. Television, movies, magazines, the Internet—these are our sacred texts. These are our shared communities. Information is our sacrament. We worship at the altar of entertainment.

Theologian Tom Beaudoin, author of *Virtual Faith: The Irreverent Spiritual Quest of Generation X*, argues that, for our generation, pop culture contains more relevant spiritual content than institutional Christianity. "I began to notice," he wrote of his spiritual journey, "how the popular culture seemed suffused with religious references. Our popular songs, music videos, and movies were about sin, salvation, and redemption, among other themes. Contrary to common perception, we appeared to have a very theological culture.... Could it be that popular culture was our religious arena?"[1]

It could be. And if Beaudoin is right, then the artists behind that culture—the actors and musicians and celebrities—are worth examining. Because if the entertainment has become our church, then the entertainers are our clergy. They're our pastors. They're our preachers.

We don't trust the guy in the suit reading to us from the Bible, banging the pulpit and shouting about the end times. We do, however, trust the guy in the baggy pants and FUBU jersey telling us what life is like, what relationships are like, where hope can be found. That's why the content of Eminem's raps matter. That's why we devour interviews with Jeff Tweedy and Dave Grohl and Jack & Meg White. That's why, in the last couple of years, Bono has been given such an influential public platform. For many of us, the songs and lyrics of these artists are our lenses for viewing the world.

Music matters, and so do the people behind it.

That's the point of this book. Here, the authors examine the spiritual lives of, to borrow a phrase from Beaudoin, our "surrogate clergy." The purpose is not to pigeonhole them into a certain faith tradition or to out these musicians as believers—we're not stamping "CHRISTIAN" on their foreheads. Nor are we out to judge the quality or sincerity of something as personal as their religious beliefs. Rather, the goal is to explore the way their spiritual paths have intersected with their art. What kind of faith is evident? *Where* is it evident? And what does it mean for the listener?

We're tackling specific questions: What do we make of the outlaw dark side and gospel fervor of Johnny Cash? How are P. Diddy's violent lyrics and behavior reconciled with his proclaimed devotion to God? Why does Lauryn Hill talk so much about Jehovah during her concerts? Why do journalists keep asking Moby to explain his self-stated love of Jesus? How does being the grandson of a voodoo priest and the son of a conservative Protestant minister inform the music of Wyclef Jean? What about Scott Stapp of Creed? Is he a rebel? A moralist? A self-involved poseur?

Two thousand years ago, the Apostle Paul described the power of the Gospel as a treasure kept in earthen vessels — something of re-markable worth stored inside a chipped, flawed, clumsy container.[2] We're all clay pots, cracked and grubby. Nobody's perfect, these artists included. But each of them has something to offer from their particular experience of faith, whether that trip has taken them down the middle of a familiar religious highway or along some barely recognizable back road of belief.

The point to remember, from a Christian perspective, is that the Spirit blows where it will. You can't tell the storm where to rage. You can't tell the wind which trees to rattle and which ones to spare. You can't direct the Spirit—but you can certainly recognize it once the gusting begins. That's when you take notice. That's when something significant occurs.

At some point, each of these musicians have encountered the winds of faith. We'd do well to listen to their stories.

Jason Boyett
Author

1. Tom Beaudoin, *Virtual Faith: The Irreverent Spiritual Quest of Generation X* (San Francisco: Jossey-Bass, 1998), 13-14.
2. 2 Corinthians 4:7

JOHNNY CASH

MAN IN BLACK

By Steve Beard

One gets the distinct impression that when Johnny Cash first lays eyes on St. Peter, he'll have a guitar slung around his neck and will be looking for a microphone. The Man in Black never seemed satisfied with any kind of retirement plan—and we are all the beneficiaries of his work ethic. "So many times, when there would be something I'd have to do that I didn't have my heart in, I'd say, 'All I ever wanted to do was play my guitar and sing a simple song,'" Cash said. "And that's still all I want to do."[1]

His 2002 release, *The Man Comes Around*, embodied the jagged and prophetic sound that has marked his career—and testified to the fact that, at age seventy, he still had more grit and bang than all the newfangled pop stars combined. One of the surprising hits on the album was Cash's rendition of "Hurt" written by dark and brooding Trent Reznor of the industrial rock band Nine Inch Nails. *I hurt myself today/ To see if I still feel/ I focus on the pain/ The only thing that's real*, Cash sang. *The needle tears a hole/ The old familiar sting/ Try to kill it all away/ But I remember everything*—a poignant reminder of his dark years in the 1960s. "I think 'Hurt' is the best anti-drug song I ever heard," Cash said. "It's a song about a man's pain and what we're capable of doing to ourselves and the

possibility that we don't have to do that anymore. I could relate to that from the very beginning."[2] He said, "I would have written something like that in the '60s, if I had been that good."[3]

When the video for the song was released, it became a fascinating crossover hit, being played on MTV, VH-1, and CMT. Director Mark Romanek spliced together one of the most vivid and moving visual portraits of Cash's illustrative career. Footage was gleaned from his early years, prison concerts, walking through the Holy Land, and hopping a boxcar. Cash was shown sitting behind a piano as well as strumming his guitar in his all-so-familiar black apparel.

Interspersed throughout the video was the backdrop of the famous House of Cash museum in Tennessee—sitting in disrepair, having never fully recuperated from flood damage. The museum served as a metaphor for Cash's physical condition—weak, willing, and in pain. Cash was seated behind a grand table spread generously with meat and fish. With trembling hand, he poured a glass of red wine over the food as he sang, *You could have it all/ My empire of dirt/ I will let you down/ I will make you hurt.*

The face of Jesus appears; first, as a portrait, and later footage is taken from *Gospel Road*, a movie on the life of Christ that Cash produced with his own finances in the 1970s. As the nails are driven in the hands of his Savior, a concert audience cheers with glee.

Never before in the history of music videos has there been such a rattling reminder of youth, aging, and the sometimes agonizing trek through the twilight years. "Mortality is a very unusual topic for this medium," Romanek said. "But I ascribe most of the power to the Johnny Cash-ness of it all."[4]

Trent Reznor was in the studio with Zach de la Rocha, the former lead singer of Rage Against the Machine, when he received the video. "By the end I was really on the verge of tears," Reznor said.

"At the end of it, there was just dead silence. There was, like, this moist clearing of our throats and then, 'Uh, okay, let's get some coffee.'"[5]

Cash's producer Rick Rubin cried when he saw it for the first time. "I spoke to (U2 singer) Bono and he compared what Johnny is doing now to what Elvis Presley did in the 1950s," Rubin said. "Then, Elvis represented a new youth culture and it shocked and terrified everyone because culture wasn't about youth before him. Now we live in a youth culture and Johnny Cash is showing the experience of a much older generation. It's just as radical."[6]

Life, death, drugs, Jesus, pain, joy, disappointment, and success were all wrapped together in that video—the essential elements of Johnny Cash's career and life's work. "Life isn't just for living, it's for singing about," he wrote in the liner notes for his 1977 album *The Rambler*. "Loneliness is real, the pain of loss is real, the fulfillment of love is real, the thrill of adventure is real, and to put it in the song lyrics and sing about it—after all, isn't that what a country singer-writer is supposed to do, write and sing of reality?"

The title track, "The Man Comes Around," has been widely heralded as one of Cash's greatest songs. Seven years ago in Nottingham, England, he had a dream where he found himself in Buckingham Palace in the presence of Queen Elizabeth, who was sitting on the floor. She looked at him and said, "Johnny Cash, you're just like a thorn tree in a whirlwind."

The dream slipped his mind for a few years, but then it began to vividly haunt him. Stumped by the peculiar phrase, he finally ran across the word "whirlwind" in the Bible, leading him on a lengthy hunt through concordances and reference books. He ended up going on an extensive study of Judgment Day and the Book of Revelation.

"I've wanted to write a spiritual that would be worthy of recording," he said. "I worked really hard on this song. I worked for five or six months on this song. I finally realized where I was going with it—kind of a spiritual odyssey of the apocalypse. This is my apocalyptic song."[7]

The song is about the day of reckoning and the notion that there will be an accounting for the way in which we live on earth. "It's a gospel song," Cash collaborator Marty Stuart said of the song. "It is the most strangely marvelous, wonderful, gothic, mysterious, Christian thing that only God and Johnny Cash could create together"—perhaps the finest tribute that can be paid to a songwriter.[8]

Everybody won't be treated the same, Cash sang, *There'll be a golden ladder reaching down when the man comes around.* He has seen that golden ladder swinging down from heaven on several occasions in his latter years. Perhaps that is why death does not rattle him. "To tell you the truth, I don't think about death at all," he said. "What is there to think about? I enjoy my life now."[9]

In 1997, Cash was in a coma for twelve days. Doctors told the family to expect the end. But June Carter Cash, his wife, had different plans. She got on the Internet and asked fans around the world to pray for Cash on an upcoming Tuesday evening. "On that night—while fans prayed around the world—Cash's family gathered around his bed in the intensive care unit, held hands, and joined in prayer," reported *Billboard* magazine. "Within hours, he finally emerged from his coma."

"It was incredible," said Cash's longtime manager, Lou Robbin. "He was in critical condition at that point, and the next morning he had turned the corner." June said she had no other choice but to pray: "They really thought they were gonna lose him—we all thought we were losing him. He was in this coma—just down so far that there seemed to be no way to reach him—and I couldn't think of anything but to pray. So we prayed, and within a matter of hours, he just started squeezin' my hand."[10]

COOL AS SIBERIAN STEEL

Johnny Cash is one of the most significant patriarchs in modern American music. Launched into fame because of hits such as "Folsom Prison Blues," "Ring of Fire," and "I Walk the Line." He has sold more than 50 million records and won eleven Grammys. He is the only person to be inducted into the Rock and Roll Hall of Fame, Country Music Hall of Fame, and the Songwriters Hall of Fame. Cash worked with legends such as Elvis and Dylan and performed before presidents and prisoners.

He has written books, hosted a popular television show, starred in and produced movies, and has recorded 1,500 songs that can be found on 500 albums. He remains today, the crowned king of blue-collar troubadours. Cash has the lurching height of a NBA forward, the distinctive facial features of a cleanly-shaven Abe Lincoln, the swagger of John Wayne, and the perceived moral authority of Moses.

Few things divide parents and their kids like popular music. Enmity between the music of one generation and that of the next seems to be a fact of life. Perhaps that is one of the reasons God gifted Johnny Cash. Like no other artist, he seems to have an uncanny ability to bridge the chasm between age groups. Cash has had a special magnetism spanning five decades of popular culture. He is, after all, an American original with few peers. "Locust and honey ... not since John the Baptist has there been a voice like that crying in the wilderness," U2's Bono summed it up. "The most male voice in Christendom. Every man knows he is a sissy compared to Johnny Cash."[11]

Cash's cross-generational appeal may have a lot to do with the fact that he writes songs the man on the street—or perhaps more appropriately, the guy hanging out in the alley—can relate to. He loves prisoners, the working man, and the welfare mother—those found on the outskirts. "Those are my heroes: the poor, the down-trodden, the sick, the disenfranchised," Cash said. "Ain't no end to street people. There's no end to the people of the margins. There's no end to the people who can relate to that."[12]

His songwriting repertoire includes tales of injustice and stories of redemption. His recent three-album collection is titled *Love God Murder*. What you see is what you get with Cash. He is as cool as Siberian steel. When he sings, you can almost taste the hillbilly moonshine, smell the sulfur of a smoking gun, and feel the drops of blood off the thorny crown of a crucified Christ.

CAN YOU HEAR THE ANGELS SING?

Cash was brought up as a Depression-era Arkansas farm boy. His family scraped at twenty acres of government-granted land, depending on soil and sweat to eek out a living. He had Baptist blood racing through his veins and the echoes of Pentecostal fire and brimstone preaching reverberating through his soul. He came from a white trash culture that depended on the white light of religion.

"The first preachers I heard at a Pentecostal church in Dyness, Arkansas, scared me," Cash wrote in the liner notes of his album *Unchained*. "The talk about sin and death and eternal hell without redemption, made a mark on me. At four, I'd peep out of the window of our farmhouse at night, and if, in the distance, I saw a grass fire or a forest fire, I knew hell was almost here." That deep sense of everlasting accountability was etched deep into the soul of Cash.

The young Cash loved music, especially hearing his mother Carrie singing gospel songs in the cotton fields or hearing her strum her guitar and singing "What Would You Give In Exchange for Your Soul?" by the Monroe Brothers. "The music in the Pentecostal churches in the early years was wonderful. They were more liberal with the musical instruments used," Cash recalled. "I learned to sit through the scary sermons, just to hear the music; mandolins, fiddles, bass, banjo, and flattop guitars. Hell might be on the horizon, but the wonderful gospel-spiritual songs carried me above it."[13]

While Jewish boys reach their age of religious responsibility at thirteen for their bar mitzvah, Baptist boys in Cash's family had to make the decision at twelve. Once the time had come, he already knew that he had reached "the age of moral and spiritual accountability. So while the congregation sang the invitational hymn, 'Just As I Am,' I walked down the aisle of the church and accepted Jesus Christ as my Lord and Savior."[14]

Only a few months after that experience at the altar, he was confronted with the horrible death of his older brother Jack. While he was cutting fence posts, one got tangled up in the swinging saw and jerked him into it, cutting him severely. Jack was rushed to the hospital, but there wasn't much that could be done. His mother and father were on their knees praying when Jack awoke and asked, "Why is everybody crying over me? Mama, don't cry over me. Did you see the river?"

"No, I didn't, son," Carrie replied.

"Well, I thought I was going toward the fire, but I'm headed in the other direction now, mama. I was going down a river, and there was fire on one side and heaven on the other. I was crying, 'God, I'm supposed to go to heaven. Don't you remember? Don't take me to the fire.' All of a sudden I turned, and now, mama, can you hear the angels singing?"

"No, son, I can't hear it."

Jack began to squeeze her hand and said, "But mama, you've got to hear it." The tears began to fall from his eyes as he said, "Mama, listen to the angels. I'm going there, mama." The family at his bedside listened with stunned attention.

"What a beautiful city," he said. "And the angels singing. Oh, mama, I wish you could hear the angels singing." Those were Jack's last words before he died.[15]

"It was like a burden had been lifted from all of us," remembered Cash, "and it wasn't just the eight-day burden of fighting for Jack's life. Rather, we watched him die in such bliss and glory that it was like we were almost happy because of the way we saw him go. We saw in our mind's eye what he was seeing—a vision of heaven."[16]

That vision would be long lingering in his psyche and spirit. "The memory of Jack's death, his vision of heaven, the effect his life had on the lives of others, and the image of Christ he projected have been more of an inspiration to me, I suppose, than anything else that has ever come to me through any man," he would say.[17]

WALKIN' THE LINE

Cash's launch into fame and notoriety began while he was still in his twenties. He began recording for the now legendary Sun Records in Memphis, Tennessee—a creative convergence of pop, country, and rhythm and blues. Sun was a virtual Cape Canaveral of rockabilly stars, launching names such as Elvis Presley ("That's All Right, Momma"), Carl Perkins ("Blue Suede Shoes"), Jerry Lee Lewis ("Great Balls of Fire"), Roy Orbison ("Ooby Dooby"), and Cash ("I Walk the Line") into music history.

Cash describes the Sun years as "heady times." He recalls one particular tour he took with Lewis, Perkins, and Presley (once dubbed the Million Dollar Quartet). The four of them were in a car when Lewis started preaching to them about how they were all going to hell (he was fresh out of Bible school).

Cash asked him, "Well, what about you?"

Lewis said, "Well I'm going to hell too. We're all out here doing the devil's work."

"I'm not doing the devil's work," Cash said. "I'm doing it by the grace of God because it's what I want to do."[18] As a matter of fact, one of the reasons Cash left Sun in 1958 was to have the freedom to record gospel songs.

WRESTLING WITH DEMONS

Cash began popping pills as his success began to blossom in 1958. At first, he looked upon them as a divine gift. "I honestly thought it was a blessing—a gift from God."[19] But it did not take him long to realize that he was deceiving himself and that the drugs were charms of the devil, luring him deeper into retreat mode from unresolved issues in his life. "Drugs were an escape for me, a crutch—a substitute for what I now feel. I was looking for a spiritual high to put myself above my problems," he recalled, "and I guess I was running from a lot of things. I was running from family, I was running from God, and from everything I knew I should be doing but wasn't." The times were tough. "I wound up living from high to high, and the highs got higher—but the lows got lower. So low, sometimes, that I realized I was at the bottom, and that if I didn't stop I would die."[20] He almost did—many times.

His first marriage crumbled under the weight of his manic touring schedule and an ever-increasing hunger for amphetamines. When he would come home, Cash argued with his wife, got stoned, and drove off—usually wrecking whatever he was driving. "I totaled a lot of vehicles, and I guess I must've broken twenty bones in my body—my toes, my jawbone, my nose, my fingers, my elbow, my foot, my kneecap," Cash said. "I don't know why I didn't kill myself then. I think it was because God was really good to me, which is why I'm where I am now spiritually."[21]

Cash was wrestling with his demons—quite literally. He can remember going to the desert and conversing with the voices in his head. "I'd talk to the demons and they'd talk back to me—and I could hear them. I mean, they'd say, 'Go on, John, take twenty more milligrams of Dexedrine, you'll be all right.' And I'd say, 'Yeah, but I've already had forty today.' And they'd answer, 'Take twenty more, it'll be good for you, it'll make you feel just fine.' So I'd take 'em and then continue talking back and forth to the demons inside me."[22]

For good reason, Cash thought that he was going crazy. Hauntingly, he recollected the day he sat behind the wheel of his camper truck and looked at himself in the mirror. "I put my hand over my face and peeped through my fingers at myself and said, 'Let's kill us.' And then I said, 'I can't be killed. I'm indestructible.' Well, I looked myself right in the eye and said, 'I dare you to try.'" He pressed the gas peddle and began to speed down the mountain until the truck flipped over twice. Remarkably he only broke his jawbone. "It was really a battle that raged within me for a long time—but somehow I survived."[23]

Throughout this entire time, he never stopped singing gospel songs. He was stoned on amphetamines while he sang "Were You There When They Crucified My Lord," one of his most beloved songs. "I used to sing all those gospel songs, but I really never felt them," he said. "And maybe I was a little bit ashamed of myself at the time because of the hypocrisy of it all: There I was, singing the praises of the Lord and singing about the beauty and the peace you can find in Him—and I was stoned." He was in a drug-addled hell, but these old gospel songs were etched in his DNA. "They were the first songs I ever heard—and I know this sounds corny, but they're the songs my mother sang to me."[24]

The legendary Carter Family, musical pioneers of folk, country, and bluegrass music, performed a number of those songs from his childhood. Some of their hits included "Keep on the Sunny Side," and "Wabash Cannonball." Cash became acquainted with members of the musical family, especially Maybelle and Ezra "Eck" Carter. They cared deeply for the man that would eventually marry their daughter, June. Understanding his addiction, they did everything they could to help him beat it. They even invited Cash to stay in their home when he was in town.

Sometimes he would burst into the house drugged out of his mind. Eyes bulging and legs flailing, he would pace around the house. Maybelle would quietly and calmly try to talk him into going to bed. All the while, Eck would say, "The Lord's got his hand on Johnny Cash and nothing's going to happen to him. The Lord's got greater things for him to do."[25]

Eck Carter may have seen the hand of the Lord on Johnny Cash, but everyone else saw a legendary country outlaw. "I was backstage at the Grand Ole Opry in Nashville when I met him in 1965," said Kris Kristofferson, whose career Cash helped to launch. "It was back in his dangerous days, and it was electric. He was skinny as a snake, and you just never knew what he was going to do. He looked like he might explode at any minute. He was a bad boy, he stood up for the underdog, he was exciting and unpredictable, and he had an energy onstage that was unlike anybody else."[26]

Others weren't so thrilled. Country singer Jimmy Dean once complained that Cash was undercutting Dean's tours because he and his band kept getting turned down from hotels Johnny had trashed.

Legendary country guitarist and songwriter Merle Travis said, "I'm amused by him as a pet coon. I'm impressed with him like a snake behind glass. He's that unique to me ... Even though he's a kaleidoscope of a thousand different ideas, he's a straight line. There ain't no twilight and there ain't no dusk to Johnny Cash. He's like a sunny day, or he's completely dark."[27]

Cash's reputation as a rebel grew even more legendary when he was banned from the Grand Ole Opry after smashing all the footlights with his mike stand in 1965. He wrapped June Carter's Cadillac around a utility pole—totaling the car, breaking his nose, and knocking out four of his teeth. Cash also accidentally burned down more than five hundred acres of national forest in California (he was fined $85,000). And then, there was the time when he got busted for smuggling 475 Equanil and 688 Dexedrine tablets across the Mexican border.

Amazingly, the Carters were there for him even in his most self-destructive state, opening their home and hearts to him like he was one of the family. "You know when he'd come to the house, he'd come starved," Maybelle said. "I'd always see he got something to eat, and if his clothes needed washing, I'd see to that, because John did a lot for me. We had to stick by him. His people weren't here. He was alone."[28]

Eventually Cash bought a mansion in Hendersonville, Tennessee, just outside Nashville. He would get the pills by the hundreds and hide them around the house in socks, between boards in the floor, and in the ceiling tiles. The Carters would spend hours searching the house for his hidden stashes.

A defining moment for Cash occurred in October 1967 when he had been arrested for the seventh time and woke up behind bars in Lafayette, Georgia. Apparently, he had been out pounding on someone's front door after having wrecked his Jeep in the woods of north Georgia. The next day, Sheriff Ralph Jones released the singer and said, "Here's your money—and here's your dope ... Now get out of here and go kill yourself." Cash was startled. "What? What do you *mean*, 'go kill myself?'"

The sheriff told him, "You got the power to do it and you're trying to, so go ahead and finish the job. You don't have far to go." Cash responded, "I don't want to kill myself." Unrelenting, Jones said, "Of course you do. You almost did. When we brought you in here I called a doctor and he gave you a shot and put you to sleep. But he said you evidently want to kill yourself, so there's your dope—go ahead and do it." The sheriff's disappointment and indignation stung even more when he said, "My wife and I have every record you have made, and it broke my heart when they brought you in here."[29]

Cash returned home feeling depressed and defeated. "By early October 1967, I'd had enough," he recalled. "I hadn't slept or eaten in days and there was nothing left of me."[30] He tried to end his life by crawling into the Nickajack Cave on the Tennessee River in hopes of getting lost and dying. He crawled for several hours until his flashlight went out and he was trapped in the darkness, left to contemplate. "I was as far from God as I have ever been. My separation from Him, the deepest and most ravaging of the various kinds of loneliness I'd felt over the years, seemed finally complete. It wasn't. I thought I'd left Him, but He hadn't left me. I felt something very powerful start to happen to me, a sensation of utter peace, clarity, and sobriety."[31]

Although he didn't hear an audible voice, he sensed the presence of God. "There in the Nickajack Cave I became conscious of a very clear, simple idea: I was not in charge of my destiny." Cash began crawling in the deep darkness of the cave's belly. "I started crawling in whatever direction suggested itself, feeling ahead with my hands to guard against plunging over some precipice ... I began to

see light, and finally I saw the opening of the cave."[32]
Like the biblical character Jonah many thousands of years ago, Cash emerged from the belly of the beast after tumultuous soul-searching. He told June he wanted to kick the pills. Psychiatrist Nat Winston, then Tennessee's commissioner of mental health, was summoned, and he began to meet with Cash. He told Johnny that he would help save his life if Cash really wanted to save it.

Winston showed up every day for a counseling session at 5:00 P.M. when he got off of work. "John," he said, "I'm a doctor, I'm a psychiatrist, and I've seen a lot of people in the shape you're in. And frankly, I don't think there is much chance for you. I've never known of anyone as far gone as you are to really whip it. Only you can do it, and it would be a lot easier if you let God help you."[33]

Despite his best intentions to get clean, Cash continued to stash pills around the house. The spirit was willing, but the flesh was weak. Less than a week into detox, Winston came out to the house and asked him how he was doing. Cash said he was doing great. The doctor knew better and said, "No, you're not. You're lying." He asked Cash where the pills were. "You want to flush them," Winston asked, "or do you want me to just leave and you keep taking them?" The pills were flushed.[34]

Maybelle, Eck, and June moved into the Hendersonville mansion. They circled around Cash's bed and began to pray. He went through withdrawals for weeks, suffering nightmares and torturous stomach cramps. When he was not sleeping, he was tearing up the place looking for drugs. This episode of breaking the addiction took thirty-two days.

"My liberation from drug addiction wasn't permanent," he wrote in his 1997 autobiography *Cash*. "Though I never regressed to spending years at a time on amphetamines, I've used mood-altering drugs for periods of varying length at various times since 1967:

amphetamines, sleeping pills, and prescription painkillers."[35] Looking back on those difficult years in the 1960s, Cash said that the drugs "devastated me physically and emotionally—and spiritually. That last one hurt so much: to put myself in such a low state that I couldn't communicate with God. There's no lonelier place to be. I was separated from God, and I wasn't even trying to call on him. I knew that there was no line of communication. But he came back. And I came back."[36]

The degree of freedom that Johnny has enjoyed is attributed to God, June, Maybelle, and Eck Carter. Nevertheless, Cash admitted, at age 70, that the demons still lurk. "They don't come knocking on a regular basis. They just kind of hold their distance. I could invite them in: the sex demon, the drug demon. But I don't. They're very sinister. You got to watch 'em. They'll sneak up on you. All of a sudden there'll be a beautiful little Percodan laying there, and you'll want it."[37]

RING OF FIRE

Standing by his side in the worst of times was June Carter. When they met for the first time backstage at the Grand Ole Opry in the late 1950s, June was singing backup for Elvis. "I want to meet you. I'm Johnny Cash," said the tall, lanky Man in Black. She responded by saying, "Well, I ought to know who you are. Elvis can't even tune his guitar unless he goes, *Everybody knows where you go when the sun goes down*." It was a line from one of Cash's first hits, "Cry, Cry, Cry." During their tour, Elvis would drag June along as he popped coins in the jukeboxes throughout the South to hear Cash's songs.

As Cash grew closer to the Carter Family, his heart was thumping for June. On the road, she was the one who had diligently tried so hard to keep him off the drugs. They fell in love while they were still married to other people. "I used to go to church about every day for a year," June recalled. "I used to get out my Bible and look through it. I used to wear out my knees and pray."[38]

Love is a burning thing, Cash would sing, *And it makes a fiery ring/ Bound by wild desire/ I fell into a ring of fire.* June Carter and her cousin Merle Kilgore wrote that song, but it best typifies the relationship between Johnny and June.

"One morning, about four o'clock," June said, "I was driving my car just about as fast as I could. I thought, 'Why am I out on the highway this time of night?' I was miserable, and it all came to me: 'I'm falling in love with somebody I have no right to fall in love with.'" She was frightened of his way of life, having seen first-hand the way that lifestyle killed country legend Hank Williams. She thought to herself, "I can't fall in love with this man, but it's just like a ring of fire."[39]

Both Johnny and June knew what was brewing: "We knew what was going to happen: that eventually we were both going to be divorced, and we were going to go through hell. Which we did," recollected Cash. "But the 'ring of fire' was not the hell," he clarified. "That was kind of a sweet fire. The ring of fire that I found myself in with June was the fire of redemption. It cleansed. It made me believe everything was all right, because it felt so good."[40]

June took on the responsibility for keeping Cash alive. "She'd take my drugs and throw them away, and we'd have a big fight over it. I'd get some more, and she'd do it again," he said. "I'd make her promise not to, but she would do it anyway. She'd lie to me. She'd hide my money. She'd do anything. She fought me with everything she had."[41]

The two of them would sing, *We got married in a fever/ Hotter than a pepper sprout*, for their hit "Jackson," and it served as a good descriptor of their marriage. "I think all this free love is a passing plaything," said Cash in a 1971 interview with *Redbook* magazine. "June and I found what we want in this world, and it's beautiful, the love we have for each other ... I don't think there's anything in this world that could destroy my marriage to June."

Cash admitted that he did notice other women and that June understood his wandering eyes. "We'll be driving along and see a girl in a short skirt and I'll turn completely around in my seat and say, 'Wow!' and she'll say, 'Get a good eyeful, honey. Oh ain't she pretty? Don't let her get by without seein' everything she's showin', honey.' But that's as far as it goes," Cash said. "I still look because I like to see a pretty woman. But I couldn't share June with anyone. It's a spiritual bond we have and it would be sin for anyone to come between us."[42]

Nearly twenty years later, Cash would tell *Rolling Stone* that "unconditional love" was the glue of his marriage. "You hear that phrase a lot, but it's real with me and her. She loves me in spite of everything, in spite of myself. She has saved my life more than once," he said. "She's always been there with her love, and it has certainly made me forget the pain for a long time, many times. When it gets dark, and everybody's gone home and the lights are turned off, it's just me and her."[43]

PRISON BOUND

By the time June and Johnny got married in 1968, he was riding high on the live recording of *Johnny Cash At Folsom Prison*. This was a renaissance time for the couple. They were hosting singers and songwriters in their home, events that would have made record executives shiver in jealousy. "The most memorable night," Cash said, "was when Kris Kristofferson sang 'Me and Bobby McGee,' Bob Dylan sang 'Lay, Lady, Lay,' Joni Mitchell sang 'Both

Sides Now,' Graham Nash sang 'Marrakesh Express,' and Shel Silverstein sang 'A Boy Named Sue'—all in the same night."[44] Of course, Cash performed "A Boy Named Sue" as a fluke (at the insistence of June) for the album *Live at San Quentin*, released in 1969.

The prison albums were some of Cash's most successful work. Merle Haggard remembered, "I was in the prison band in San Quentin when I first saw Johnny Cash. I was impressed with his ability to take five thousand convicts and steal the show away from a bunch of strippers. That's pretty hard to do."[45] Cash has long been identified with men behind bars ever since he wrote "Folsom Prison Blues" (which he was inspired to write after watching a documentary on the prison while he was in the Air Force in Germany).

"My biggest selling albums have always been the prison albums," he said. "I think there's a little bit of criminal in all of us. Everybody's done something they don't want anybody to know about. Maybe that's where it comes from."[46] He recalled the time when an inmate at the Tennessee State Prison told him, "I believe I can make it another five years. I know somebody out there cares, cares enough to come in here and sing for us."[47] Cash walked a paradoxical line as he played in prisons and identified with the inmates, while at the same time supporting organizations that assisted families of slain police officers. This same irony was evident in his performing for American troops while simultaneously protesting the Vietnam War.

Cash's popularity served as a springboard to his own network television variety program, *The Johnny Cash Show* (1969-1971), which he used to host vastly diverse musical talents such as Bob Dylan, Louis Armstrong, Pete Seeger, Linda Ronstadt, Mahalia Jackson, and The Who.

Cash ruffled feathers when he made a public profession of his Christian faith on his television show. "It wasn't something I was driven to do by an urge to convert anybody or spread the word of the Lord; I did it because people kept asking me where I stood, in interviews and letters to the network, and I thought I ought to make it clear that yes, I was a Christian." Cash sang gospel songs on the show because they were an indispensable part of who he was. While he was introducing one of his gospel songs, he said, "I am a Christian." This simple statement brought a rebuke from his ABC producer, telling him that he should not be talking about God and Jesus on network television.

Cash told him, "You're producing the wrong man here, because gospel music—and the word 'Gospel' means 'the good news about Jesus Christ'—is part of what I am and part of what I do. I don't cram anything down people's throats, but neither do I make any apologies for it, and in a song introduction, I have to tell it like it is." He made it clear that he was not going to back down, and if they didn't like it, they could always edit it out. "They never did edit me that way," he recalled, "and I never made any big fuss with them about it after that; I just went on doing what I was doing."[48]

Cash has always loved and taken gospel music very seriously. "I don't preach to people. I don't ever push it on anybody, and I wouldn't sing a gospel song on any show if I didn't think the people would enjoy it," he said. "They seem to enjoy those as much or more than anything else. It's not that I'm proselytizing. I'm not out there tryin' to convince people, just to spread a little good news."[49]

Cash has always allowed faith to play as big a part in his music as it plays in his own personal life—no more, no less. In 1971, Cash released *The Holy Land*, an album inspired by a pilgrimage to Israel. Two years later, he produced *The Gospel Road*, an album and motion picture that he produced in the Holy Land based on the life of Jesus. The film was inspired by a dream that his wife had in the late 1960s of Cash standing on a mountaintop in the Holy Land talking about Jesus. He was also inspired by a conversation he had with Billy Graham a few years later, during which the evangelist complained that young Americans were forsaking church attendance because they couldn't relate to the music. Graham said that the latest thing that young people were hearing those days was songs such as "Bringing in the Sheaves" and "How Great Thou Art"—not exactly the kind of tunes that inspired the younger generation.

The movie was released through the Billy Graham Evangelistic Association. "I'm not looking to make money on this," Cash told the *New York Times* regarding the movie. "This is my expression of faith."[50]

Cash has also had a lifelong intellectual curiosity with ancient history, culture, and religion. He read Lloyd C. Douglas' *The Robe*, a fictional account about a Roman solider who won Christ's robe after his crucifixion, as well as T.B. Costain's *The Silver Chalice*, about a young man who is asked to create a silver chalice with the likeness of Jesus. Both of these books, though fictional, fed into Cash's interest to the apostolic time period.

Back when he lived with the Carters before he married June, Johnny and Eck used to read writings by Flavius Josephus, the prolific Jewish historian (A.D. 37-101). They also worked through texts by Pliny the Elder (died A.D. 79), a Roman nobleman and historian, and Edward Gibbon (1737-1794), the British author of *The History of the Decline and Fall of the Roman Empire*. "We spent hours and hours talking about those books," Cash said. "On Sundays, we'd sit and talk about the Bible. I never asked him why he never went to church, and he never asked me. That was our church, right there—those books, those walls, those conversations."[51]

In 1986, Cash wrote *Man in White*, a novel about the conversion of the Apostle Paul, using his extensive research of the history and culture of the New Testament era. He was annoyed when novelist

Barry Hannah called *Man in White* a "highly literary effort" in *Spin* magazine and also said, "off the top I'd guess Cash didn't write it at all."[52]

Cash had worked hard to integrate his faith with his talents, but at the very core, he really just wanted to be in righteous standing with "The Man upstairs." Cash said there are three different kinds of believers. "There's preaching Christians, church-playing Christians, and there's practicing Christians—and I'm trying very hard to be a practicing Christian," he said. "If you take the words of Jesus literally and apply them to your everyday life, you discover that the greatest fulfillment you'll ever find really does lie in giving. And that's why I do things like prison concerts. Compared to that, projects like the television series I did, for example, have very little meaning for me."[53]

Long before the slogan WWJD became a popular bracelet, the question of "what would Jesus do?" was the theme of a book called *In His Steps*, written in 1896 by Charles M. Sheldon. Cash read the book in the 1970s, and it had an effect on the kinds of questions he had to ask himself. In a 1979 interview, Cash described what happens when a congregation tried to respond to the book's message: "They started putting their Christianity into action," he observed. "Stopped separating themselves in their beautiful white sepulcher of a church from the poor people, the hungry people in the slums and the ghettos." This is the vision of Christianity that Cash relished, and it is the one that caused him frustration when he did not see it fulfilled. "Like I say, the churches are full, but the slums and the ghettos are still full, and for the most part, the churches and the needy haven't quite gotten together yet," he believed. "And until more people in the Church realize the real needs of the people, and go out rather than going in ... I mean, to go into church is great, but to go out and put it all into action, that's where it's all at. And I haven't seen a lot of action."[54]

AMERICAN LEGEND

Johnny Cash's career took on a whole new lease on life when he met Rick Rubin in 1993 backstage at the Viper Room in Los Angeles. Rubin made his name as the eclectic producer of LL Cool J, Public Enemy, Slayer, and the Beastie Boys. "It was like deja vu with my Sun days when Rick said, 'Just come in, sit down with your guitar and sing me the songs you want to record. That's what Sam Phillips said," Cash remembered. "Sam Phillips said, 'Come in and play anything that you like.' So I started singing my songs, Hank Snow songs, Carter Family songs, a little bit of everything."[55]

For his part, Rubin recognized that Cash was still a hugely untapped artistic resource. "He's a timeless presence," he said. "From the beginning of rock 'n' roll there's always been this dark figure who never really fit. He's still the quintessential outsider. In the hip-hop world you see all these bad-boy artists who are juggling being on MTV and running from the law. John was the originator of that."[56]

Of course, Cash's most well-known line is, *I shot a man in Reno/ Just to watch him die.* That bad-boy reputation was played up when *American Recordings* was released in 1994. Stories of his pill-popping past began to re-emerge about the same time that T-shirts appeared with the famous 1969 photograph of Johnny flipping off a camera in an angry fit. "I understand them obsessing on the dark side," Cash said. "Everybody's got a dark side ... Americans have a history of upholding their outlaw heroes, of holding them up as people to be admired and emulated."[57]

Quentin Tarantino, famous for his movies *Reservoir Dogs* and *Pulp Fiction*, wrote the liner notes to Cash's collection of songs on *Murder*. "With their brutal sheriffs, pitiless judges, cheating tramps, escaped fugitives, condemned men, chain gang prisoners, unjustly accused innocents, and first-person protagonist who shoots a man just to watch him die," he wrote, "Cash songs ... are poems of the criminal underclass." Tarantino goes on to point out, however, that when Cash tells a story, "he tells it not with bravado but [with] an overwhelming sense of regret."

While Cash understood the draw to his outlaw image, he was also anxious to clear up misconceptions. "I'm an entertainer. 'I shot a man in Reno just to watch him die' is a fantasy. I didn't shoot anybody in Reno—and I didn't kill Delia," he said emphatically, referring to one of his gruesome songs. "But it's fun to sing about those things. Murder ballads go way back in country music."[58] As he said on his *Murder* album, "These songs are just for listening and singing. Don't go out and do it."

SIN AND REDEMPTION

On the *American Recordings* album, Cash was photographed with two dogs. He named them Sin and Redemption, fitting benchmarks in his life. "Sin is the black one with the white stripe; Redemption is the white one with the black stripe," he told *Rolling Stone*. "That's kind of the theme of that album, and I think it says it for me too. When I was really bad, I was not all bad. When I was really trying to be good, I could never be all good. There would be that black streak going through."[59]

Back in the 1970s when he was becoming more serious about his faith, Cash said it was Billy Graham who advised him to keep singing "Folsom Prison Blues" and "A Boy Named Sue," and "all those other outlaw songs if that's what people wanted to hear—and then, when it came time to do a gospel song, give it everything I had. Put my heart and soul into all my music, in fact; never compromise; take no prisoners."[60] Cash subsequently sang in the sold-out honky-tonks of the world and the jam-packed arenas of evangelistic crusades—never allowing himself to be too easily pigeonholed by the holy or the heathen.

"Johnny Cash doesn't sing to the damned, he sings with the damned, and sometimes you feel he might prefer their company," wrote Bono on the liner notes of Cash's *God* collection. "Johnny Cash is a righteous dude, and he keeps righteous company with June Carter Cash and the Carter Family, but it's the 'outlaw' in him we love ... the 'thief' who would break and enter your heart, and leave you with a nagging question, 'Were you there when they crucified my Lord?'"

Cash is destined to remain a spiritual enigma who fears only two things in life: God and drugs. He is one part outlaw and one part Old Testament prophet who sings about murder and Judgment Day on the same album. "I believe what I say, but that don't necessarily make me right," he said. "There's nothing hypocritical about it. There is a spiritual side to me that goes real deep, but I confess right up front that I'm the biggest sinner of them all."[61]

His momma used to tell him, "God has his hand on you. Never ignore the gift." Thank the Lord he didn't.

1. Anthony DeCurtis, "Johnny Cash Won't Back Down," *Rolling Stone*, October 26, 2000.
2. Quoted on JohnnyCashMusic.com.
3. Brian Mansfield, "Johnny Cash Puts a 'Hurt' on Video," *USA Today*, January 31, 2003.
4. Mark Binelli, "Johnny Cash Makes 'em Hurt," *Rolling Stone*, February, 20 2003.
5. Ibid.
6. "'Man in Black' at age 70 is new MTV star," Associated Press, February 17, 2003.
7. Luke Torn, "Still Keeping His Eyes Wide Open," *Wall Street Journal*, November 15, 2002.
8. Andrew Dansby, "Cash Comes Around this Fall," *Rolling Stone*, May 31, 2002.
9. Jason Fine, "A Day In the Life of Johnny Cash," *Rolling Stone*, December 12, 2002.
10. *Billboard*, March 30, 2002
11. Bono, God, Columbia/American/Legacy, liner notes.
12. Bill Friskics-Warren, "The Man in Black and White and Every Shade in Between," *No Depression*, November-December 2002.
13. Johnny Cash, *Unchained*, (American Recordings), liner notes.
14. Ibid.
15. Johnny Cash, *Man in Black*, (Grand Rapids: Zondervan 1975), 47-48.
16. Ibid.
17. Ibid.
18. Bill Friskics-Warren, "The Man in Black and White and Every Shade in Between," *No Depression*, November-December 2002.
19. Interview with CNN's *Larry King Live*, November 26, 2002.
20. Larry Linderman, "Penthouse Interview: Johnny Cash," *Penthouse*, August 1975.
21. Peter McCabe and Jack Killion, "Interview with Johnny Cash," *Country Music*, May 1973.
22. Ibid.
23. Ibid.
24. Ibid.
25. Mark Zwonitzer with Charles Hirshberg, *Will You Miss Me When I'm Gone? The Carter Family and Their Legacy in American Music*, (New York: Simon & Schuster 2002), 358.
26. Anthony DeCurtis, "Johnny Cash Won't Back Down," *Rolling Stone*, October 26, 2000.
27. Mark Zwonitzer with Charles Hirshberg, *Will You Miss Me When I'm Gone? The Carter Family and Their Legacy in American Music*, (New York: Simon & Schuster 2002), 345.
28. Ibid.
29. Ibid. As well as Larry Linderman, "Penthouse Interview: Johnny Cash," *Penthouse*, August 1975.
30. Johnny Cash with Patrick Carr, *Cash*, (New York: Harper/San Francisco, 1997), 170-171.
31. Ibid.
32. Ibid.
33. Ibid.
34. Interview with CNN's *Larry King Live*, November 26, 2002.
35. Johnny Cash with Patrick Carr, *Cash*, (New York: Harper/San Francisco, 1997), 174.
36. Anthony DeCurtis, "Johnny Cash Won't Back Down," *Rolling Stone*, October 26, 2000.
37. Jason Fine, "A Day In the Life of Johnny Cash," *Rolling Stone*, December 12, 2002.
38. Mark Zwonitzer with Charles Hirshberg, *Will You Miss Me When I'm Gone? The Carter Family and Their Legacy in American Music*, (New York: Simon & Schuster 2002), 358.
39. Anthony DeCurtis, "Johnny Cash Won't Back Down," *Rolling Stone*, October 26, 2000.
40. Ibid.
41. Ibid.
42. Dorothy Gallagher, "Johnny Cash: 'I'm Growing, I'm Changing, I'm Becoming,'" *Redbook*, August 1971.
43. Anthony DeCurtis, "Johnny Cash Won't Back Down," *Rolling Stone*, October 26, 2000.
44. Mark Zwonitzer with Charles Hirshberg, *Will You Miss Me When I'm Gone? The Carter Family and Their Legacy in American Music*, (New York: Simon & Schuster 2002), 358.
45. Merle Haggard, *The Essential Johnny Cash*, Columbia/Legacy, liner notes.
46. Richard Skanse, "The Man in Black Turns Seventy," *Rolling Stone*, February 21, 2002.
47. Peter McCabe and Jack Killion, "Interview with Johnny Cash," *Country Music*, May 1973.
48. Johnny Cash with Patrick Carr, *Cash*, (New York: Harper/San Francisco, 1997), 274-275.

49. Bill DeYoung, "Talk Talk: American Music Legend, Johnny Cash," *Goldmine*, July 19, 1996.
50. George Vescsey, "Cash's 'Gospel Road' Film is Renaissance for Him," *New York Times*, December 13, 1973.
51. Mark Zwonitzer with Charles Hirshberg, *Will You Miss Me When I'm Gone? The Carter Family and Their Legacy in American Music* (New York: Simon & Schuster 2002) 358.
52. Nick Tosches, "Chordless in Gaza: The Second Coming of John R. Cash," *Journal of Country Music*, 17, no. 3, 1995.
53. Peter McCabe and Jack Killion, "Interview with Johnny Cash," *Country Music*, May 1973.
54. Patrick Carr, Johnny Cash's Freedom, Country Music, April 1979.
55. Bill Friskics-Warren, "The Man in Black and White and Every Shade in Between," *No Depression*, November-December 2002.
56. Anthony DeCurtis, "Johnny Cash Won't Back Down," *Rolling Stone*, October 26, 2000.
57. Bill Friskics-Warren, "The Man in Black and White and Every Shade in Between," *No Depression*, November-December 2002.
58. Anthony DeCurtis, "Johnny Cash Won't Back Down," *Rolling Stone*, October 26, 2000.
59. Janice Dunn, "Q&A with Johnny Cash," *Rolling Stone*, June 30, 1994.
60. Johnny Cash with Patrick Carr, *Cash* (New York: Harper/San Francisco, 1997) 281.
61. Jason Fine, "A Day In the Life of Johnny Cash," *Rolling Stone*, December 12, 2002.

SEAN "P. DIDDY" COMBS

GOD'S CHILD

By Jason Boyett

He sat quietly. He wore a conservative, blue pinstriped suit and tie. Gone were the multi-carat earrings, platinum jewelry, Bentleys, sunglasses, and strutting entourage. The world-famous girlfriend was gone, as was his legendary aura of complete control. This was not the Hamptons, or his midtown restaurant, or a Sean John fashion show, or a Bad Boy recording studio. This was a Manhattan courtroom with a real jury and the very real threat of a fifteen-year prison term.

He was out of his element. Gagged by a court order and barred from the media, he felt like Job: wealthy, powerful, devout, and inexplicably thrown into a destructive, downward spiral. Over the course of his seven-week trial, the crowd of onlookers often saw him clutching a miniature copy of the New Testament, holding it to his chest as he strode through the gauntlet of paparazzi and into the courtroom.

The slim Bible was frayed around the edges, worn with use. He thumbed through it constantly between rounds of testimonies and cross-examinations. This was early 2001.

That spring, a Manhattan jury acquitted rap superstar/mogul/ producer/trendsetter Sean "Puffy" Combs of four counts of illegal possession of a gun and a single count of bribery for his alleged involvement with a 1999 nightclub shooting. Combs breathed a public sigh of relief, gave credit to God, and vowed that the experience had changed him. When the bullets struck those three people at Club New York, his mainstream, suburbia-approved image had dropped into hip-hop purgatory, somewhere between Young MC and Flava Flav. Combs needed a rebirth, a resurrection.

Goodbye, Puff Daddy. Hello, P. Diddy.

A Saul-Paul conversion? A modern Damascus Road experience? Maybe. Or perhaps it was just another calculated move by a master promoter, just one more shiny silver suit. Whatever the case, Puffy's name change carried with it the glimmer of symbolism, a willing renunciation of the preceding years. He dropped the pseudo-thug act and began the long dance back into the arms of his white teenage audience. In 2003, he returned to prominence with a new multimillion-dollar distribution deal, a hit reality show, and a growing influence in the fashion world—to say nothing of the music. Sean Combs was back.

THE MAKING OF A BAD BOY

It started in Harlem, where Sean Combs was born the first of two kids in 1970. His mother, Janice, was a former model, an attractive "fly girl of the neighborhood,"[1]—as Puffy once described her in *Rolling Stone*—who hooked up with the flyest guy in the neighborhood, a certain Melvin Combs. In the seventies, Harlem was known for its rough edges. Nearly half a million people, mostly African-Americans, shared six square miles of urban battleground, barely getting by in decaying houses, brownstones, and subsidized apartment projects.

That's why everyone in the neighborhood knew with some certainty that Melvin Combs didn't exactly come by his money via legitimate means. The Combs family, after all, was the only one around piling into a Mercedes and sporting furs. A drug dealer and numbers runner, Melvin ruled the community until January 26, 1972, when he was shot in the head on Central Park West. He was respected on the streets—despite his line of work, despite his violent end—as something of a Robin Hood figure, a man who made a living from the community but also gave back to it as well. People remembered Melvin Combs as a good man.

Young Sean hardly remembered him at all, though. After his father's death, he moved with his mom and younger sister into his grandmother's housing development. His grandmother was a major spiritual influence on him, emphasizing the importance of the Christian faith in his daily life. He held onto those personal beliefs, if not the religious trappings that often accompany them. "I believe in God," he once told the editors of *Muse*, a Dublin-based entertainment webzine. "He's my father. He's my saviour. I'm not into following religion. I don't care if you're Catholic, Protestant, Jewish, whatever you are. I just believe in the love of God, and just try and live by those spiritual rules."[2]

Combs was a devout Catholic as a child, attending church every Sunday and serving as an altar boy. Still, the neighborhood was a tough one, and not even an altar boy was immune to the negative influence of Harlem's street life. So in 1982, Janice moved Sean and his sister, Keisha, to the working-class suburb of Mount Vernon, north of the Bronx, to escape the clutches of the 'hood. She enrolled Sean in Mount St. Michael Academy, a private Catholic school. Even so, he kept his connection to the streets, spending time in Harlem at an after school program where, according to biographer Ronin Ro, he "immersed himself in hip-hop … dancing in clubs, rocking in then-fashionable polka dot shirts, and answering to the nickname Puffy."[3] He developed into a great dancer, and by the end of his senior year, he had already been exposed to the high-powered world of music entertainment, performing in videos by Doug E. Fresh, Babyface, and the Fine Young Cannibals. He was enthralled by the well-dressed executives who held sway on these video sets with their limousines and cell phones and briefcases.

Following graduation, Combs headed to Howard University, the prestigious African-American institution in Washington, D.C. He was a bright student who made average grades, preferring to put most of his energy and intellect into a thriving social scene—one he helped create. When Combs arrived, the Howard nightlife was no-ticeably lacking the vitality of the hip-hop scene back in New York, so the burgeoning entrepreneur in him vowed to do something about it. Puffy became a party planner, renting a local basement or area gym and selling tickets. He'd seek out up-and-coming rap acts, occasionally coaxing bigger names like Slick Rick or Heavy D to drop by when they were in town for a show. Puff's parties became the place to be around Howard and D.C., and soon industry execu-tives were mingling with the underclassmen.

By the age of nineteen, Sean had used the connections made at those events to scratch his way into an unpaid internship for Andre Harrell, a powerful executive at Uptown Records. Within months, Puff was Harrell's right-hand man. He dropped out of the univer-sity, took up residence at Harrell's New Jersey mansion, and began schmoozing 24-7. That's when things really started rolling. Harrell promoted him to Uptown's head of artists and repertoire in 1991, then gave Puffy the freedom to create his own record label, based on his success developing artists like Father MC, Jodeci, and Mary J. Blige. Bad Boy Entertainment was born. In less than two years, Combs had gone from intern to boss.

The business relationship between Puffy and Harrell eventually strained amid clashing egos and predictable power plays. Harrell fired him. Puffy took it all in stride and relocated Bad Boy to Arista in a $15 million deal, one that would last until Arista parted ways with Combs in 2002. As fate would have it, the relationship would come full circle: Harrell soon went to work for Puffy as the president of Bad Boy.

Success came easy and early for Sean Combs. By the time he hit his twentieth birthday, he'd earned his first million. The rest was gravy. "After I achieved that, the thrill was gone," he told VH1. "It was a good feeling, but more money brings more problems."[4]

MO' PROBLEMS

After the March 1997 shooting death of Notorious B.I.G.—the baddest boy of Puffy's Bad Boy Entertainment—Combs sat down with Mikal Gilmore of *Rolling Stone*. He was in the middle of filming a posthumous video for Biggie's "Mo' Money, Mo' Problems" and was flanked by heavy security. During the interview, Combs fiddled with a gold Jesus medallion around his neck and discussed the existence of evil in the world.

"Do you ever feel in danger?" Gilmore asked. Puffy indicated a monstrous tattoo on the inner side of his lower right arm. It was a reproduction of Psalm 23: "Though I walk through the valley of the shadow of death, I will fear no evil."

"I believe in God," he told the reporter. "He's my best friend. If I truly believe and have faith, why would I be afraid to meet God? I mean, what would I fear? If something happens to me, he's just calling me to leave."[5]

One might also argue that when something happens to Sean Combs—particularly something negative—it's not God's call but a simple matter of life balancing the scales. Throughout his career, death and violence have surrounded the man to a remarkable extent. Some see these tragedies as karmic retribution, others as examples of the power of faith to sustain. Whatever the case, they each seem to have served as spiritual touchstones in his life, markers of a faith that's been tried, tested, and found solid. Maybe the Job comparison is right.

CELEBRITY BASKETBALL

In 1991, a tragic episode at a celebrity basketball game promoted by Puffy left nine people dead. The game, featuring hip-hop artists Heavy D, Father MC, Jodeci, Big Daddy Kane, and members of Run-DMC and Boyz II Men, among others, was organized at City College of New York (CCNY) to raise awareness of the AIDS crisis. Puffy's promotional savvy and the big-name nature of the event were a huge draw. Too huge. The CCNY gym had a seating capacity of 2,700, but as many as 5,000 attendees showed up. Anticipation was high, space was scarce, and tempers flared. When the crowd attempted to squeeze through the gym's single open entrance prior to tip-off, chaos ensued. Dozens of helpless people were pinned against each other, trapped by the rest of the facility's locked doors. Eight people were crushed to death by the stampede. A ninth victim died later at the hospital. Twenty-eight more were injured.

Puffy, the promoter and organizer of the game, shouldered a great deal of blame for his mismanagement of both the event and the venue. The media jumped on him, attributing the carnage to a "fool named Puff Daddy," as the *New York Post* memorably reported. Combs' fast-track career seemed to be over until Harrell, his boss at the time, arranged for a team of high-profile lawyers to defend him. They began asking public questions and assigning culpability, turning the focus to the school's security force and administration. Puffy, they said, had no responsibility as promoter to control the crowd. The strategy worked. He got off free and clear, though his name remains connected to the tragedy still today.[6]

While he never faced any actual legal challenges, the self-imposed moral burden of the tragedy took its toll. Puffy suffered from bouts of depression and even suicide. In the valley of the shadow of death, he found strength in prayer. "Believing everyone had turned against him," biographer Andrew Cable wrote, "he started talking to God more and more. His belief in the Lord grew deeper and deeper, and carried him through the crisis."[7]

EAST VS. WEST

Over the course of a few years in the mid-nineties, a well-documented rap rivalry erupted between Puffy's East Coast Bad Boy stable (home to Christopher Wallace, a.k.a. the Notorious B.I.G.) and Marion "Suge" Knight's artists at Death Row Records in L.A. (home to Tupac Shakur). The feud, which started harmlessly enough as playground rap dissing on competing albums, soon escalated into an industry-wide civil war. It culminated in death.

In 1994, Shakur was shot five times in the lobby of a New York recording studio. Combs was in the building at the time, working a recording session on the eighth floor. Shakur survived, but publicly questioned Puffy and Biggie's proximity to the shooting. He accused them of setting up the hit. A few awards-show insults later, a Death Row bodyguard was assaulted and killed at an Atlanta nightclub where Puffy and entourage were present.

The bad blood came to a boil in September of 1996. Sitting at a Las Vegas traffic light in the passenger seat of Knight's vehicle, the twenty-five-year-old Shakur was offed in a gangland-style assassination. Wallace met a similar fate six months later—he was killed in an SUV parked outside a *Vibe* magazine party in Los Angeles. Puffy was a few cars behind him in the motorcade when the shots rang out. Neither crime has been solved, nor have police named any suspects or made any arrests in connection with the killings.[8]

Puffy was devastated about losing Biggie, the top artist in his crew and his closest friend. He was equally devastated that his name continued to surface in connection with Tupac's demise. "That's insane," he told *Rolling Stone*. "Why would I have anybody killed? I have too much to lose. I fear God too much."[9]

Ironically—or, as some would say, tastelessly—Wallace's death was a major stepping stone in Puffy's rise to national prominence. His Biggie tribute song, "I'll Be Missing You," entered the *Billboard* charts at number one. At the time, it was only the fifth title in the history of the Hot 100 to do so. Based on an extensive sample of the classic "Every Breath You Take," by The Police, the song wrapped around a stirring chorus by Biggie's widow, Faith Evans. Puffy's contribution was a handful of trite "uh-huh"-laden rhymes like the following: *It's kinda hard with you not around/ Know you in heaven smilin' down/ Watchin' us while we pray for you/ Every day we pray for you*.[10]

Despite Puffy's superficial mumblings, "I'll Be Missing You" was the best-selling single of 1997, endearing Sean Combs to the media and cementing his kid-tested, suburb-approved image.

STEVE STOUTE

Queens-based rapper Nas tapped Puffy to appear in his 1999 video for "Hate Me Now," which featured a shirtless Nas carrying a cross on his back through a jeering crowd. Combs was asked by director Hype Williams to join the rapper in the crucifixion scene. Puffy complied, allowing himself to be placed on a huge cross, where he screamed the words of the chorus: *You can hate me now*. He mouthed additional dialogue: *I think I like this*. Ronin Ro wrote that many on the set reported that Puffy was excited about the overt sequence and didn't have reservations until he saw the scene as it was being edited.[11]

Whatever the case, Combs got nervous about the religious implications and consulted with his minister, Hezekiah Walker, of the Brooklyn-based Love Fellowship Tabernacle (the so-called "hip-hop church"—home to Foxy Brown, Lil' Kim and a number of other hip-hop luminaries). He decided the mock crucifixion was borderline blasphemous, and asked Nas' manager Steve Stoute to remove it from the video's final cut. Unfortunately, a copy of the video had already been released by Nas' label to MTV. A few days later, Combs saw the offensive cut air on *Total Request Live*, complete with crucified Puffy. He went ballistic.

"I was not trying to portray Jesus, but when I saw the new video I felt like it [looked that way] and I don't feel comfortable with that," he told leading hip-hop publication *The Source*. Money, women, and friends will come and go, he said, but "God will always be there. He gonna love me now matter what. And that had me scared to death, 'cause no matter what I do, I can always go to church. If I disrespect God and make a mockery of God, I can't even go to church."[12]

So, according to reports, Combs and two of his bodyguards approached Stoute at his private Universal Records office, where they allegedly attacked the exec with a chair, a telephone, and a champagne bottle, among other objects. The office was ransacked, and Stoute was left curled into a bloody heap on the floor. Stoute—who was treated for a broken arm and jaw—pressed charges. Two days later, Combs turned himself in to the NYPD.

"Basically I didn't want to be up on the cross," he told Stephen Jones of British industry publication Dotmusic.com. "It was against my religious beliefs. I got upset and handled myself inappropriately. I had no right to touch anybody and basically I f---ed up ... I was extremely embarrassed about my actions. Sometimes I've just gotta be Sean. Sometimes I'm just a human being who is gonna be mad."[13]

Despite "just being Sean," Combs could have faced up to seven years in prison had he been charged with the more serious crime of assault. Instead, he eventually settled the dispute, pleading guilty to misdemeanor second-degree harassment in connection to the attack. He got off easy: As punishment, he was sentenced to attend a one-day anger management class.

THE TRIAL

Sean Combs' most public controversy was alluded to at the beginning of this chapter: the 2000 shooting of three people at a Manhattan nightclub and the media circus that followed it, after which Sean Combs was so certain the public was tired of hearing about "Puff Daddy" he dropped the name. Following the trial, he announced he was changing his professional name, within the month, to "P. Diddy." The statement was criticized by some as utter silliness. Others ranked it high on the pretension meter, right below the well-documented symbolic branding of The Artist Formerly Known As Prince.

Combs was serious, though, forecasting a new direction for himself and his label and downplaying the perfunctory gun-and-ho bravado that was a Bad Boy staple. Things are different when the rhyme becomes real.

Late in the evening on December 27, 1999, Combs and his then-girlfriend, Jennifer Lopez, headed to Club New York in midtown Manhattan. Puffy's newest protégé, Jamal "Shyne" Barrow, a gold-toothed rapper who fit the Bad Boy formula, was also present.

According to reports (many of which were contradictory), Combs and another club-goer got into a disagreement. The crowd surged, heated words were exchanged, and suddenly shots rang out. Some witnesses claimed both Puffy and Shyne had been holding guns at the time of the shooting. Others identified Shyne alone as the shooter.

At any rate, Combs' behavior following the incident suggested little in the way of innocence. As Shyne ran from the building only to be immediately arrested by two police officers in the vicinity, Combs and Lopez hopped into their chauffeured Lincoln Navigator and sped away from the scene. A police car tailed them, finally bringing them to a stop—eleven disregarded stoplights later. A 9mm handgun was found under the front seat. Another was found outside the club; witnesses claimed it had been thrown from Puffy's vehicle.

Combs, Lopez, their chauffeur, and Puffy's bodyguard were all brought in for questioning. Lopez was eventually released, while the other three were arrested. Combs was charged with four counts of illegal weapons possession as well as a one count of bribery, having been overheard offering an expensive ring to the chauffeur in exchange for confessing to ownership of the gun. Shyne was charged with three counts of attempted murder and a half-dozen other lesser offenses.

Several months of O.J.-like scrutiny followed—Johnnie Cochran even got involved in Puffy's defense—and Combs was eventually acquitted of all charges stemming from the incident. He broke down in tears as the "not-guiltys" were announced. Shyne, meanwhile, was found guilty of five of the eight charges against him. He is currently serving out a ten-year jail sentence in New York State.

Combs approached a bank of microphones as he left the courthouse just minutes after his acquittal. His thoughts turned heavenward. "I give all the glory to God," he said. "If it wasn't for God,

I wouldn't be able to walk out here."[14] In recounting each of the incidents—the stampede at CCNY, the death of Biggie, the Stoute assault, and the 2001 trial—Combs has declared openly and often that faith in God had been his salvation, that prayer had given him the strength to endure. He once told an interviewer that the book that had influenced his life the most was the Bible. Of significant meaning to him was the story of Lazarus, the dead man resurrected by a weeping Christ—in fact, Combs has been known to wear a gold Lazarus piece around his neck. "I've risen from the dead a couple of times, just through all this stuff I've been through, man."[15] In an interview with *The Source*, he wondered aloud if his struggles in the present were readying him for bigger things in the future: "Spiritually I'm as strong as I have ever been. Going through a certain amount of pain just makes you stronger. I've made a lot of mistakes in my life, and I've had a lot of successes, and I've learned from both sides of it."[16]

But despite his positive outlook and perseverance, each symbolic rebirth was accompanied by a dark side. Sean Combs had become wealthy, famous, and influential, but at what cost? The realization that he had gained notoriety for his association with controversy and violence weighed on him. As he told *Rolling Stone* following Biggie's death: "Sh-- is f---ed up. I've gotten my fame through tragedies. My successes have been overlooked. You think that's pleasant for me?"[17]

NOISE FOR GOD

Consider: Born into humble circumstances, he rises to prominence almost immediately, relying on an intense combination of discipline, determination, and faith. He reaches the pinnacle of power faster than anyone expects, yet bloodshed and controversy follow him every step of the way. He grieves over the murder of his best friend, yet turns that heartbreak to his advantage. Remarkably creative, born with an ear for music and a knack for poetry, he gains the heart of a nation almost overnight.

The man claims God's blessing on his life, yet slips seamlessly into a less-than-spiritual lifestyle. He has a weakness for women and has fathered children under questionable circumstances. He's said to have been directly involved in at least one execution, possibly more. He battles depression and speaks often of death. His poetry alternates between piety and unnerving violence. His life remains a mass of contradictions: devout yet ridiculously self-absorbed, a believer in God but a greater believer in his own authority. He dances ecstatically and exhorts his followers to lift their hands to the Lord Almighty. He worships with gusto. He sins with gusto, too.

And so, to the religious, the question remains: What do we do with the man described above? What do we do with King David of Israel?

The answer is obvious: We hold him up as an icon of faith, a warrior for Jehovah, a man after God's own heart. We recognize his flaws but overlook them. David, after all, was God's chosen, the forerunner of Christ. He slew giants. He captured the heart of a nation and turned it towards the Lord. He ruled with divine authority.

Of course, he also pulled a peeping Tom—or rather, Dave—on Bathsheba. He gained access to her via his authority, slept with her, got her pregnant, then arranged to have her husband killed in battle. Of deeply flawed biblical figures—and there are a bundle—David leads the list. Yet for thousands of years, the people of God have embraced him.

But Sean "Puff Daddy/P. Diddy" Combs? Like the name situation, it's a little more complicated than that. His faith seems as complex and contradictory as David's.

Had you attended a "Puff Daddy and the Family" concert on the *No Way Out* tour in 1998, you most likely would have heard Sean Combs open the evening by addressing the crowd like a revivalist: "If it wasn't for God, y'all wouldn't be here tonight. Make some noise for God."[18] These calls to worship would have been followed by a barrage of blatant sexuality and innuendo, risqué oral sex banter between Puffy and a barely dressed Lil' Kim, and Puffy-led audience chants of "F--- you!" The backdrop for the mid-show chatter was the music, which featured a constant glorification of money, drugs, violence, and outright hedonism.

Had you attended the 1997 MTV Video Awards, you would have seen Puff Daddy and Faith Evans perform their mega-hit "I'll Be Missing You," with Combs flanked by a bevy of nubile dancers shaking substantial amounts of booty. A few minutes later, you would have also seen Combs and the rest of the Bad Boy family politely turn away from the stage when self-professed antichrist Marilyn Manson performed, a silent protest as a witness of their Christian faith.

Watch any episode of *Entertainment Tonight* or pick up any celebrity glossy, and you'll see Combs flashing his ghetto-fabulous millions around like Monopoly® money. There's the house in the Hamptons, the jewelry-laden entourage, the private jet, the celebrity-rich parties, and the photo-ops with Donald Trump. But look past the paparazzi, and you'll see the time he puts in at Daddy's House Social Programs, Inc., a non-profit organization he founded—and which he finances—to work with disadvantaged urban youth in New York. You'll see him giving food to the hungry and homeless every year through a number of charities. You'll admire his work in Africa, where he puts his worldwide popularity to work in the fight against AIDS.

And if you listen to any of his albums at length, you'll hear enough four-letter words, "b-tches-and-ho's" misogyny, and gun-wielding posturing to send a Sunday school teacher to her grave. You'll also hear a lot of God-centered gratitude, confession of sin, and unabashed professions of faith: "I love you, Jesus," he voices in the *Forever* cut "Best Friend." Still, this ain't Bill Gaither—anyone who goes looking for church music on a P. Diddy album will likely be disappointed. Or furious.[19]

As an industry giant, he has readily defended the explicitness of his albums and those of the Bad Boy family, saying that his raps' lyrics were reality-based and expressed the vital viewpoints of the street. Yet as a father, he has worked tirelessly to keep his children from hearing the explicit themes and lyrics found in his songs. And not just *his* children. One writer, on the set of a posthumous Notorious B.I.G. video shoot, recounted a moment on tour when Puffy sprinted the length of a tour bus—in his underwear, no less—to prevent Biggie's four-year-old daughter from hearing a profanity-laced track by her late father.[20]

When Combs thanks God—in his raps, in CD liner notes, upon accepting awards—he means it. The person of Jesus Christ is real to Sean Combs. There's a scene in his "Victory" video where a wall-mounted figure of Christ turns his head and looks down on him. Puffy's Jesus is alive, approving, and active in his life. Like it or not, Combs is a tireless, if unorthodox, believer.

For conservative, white, religion-drenched middle America, this is the height of blasphemy. Artists who declare a belief in Jesus Christ don't beat up record executives or wave guns around. They don't drop four-letter bombs into their music, much less their everyday conversations. They don't hoist themselves onto crosses in crucifixion-parodying videos. They don't bookend morally bankrupt lyrics with sincere shout-outs to the Almighty.

And they most certainly don't look like P. Diddy. Do they?

There's a street spirituality, though, that doesn't often rear its head in the Bible Belt. In a Washington, D.C., memorial service following the 1996 shooting death of Tupac Shakur, Baptist pastor Willie Wilson raised a few eyebrows with the following words: "Hip-hop artists, in many instances, are the preachers of their generation, preaching a message which, too often, those who have been given the charge to preach prophetic words to the people have not given. The Tupacs of the world have responded and in many instances have reflected ... that Scripture that comes to mind: 'If you don't speak out, then the rocks will cry out.' I think in a very real sense these pop artists are the rocks that are crying out with prophetic voices."[21]

Michael Eric Dyson, a professor of African-American studies and an ordained Baptist minister with a Ph.D. in religion and philosophy—and who relayed the anecdote above—has written extensively on the seemingly incompatible connection between hip-hop culture and the church. That unique relationship is at the heart of Combs' story. "Some of the most hardcore rappers are more God-intoxicated than some believers in religious circles," Dyson wrote. "To a remarkable degree, many hardcore rappers, as profane and as vulgar as they can be, are figures who by virtue of their meditations on fate, judgment, death, and God force us to contend with the ultimate truths and proclamations of the Gospel."[22]

Sean Combs is many things to many people. To some, he's a master promoter, a mogul who made it big because he was driven and profoundly capitalistic, not because he had anything to offer as an entertainer. To others, he's a shameless copycat who made millions from sampled music cribbed from more talented artists. He's nothing if not mediocre. And lucky.

He's a rapper, producer, dancer, marketer—and yes, he's a preacher. Just not a typical one. Combs doesn't fit within the safe walls of the church. For all the shiny suits he's known to wear, none is the traditional suit of religion, at least not one recognized by the average pew-sitter. But the "truths and proclamations of the Gospel"? The meditations on fate, judgment, death? Diddy's got 'em. He's lived among them for years. The result of that life is the earthen vessel the Apostle spoke of in 2 Corinthians, an extraordinarily flawed container wrapped around something of great value. What that something is, exactly, is not always distinguishable. But there's no denying it's there, and Puffy knows it.

There's a large tattoo on his neck, just above his shirt collar. It reads, simply, "God's Child."

1. Mikal Gilmore, "Puff Daddy," *Rolling Stone*, August 7, 1997, 54.
2. "Puff Daddy," Leagues, Muse. *http://www.muse.ie/170300/puff.html*, March 17, 2000.
3. Ronin Ro, *Bad Boy: The Influence of Sean "Puffy" Combs on the Music Industry* (New York: Pocket, 2001), 7. Combs has consistently been evasive about his stage name—at least his first one—but once admitted it's related to his notorious temper: As a child, he used to "huff and puff" whenever he'd get angry.
4. VH1 Interview, "Q&A with P. Diddy," *Say It Loud*. *http://www.vh1.com/shows/events/say_it_loud/puffdaddy.jhtml*.
5. *Rolling Stone*, August 7, 1997, 52.
6. In 1999, Combs and co-promoter Heavy D were found negligent by the New York Court of Claims, which considered them responsible for overbooking the event. No criminal files were charged, but a number of civil lawsuits were subsequently generated, many of them ongoing.
7. Andrew Cable, *A Family Affair: The Unauthorized Sean "Puffy" Combs Story* (New York: Ballantine, 1998), 42-43.
8. 2002 saw the release of two high-profile analyses of the shootings. Nick Broomfield's documentary, *Biggie and Tupac*, suggested that Suge Knight arranged both Tupac's and Biggie's murders. Meanwhile, a lengthy *L.A. Times* exposé concluded that Wallace signed off on Tupac's murder, paying $1 million for the hit and even supplying the gun.
9. *Rolling Stone*, August 7, 1997, 53.
10. Puff Daddy & The Family, "I'll Be Missing You," *No Way Out*, songs published by Justin Combs Publishing, EMI April Music, Butter Jinx Music, BMG Songs and Yellow Man Music, 1997.
11. *Bad Boy*, 145.
12. Selwyn Seyfu Hinds, "Me, Machine: The Curious Case of a Man Called Sean," *Da Capo Best Music Writing 2000*, Eds. Peter Guralnick & Douglas Wolk (New York: Da Capo, 2000), 64. First published as the cover story in the September 1999 issue of *The Source* magazine.
13. Stephen Jones, "Dotmusic Interview: Puff Daddy," Dotmusic.com (July 21, 1999).
14. *Bad Boy*, 206.
15. *A Family Affair*, 43.
16. *Da Capo Best Music Writing 2000*, 63.
17. *Rolling Stone*, August 7, 1997, 72.
18. Katie Lindgren, "With Prayer and Vinyl Suits, Puff Daddy Rouses Elm City," *Yale Daily News*, March 23, 1998.
19. Though it should be noted that, since early 1999, Combs has been promoting the imminent release of his church-friendly Bad Boy gospel album, titled *Thank You* and featuring Hezekiah Walker and the Love Fellowship Crusade Choir, Faith Evans, Brandy, Kelly Price, Boyz II Men, and others. For unknown reasons, the much-anticipated release has been pushed back countless times, and is still unavailable as of summer 2003.
20. *A Family Affair*, 194.
21. Recounted by Michael Eric Dyson, *Holler If You Hear Me: Searching for Tupac Shakur* (New York: Basic Civitas Books), 202.
22. Dyson, *Open Mike: Reflections on Philosophy, Race, Sex, Culture and Religion* (New York: Basic Civitas Books), 309.

STRIPPED-DOWN SPIRITUALITY

By Denise Washington

At the 1999 Grammys, millions watched twenty-three-year-old Lauryn Hill gracefully cradle an award for her debut solo album, *The Miseducation of Lauryn Hill*. With a Bible in hand, she read Psalm 40:3 to a captivated audience. Hill boldly declared her faith to world in the form of a humble, yet passionate, acceptance speech.

Four years, five Grammys, and a five-time platinum status later, Hill found herself in a swirl of intense touring to accommodate new fans, increased media appearances, and long periods of time away from her family. Suddenly, her existence as a hip-hop diva meant that she was responsible for keeping certain people in jobs and livelihoods. Roadies, crew, and hair and makeup stylists all depended on her. It was all too overwhelming. With that burden becoming too hard to carry, she broke down emotionally and spiritually. She took a sabbatical, what she termed as "emotional rehab," in order to reconnect with God.

"I firmly believe [the reason] why I rose to the status that I did because I was so driven for validation," she told *Essence* magazine.[1] "The passion was good; it was just in the wrong direction. That passion should have been in the direction of gratitude and acknowledgement of everything God has done, instead of 'I'm going to get everything I want, right now.' God has given me what I needed even though it wasn't what I wanted at the time. I trust that whatever God wants me to do, He's going to provide."

A rested Hill returned to reveal a scaled-down, more raw and earthy side. She brought with her a group of austere songs that revealed the struggles and the lessons she had learned. The common thread of the songs focused on her rejuvenated relationship with God. Hill performed the songs on a *MTV Unplugged* session dressed in T-shirt, jeans, and baseball cap with her guitar. In the performance, tears streamed down her face as she sang about a "wonderful and merciful God" and the strength God has given her to endure.[2] The live performance resulted in a double CD called *Lauryn Hill: MTV Unplugged No. 2.0*. Some critics applauded the lyrics and called them "passionately spiritual songs that were stripped down with no conventional 'hooks.'"[3]

Hill had shed all the components that made her a pop idol. Writer Saada Branker approved of this boldness. "It's fine if critics think the songs run too long. It's even all right if they expected more polish to her work. But, for an unplugged version, fans are getting just that. No pretty packaging or slick studio edits. This ain't Britney or Mary J. or even Whitney Houston. It's Lauryn Hill."[4]

Other critics weren't so enamored. The graphic honesty and raw vulnerability had sacrificed marketplace sensibilities and fan expectations. Hill's artistic shift and spiritual declaration concerned writer Pearl Cleage from *Essence* magazine. "I worry about the 27 year old's willingness to speak from the heart about how passionately she had rededicated her life to God," Cleage wrote. "Surely, she must know that even in these days when no celebrity life is private, it's considered unwise to talk too much about God. A passing reference is all right. An excited awards-night acknowledgement among thank-yous to agents and managers is perfectly fine. A sentence in the liner notes right along with parents and producers is almost expected, but anything more is immediately suspect to some."[5]

Hill's personal life has also been suspect. Despite her declarations of faith, Hill's public family life sparked controversy. Having children out of wedlock and living with her boyfriend in her parents' house struck a bitter chord with some in the African-American community. Writer Debra Dickerson expressed her disapproval in an article for Salon.com. "Hill, the rhapsodic Christian proselytizer, is not everybody's idea of a black female role model. For one thing, she often dresses hoochie-style. Worse, she has two out-of-wedlock children with her live-in boyfriend, Rohan Marley (one of Bob's many children). Hill may embody the best of young black womanhood to some people, but to others she's just a hypocrite or worse, a danger to the community's endangered morals with her hip-hop halo."[6]

Dickerson also referenced an acceptance speech Hill gave at the *Essence* awards ceremony in June 1999. Hill tearfully said, "I want to let young people know that it is not a burden to love Him, and to represent Him, and to be who you are—as fly and as hot and as whatever—and to still love God and to serve Him. It is not a contradiction."[7] In Dickerson's eyes, Hill's life and Christian beliefs were a contradiction.

Some of the controversy emerged from the issue of illegitimacy within the African-American community. Writer Debra Dickerson cited a *Newsweek* poll where 55 percent of black Americans admire Hill. But when asked what they consider a "big problem," 78 percent mentioned teenagers having children, 63 percent cited "people not following religious and moral values," and 51 percent said couples parenting out of wedlock.[8] Dickerson said, "The hardcore black Protestantism many of us were raised on, with its many prohibitions regarding dress, deportment and lifestyle, makes Hill hard to accept."[9] For critics like Dickerson, it was difficult to reconcile Hill's secular lifestyle mixed with a sacred commitment to God. But, according to writer Teresa L. Reed, this issue of separating the secular from the sacred emerged only after the African-American church adopted European church styles and norms. The two existed equally in pre-slavery Africa. The Church, especially Black Protestantism, adopted strict moral and behavioral codes that still exist today. Any deviation from this norm fuels the criticism, despite artists like Lauryn Hill who frequently express their faith. For them, her "immoral" lifestyle weighed heavier than her music's impact and her philanthropic contributions to the community. Writer Teresa L. Reed contended, "Despite our attempts to polarize the sacred from the secular, we always end up praying to, thinking about, and preaching about God in our secular music forms. Perhaps we are no more able to conceive of music apart from religion—or vice versa—than were the Africans from who we descend."[10]

Others also agree with Reed, especially on what constitutes a role model. Writers Andy Crouchman and Nate Barksdale covered this subject in the article "Roaring Lambs or Bleating Lions." "Evangelical Protestants, of course, are adept at dealing with the problem of professed Christians who don't measure up to Christian ideals. When an evangelical says 'Christian,' he is actually using code for something much more specific such as 'active, church going, born-again Christian.' Hence, Greenville College is a 'Christian' college while Notre Dame is not. Michael W. Smith is a 'Christian' artist, while Lauryn Hill is not. Is America awash in Christian voices? Well, not exactly, goes the reply—we meant *Bible believing* Christians. Committed Christians. *Real* Christians. Christians like us."[11]

No matter how the critics deconstructed her life, Hill's music resonated among fans that did not view her lifestyle as mirroring or contributing to problems plaguing the African-American community. Author Joan Morgan explained, "They're celebrities, not role models. There is a difference. You can't put the weight of the black community on Lauryn. There was no Lauryn Hill when I was in high school, yet me and my two friends were the only ones who did not get pregnant. Lauryn's a positive influence, if anything. Teenagers see her with her man by her side and solid ground under her feet. Why can't that be the influence she has?"[12]

In an interview with *Jet* magazine, she spoke about how her faith combined with fame trapped her. Her release came through her art. "I'm a mess, but God is dealing with me every day. That's what all these songs are about: problem, cause and solution," she said.[13]

BIRTH OF A DIVA

Growing up in a devout Methodist home, God has always played a major part of Hill's life. Born on May 25, 1975, in South Orange, New Jersey, Hill cut her teeth on old school R&B songs on her parents' 45s. Daughter to a management consultant and an English teacher, Hill lived with her parents and brother on the cusp of the projects and suburbia. Her family attended the Methodist church, where her parents taught Hill the importance of faith and about black history and civil rights. Like most young African-American girls in the church, Hill sang in the gospel choir and gospel groups with her family. "When I was younger I was very much in touch with God. I used to talk to Him every night," she said.[14] But along with a childlike faith existed a fear of the dark in a young Lauryn. In *Heart of Soul: The Lauryn Hill Story*, the writers saw this experience as "the fear of darkness and the search of enlightenment as a recurring theme in the life and work of Lauryn Hill."[15] Also, during this time, Hill perfected her music and performance skills as musical influences like Curtis Mayfield, Aretha Franklin, Nina Simone, and Billie Holiday fueled her creativity.

At thirteen years old, Hill sang at Amateur Night at the Night at the

Apollo, but she suffered through a dismal performance. She lost but was not deterred. Soon she met Prakazrel Michel, a.k.a. Pras. Impressed with Hill's vocal abilities, Pras brought her into a hip-hop group he was piecing together called Time. Pras told *Rolling Stone*, "She was cool. I believe—because I'm a spiritual person, and I grew up in the church—everything happens for a reason. Not to say that we wouldn't be successful, but it would've been a whole different thing."[16]

Even though she performed with the group, Hill carved out time to be a cheerleader, class president, straight-A student, and creator of a breakfast program for at-risk students. Hill also auditioned and won a part in an off-Broadway hip-hop version of Shakespeare's *Twelfth Night*. There she caught the eye of a casting agent who sent Hill on auditions and casting calls in New York. She soon landed the part of runaway teen Kira Johnson on the soap opera *As The World Turns*.

With all of Hill's pursuits, her main love was music and performing. Time had switched lineups as Wyclef Jean, Pras' cousin, joined the group. Now called Tranzlation Crew, they performed at clubs and bars throughout New Jersey and New York, introducing a unique blend of music to audiences. At sixteen years old, Hill and Tranzlation Crew signed on with a small hip-hop label, Ruffhouse Records, a division of Columbia Records. Most labels did not know how to market a non-traditional hip-hop group, but Ruffhouse had experienced success with the Latino hip-hop group, Cypress Hill—a group that did not fit in the current hip-hop scene.[17]

Yet, the label gave the band no creative freedom during the production of their first album, *blunted on Reality* [sic]. They dictated the production of each song by adding remixes and speeding up vocals. The album lost the group's original sound. During this time, the trio changed their name to The Fugees.

Hill continued to act while working on the record. Before the album released, she played Rita Wilson, a troubled Catholic schoolgirl with a gift of singing, in *Sister Act 2: Back in the Habit*, starring Whoopi Goldberg. Even though critics panned the film, they applauded Hill's performance. She portrayed Rita with an edgy vulnerability, while her powerful voice belted out gospel medleys such as "Eye on the Sparrow" and "Joyful Joyful." On the movie set, Hill talked about God to the other actors and the crew. She said in the biography, *Heart of Soul*, "Talking about God doesn't embarrass me. It doesn't make me less cool or less popular or make me corny."[18]

A God connection permeated everything Hill touched. She remained candid about her relationship with God. According to writers Leah and Elina Furman, Hill was as deeply spiritual in her teens as she'd been in her childhood. "Having joined with the equally religious Pras and Wyclef, she [Hill] never stood in any danger of falling in with the wrong crowd," they said. "From day one, Lauryn methodically arranged her whole life around the teachings of the Good Book, drawing upon it both for strength and for wisdom."[19]

OLD SCHOOL WITH NEW FLAVA

In 1993, *blunted on Reality* finally released. Critics dissed the album for being a departure from the hip-hop and gangsta rap sound. The album received little radio play, no MTV rotation and no presence on the *Billboard* charts. Yet, despite the criticism and low sales, most fans flocked to The Fugees' mostly sold-out live concerts to see the group showcase their experimental styling and theatrical performances.

The Fugees regrouped on the second album, *The Score*, taking control of the creative reins, mixing old school soul with rap, flavoring it with reggae and a little acoustic folk. The Fugees were out to prove they were in the game for the long haul. Seeing themselves as pioneers, they ignored past criticism and remained true to their musical roots. Hill called the group revolutionary, comparing them to Jesus Christ and other musicians. "Both taught me that your thanks is not necessarily on Earth, that it's a rough path to tread. I mean, Nina Simone was a revolutionary who spoke on behalf of people who probably didn't appreciate her, and it made for a very hard almost bitter life. And Jesus Christ? Thankless job, too—you save the world but must be crucified," she said.[20]

Hill attended Columbia University while they were in the studio producing the second album. Combining school and a music career proved difficult, so the stay was brief. Focusing on the music, Hill assisted with the arranging, producing, songwriting, and rapping on the album—a major coup for a woman in a male-dominated industry.

With radio play and videos on MTV, *The Score* sold millions of copies, garnered critical acclaim, and propelled the group into superstardom. Suddenly, the media wanted to know all about Lauryn Hill, the beautiful, enthusiastic, and passionate songstress. They bombarded her with constant questions about her style, her looks, and her personal life. Yet, success and media attention did not prevent Hill from feeling empty. At the time, she was involved in a bad relationship. "One of the biggest sins you can do when you have such a tight relationship with God—I put someone before Him. I fell deeply in love and put a man before God," she said in *Heart of Soul.*[21]

Yet, Hill did not have time to reconnect with God in the way she wanted because the promotion of the album, touring, and media appearances created a frenzied life. With the release of "Killing Me Softly With His Song," a remake of the Roberta Flack song, more people bought the CD. The music crossed ethnic and socio-economical lines as additional fans embraced the music. Suddenly, the young woman from South Orange, New Jersey, was now a pop icon with pop music's built-in pressures and temptations. But Hill maintained humility. She utilized her celebrity and fame to better her community. She started the Refugee Project, a non-profit organization that consisted of a summer camp, after-school programs, and educational opportunities. She also continued to live near her family in New Jersey instead of in luxurious mansions like her other hip-hop contemporaries.

Even though Hill was part of a trio, the media focused more on her than the other members. So, as Wyclef Jean and Pras pursued side projects, Hill sought to diffuse the media attention because of the tension emerging in the group. She remained in the background so she would not upstage Wyclef Jean and Pras.

Hill's personal life blossomed when she met and fell in love with Rohan Marley, son of the late Bob Marley. Professionally, the group continued its success, winning two Grammys—Best Rap Album and Best R&B Performance by a Duo or Group for "Killing Me Softly with His Song." Hill pursued side projects of her own, producing and writing songs for Aretha Franklin and gospel artist CeCe Winans. But when Hill became pregnant, some whispered that motherhood would be career suicide. Yet she continued to tour with The Fugees until her seventh month.

When the time came from her baby boy to be born, Hill and Rohan named him Zion. She told *Vibe*, "Names wouldn't come when I was getting ready to have him. The only name that came to me was Zion, the deliverer. I was like, is Zion too much of a weight to carry? But, this little boy, man. I would say he personally delivered me from emotional and spiritual drought. He just replenished my newness when he was born. I almost felt like I was born again."[22]

THE SOLO EDUCATION OF LAURYN

With the group on hiatus and Wyclef Jean and Pras working on solo projects, Hill explored the possibility of recording her own solo album. She longed to birth a sound of her own, using influences of hip-hop, soul, and R&B. Completely departing from The Fugees' distinctive style, Hill started the journey.

Many did not support the next stage of Hill's life. Fans wanted the solo album to be *The Score, Part II*. But the detractors did not deter Hill. She wrote autobiographically, drawing inspiration and insight straight from the Bible. "There was a point where I had decided that I wasn't gonna pray anymore ... because there were some things in my life that I knew weren't good for me," she said. "But I had decided that I needed those things. I knew if I prayed, God would take them from me. So, I was afraid. I was devastatingly terrified of prayer. And, the moment that I did pray, lo and behold, he removed all the negativity. Quicker than a snap. In the same speed, He loosened my tongue and a creative voice just came and wrote," she said.[23]

Hill worked on the solo album in New Jersey and Kingston, Jamaica, at Bob Marley's studio. She collaborated with artists like Mary J. Blige, D'Angelo, and Carlos Santana, who played guitar on the song "To Zion." She also used a full orchestra to back up her vocals. In "To Zion," Hill lyrically expressed her feelings about her pregnancy and motherhood. "I wanted it to be a revolutionary song about a spiritual movement, and also about my spiritual change, going from one place to another because of my son," she said.[24]

In 1998, Hill finally released her solo album, *The Miseducation of Lauryn Hill*, the title inspired by the Carter G. Woodson book, *The Miseducation of the Negro*. Hill produced, arranged, and wrote the entire album. Some of the record executives objected, but Hill stood strong and created a powerful new sound. The album had "lush arrangements and a wide range of styles—a little hip-hop here, a two part harmony there and a dash of Jamaican patios for flavor."[25]

Songs touched on her new motherhood experience and the emotions surrounding her life in and without The Fugees. "I'm not embarrassed to expose myself in the sense that I'm human," she said in an interview with Horizonmag.com.[26] "I make mistakes and bad judgments and I've had my heart broken. I'm also not embarrassed to tell someone how happy I was that, um, you know, when I had my child, how conflicted I was, or how I happy I was. Or how much I love God. I don't feel like I have to put up a front to the people who want to hear my music. I don't want to write about things that separate me from the audience." Despite disapproval from record label executives, her songs also made many references to God and the Bible. She told *Ebony* magazine, "You have to assert yourself. I think when you're a woman you have to assert yourself even a little more. The record companies sign an act and they have ideas about how that act should sound. They think when you win with a formula, why change the formula?"[27]

Changing the formula proved successful as the album entered the *Billboard* pop chart at number one. And, by the end of the year, the album went triple platinum and received critical acclaim. For the first time, Hill could enjoy her success without worrying about making Wyclef Jean and Pras jealous. "I think it is a strong statement ... that I can make an album completely from soul and without compromise and be acknowledged for it," she told Horizonmag.com.[28]

Hill became pregnant with a second child while she and Rohan were still unmarried and lived in her parents' old house in New Jersey. When confronted about her personal life, Hill, according to the book *Heart of Soul*, said, "We're together and we're raising a family.

I don't consider myself a single mother."[29] Major acting opportunities emerged during this time also. But Hill turned down roles in movies like *The Cider House Rules*, *Beloved*, and *Mission Impossible 2* due to her pregnancy.

In January 1999, the Grammy nominations were announced. *The Miseducation of Lauryn Hill* garnered ten record-breaking nominations, including Best Album of the Year. It was the first hip-hop album in history to receive that many nominations. When the press wanted Hill's reaction, they showed up at her home in New Jersey. Not able to give the press conference, Rohan Marley spoke for her. He told the press that Hill "give thanks to all the people. And God's grace and blessing to everyone. And she gives thanks to the Father."[30]

Months later at the Grammy awards, Hill received five Grammys, breaking the record of being a female artist to win that many awards in one night. The awards boosted record sales and took the album five times platinum. At the time, Hill spoke of her success to *Vibe* magazine. "I'm very happy with a foundation, with a good man, and a child and a family—and I don't have the fear of losing my job," she said. "You know how in the office space people are sometimes hesitant to be vocal cause they could be fired for what they say. The only person who can fire me is God."[31]

Hill told *Teen People*, "I'm at peace because I'm very clear now about what really matters. God is the center of everything that I do ... every time I have an opportunity to get complacent or smug, God puts me in a situation where I have to struggle. I was really happy with the [Grammy] nominations, but my brother's girlfriend had been in labor for twenty-eight hours that day. Just at the time when I could have gotten so bigheaded, I had something so beautiful and so humble to focus on."[32]

Like a prodigal daughter, Hill had put her relationship with God aside and pursued fame and celebrity. Yet despite fan adoration and critical acclaim, she experienced emptiness. As she struggled with the music industry, motherhood, relationships, and critics, she returned to God and found the peace that she had been seeking most of her life. By stripping down her life and rearranging her priorities, Lauryn discovered that her life was meaningless without God. With a renewed sense of purpose and direction, her music beautifully expressed her feelings of love, humility, and gratitude. And, as she continues to tap into the source of her creative inspiration, fans will continue to experience the incredible talents of Lauryn Hill.

1. Pearl Cleage, "Looking for Lauryn: The Songbird Returns with Renewed Faith, Raw Emotion, and a Rediscovered Self," *Essence*, July 2002.
2. "Lauryn Hill Performs New Somber, Emotional Tunes on MTV," *Jet*, August 13, 2001.
3. Pearl Cleage, "Looking for Lauryn: The Songbird Returns with Renewed Faith, Raw Emotion, and a Rediscovered Self," *Essence*, July 2002.
4. Saada Branker, "The Rise of Lauryn Hill," Wordmag.com, June 2002.
5. Pearl Cleage, "Looking for Lauryn: The Songbird Returns with Renewed Faith, Raw Emotion, and a Rediscovered Self," *Essence*, July 2002.
6. Debra Dickerson, "Lauryn Hill: Hoochie or Hero?" Salon.com, June 22, 1999.
7. Ibid.
8. Ibid.
9. Ibid.
10. Teresa L. Reed, *The Holy Profane: Religion in Black Popular Music*, (Lexington, Kentucky: The University Press of Kentucky, 2003), 159.
11. Andy Crouch and Nate Barksdale, "Roaring Lambs or Bleating Lions?" *Regeneration*, June 4, 2001.
12. Joan Morgan, *When Chichenheads Come Home to Roost: My Life as a Hip-Hop Feminist*, interview by Debra Dickerson, Salon.com, June 22, 1999.
13. "Lauryn Hill Performs New Somber, Emotional Tunes on MTV," *Jet*, August 13, 2001.
14. Leah Furman and Elina Furman, *Heart of Soul: The Lauryn Hill Story* (New York: Ballantine Books, 1999), 15.
15. Ibid., 11
16. Alec Foege, "Fugees: Leaders of the New Cool," *Rolling Stone*, September 5, 1996.
17. Ibid.
18. Leah Furman and Elina Furman, *Heart of Soul: The Lauryn Hill Story* (New York: Ballantine Books, 1999), 58.
19. Ibid., 58.
20. Ibid., 68.
21. Ibid., 91.
22. Karen Good, *Vibe*, August 1998.
23. Leah Furman and Elina Furman, *Heart of Soul: The Lauryn Hill Story* (New York: Ballantine Books, 1999), 143.
24. Ibid., 149.
25. Melissa Ewey, "Lauryn Hill: Smashes Records and Tells How Motherhood Changed her Life," *Ebony*, November 1998.
26. Kevin Powell, "Lauryn Hill: She Knows Why The Caged Bird Sings," Horizonmag.com, November 1998.
27. Melissa Ewey, "Lauryn Hill: Hip-Hop's Hottest Star Balances Love, Motherhood and Fame," *Ebony*, May 1999.
28. Kevin Powell, "Lauryn Hill: She Knows Why The Caged Bird Sings," Horizonmag.com, November 1998.
29. Leah Furman and Elina Furman, *Heart of Soul: The Lauryn Hill Story* (New York: Ballantine Books, 1999), 152.
30. Ibid., 168.
31. Karen Good, *Vibe*, August 1998.
32. Ethan Brown, "Queen of the Hill: The Hip-Hop Superstar Speaks out on Spirituality, Family and the Future of the Fugees, *Teen People*, May 1999.

EVERYTHING IS COMPLICATED

By Jason Boyett

Let's play a game. It's called Mobidentification, and it's a two-step process. Here's how it works: Get some paper and a pencil and sit down in front of your computer. Locate and download Moby's Hollywood-heavy video for "We Are All Made of Stars," the first single released from his well-received 2002 album, *18*. Filmed on location in Hollywood, Santa Monica, and at Sunset & Vine, it's loaded with B-list celebrities.

Your first task as a viewer is to identify as many of these semi-familiar faces as possible during the video's three-plus minutes. Ready? Go.

Even the most culturally illiterate will find someone he or she can name. There's Gary Coleman and Todd Bridges from *Diff'rent Strokes*. And isn't that Mini-Me? (Bonus points if you come up with his real name, Verne Troyer.) Those with a little more pop savvy will recognize Tommy Lee, Thora Birch and Dominique Swain. Yes, that's Corey Feldman, and one of the non-Justin-Timberlake guys from N*Sync. There's Kato Kaelin. If you've ever been to L.A., you'll identify the ubiquitous Angelyne. Extra credit for pointing out Dave Navarro of the Red Hot Chile Peppers. Super extra credit if you place him with Jane's Addiction. And shame on you for recognizing porn legend Ron Jeremy.

Now for your next challenge. Add up your total of recognized celebrities, then make a list of ways to describe Moby—words or phrases that tell who or what he is. Try to match your number of labels with the number of "We Are All Made of Stars" celebs you named. Got it? This should be easy:

Electronic dance enthusiast. Militant vegan. Animal rights activist. Intellectual essayist. Thrash-metal guitarist. Computer geek. Straight-edge ascetic. Drug-free raver. Non-smoking non-drinker. Techno wizard. Accidental soundtracker. Hip-hop sampler. Trance-like composer. Manic performer. Lover of porn. Remixer extraordinaire. Little white bald guy. Commercial sellout. Christian.

Thus ends your game. Thank you for playing.

Like the rapid succession of faces mugging their way through "We Are All Made of Stars," Moby has endured an unending barrage of labels over the last dozen years or so. A few are accurate ("little white bald guy"). A handful are generally false ("commercial sellout"). Most lie somewhere in between.

The problem is this: all those labels? Moby hates them. "There are all these clichés that follow me around," he told *LA Weekly* in 1999. "Like the Christian-vegan-porn-fan-environmentalist-Puritan-Calvinist-whatever. And none of them are really true."[1]

That may be the case, but whether the labels are accurate or not doesn't matter. Once a tag pops out of the cultural label-maker, it sticks. Just ask Ozzy Osbourne. Despite the overwhelming success of his MTV reality series in 2002—and despite the subsequent overexposure of Ozzy, Sharon, Jack, and Kelly—Mr. Osbourne will always be known for a single event: biting the head off a bat once in a concert. That image will follow him through life. Forever.

Truth is irrelevant. Perception is everything. In our postmodern world, where the lines are so blurred we're not even sure what the categories are anymore, it's both astonishing and absolutely logical that Moby has been tagged with such diversity. Rather than being defined by a single event or album or song, he's somehow become all things to all people. Find a humanitarian cause, and Moby's become attached to it at one point or another. Find a genre of music, and its hooks and samples have shown up in one of his compositions. Find an automobile brand, and it's likely to have purchased one of his tracks for a commercial.

Moby's everywhere. He does everything. But who is he, really?

"There is some confusion regarding the public perception of me," he said in an interview with *The Inside Connection.* "I think some see me as a composer or musician, a DJ, a punk rocker, a sound artist. I'd like to be thought of as someone who makes music that people like."[2]

That's a worthy goal, and one in which he's found remarkable success. People like Moby's music. But they're also after something else, something more personal. It's one of those labels, a very specific one. The description that intrigues people the most isn't related to the genre-hopping music or the vegetarianism or the left-leaning political statements. Those get plenty of airtime, but read any interview with the artist and you're guaranteed to find one question without fail: the Jesus query.

So...I've heard you're a Christian.
What does it mean to be a Christian vegan?
What role does your Christianity play in your career?

Once Moby admitted to loving Jesus, that was it. Love for Christ became Moby's headless bat. But there's more to him than the Jesus angle, of course.

THE HISTORICAL MOBY

The first thing you should know is that Moby is reputedly the great-great-grandnephew of Herman Melville, author of high school literary staple *Moby Dick*. That's where the name comes from—Melville's mysterious creation, an elusive beast pursued by a deranged sea captain and his harpoon. Born Richard Melville Hall on September 11, 1965, in Harlem, he was apparently nicknamed at birth in homage to his ancestor's white whale. Two years later, his father, James Hall, was killed in an alcohol-related car wreck, after which Moby moved with his mother, Elizabeth, to Danbury, Connecticut.

Mom was a working-class hippie, and she raised her son to embrace creativity. Elizabeth Hall smoked pot, painted, and hung out with artists and musicians. She took Moby to concerts, clubs, communes, and, in 1969, to San Francisco for the Summer of Love. The emphasis on creativity stuck: Moby was taking guitar lessons by age thirteen and, a couple years later, began writing music for his own new wave/punk band, The Vatican Commandoes. By the time he graduated Darien (Connecticut) High School in 1983, the Vatican Commandoes had released their first record, *Hit Squad for God*. According to Moby's self-scribed bio at Moby-Online.com, he got his first four-track cassette recorder around the same time. "This is when I realized that I could finish songs by myself and that I didn't need to be so reliant upon other musicians."[3]

More than anything else, that recognition seems to have been a major turning point in Moby's musical development. He gravitated to New York's house music scene in the mid- to late-1980s, where he began DJing, crafting electronic music, and shopping around

demo tapes. The first few years were fruitless until Instinct Records, a new label, showed modest attention in 1989. He signed
with them. Soon, Moby had released his first single, "Time's Up,"
under the name The Brotherhood, and was performing regularly
at now-defunct clubs like Mars, the Palladium, MK, and Palace de
Beaute. A handful of other singles followed, released under a number of pseudonyms, one of which was Voodoo Child.

And then there was "Go."

An upbeat techno/house remix of the theme to the 1990-91 television series *Twin Peaks*, "Go" was released as a single in the spring
of 1991. It hit big on the rave scene, landing on the U.K. Top 10
and selling more than a million copies in the United Kingdom.
"And that's when things started to get a little bit crazy," Moby
remembered. "The rave scene was exploding and I was putting out
records that were actually selling well and I was traveling back and
forth to Europe and performing for thousands of kids slathered in
Vick's Vapo Rub® and out of their minds on ecstasy. Needless to
say it was very exciting."[4]

The success in Great Britain attracted a great deal of attention from
the music industry, and Moby soon became a much sought-after
remixer for big-name artists, including Michael Jackson, Depeche
Mode, the Pet Shop Boys, and the B-52s. A succession of American
tours with the Shamen, Orbital, and Prodigy followed.

By the time he released his major-label debut *Everything Is Wrong*
in 1995, Moby had developed a loyal cult following as an icon of
the rave scene, an internationally acclaimed producer, and the
pioneering little white bald face of techno. A collection of house,
trance, and slow near-acoustic cuts interspersed by brief forays into
hardcore and thrash punk, *Everything Is Wrong* made *Spin* magazine's list of the Best 20 albums of 1995 and landed Moby a spot on
the Lollapallooza tour. But there was a caveat: The eclectic genre-

blending of *Everything* annoyed the dance community who had earlier embraced him. It wouldn't be the first time Moby irritated a loyal fan base.

Regardless, *Everything Is Wrong* introduced Moby to an entirely new set of admirers. So naturally, he bewildered them by going bipolar with his next release, 1997's *Animal Rights*. Harsh, guitar-driven, and heavy on the speedcore and industrial grunge (to which was attached a handful of ambient instrumentals at the end), the album was alternately hailed as a return to Moby's punk roots and dismissed as the work of a sellout hoping to reserve a seat on the alt-rock bandwagon. Moby paid for the public's ambivalence as the abrasive album—recorded while he was suffering from acute panic attacks—was a bust among critics and fans alike. He was fed up with a techno scene to which he didn't really feel like he belonged and refused to make excuses for the album. "I've always loved heavy guitar stun, whether it was punk rock, speed metal, or old classic heavy metal," he told *EWire*, a BMX freestyle and music 'zine. "When I made *Animal Rights*, in some ways I wasn't thinking of it as a 'rock' record. I was just thinking of it as a record I wanted to make at that time."[5]

The personal nature of the failure, however, pushed him into a period of depression. Life refused to cooperate. On the heels of the album's release, his mother was diagnosed with lung cancer, from which she eventually died. The brief *Animal Rights* tour alienated Moby's core fans. Hoping to hear from the prime minister DJ of techno, they were utterly disappointed to see him strap on a guitar and crank up the reverb. The media wasn't interested, either. On a visit to the U.K. to do press for the album, only two journalists—*two*—showed any interest.[6]

Moby's response was a modest return to the electronic music that had first set his table. Under his old Voodoo Child moniker, he released *The End of Everything*, a soothing orchestral album. Around that same time, he was taking a variety of offers to score major motion pictures, which culminated in *I Like to Score*. This collection of lush, pulsing soundtrack work included music from *Heat* and *The Saint*, as well as a rejected retooling of the James Bond theme for *Tomorrow Never Dies*. Though it encountered moderate success, response was not as high as he'd hoped. For the most part, Moby had been written out of popular music.

He knew it, too. According to *Rolling Stone*, in March of 1999, Moby sat down in Sara Delano Roosevelt Park on New York's Lower East Side and convinced himself he'd blown it in the music business. He had just finished mixing and sequencing a new album of music he enjoyed but which he assumed would be another failure. It was unlike anything else in the marketplace. In an era where prepackaged teenybop boy bands and Britneys were ruling the charts, he had serious doubts about the unconventional music of a thirty-five-year-old. He recalled thinking to himself, "When this record comes out, it will be the end of my career. I should start thinking about what else I can do." He decided then and there, sitting near a bunch of weathered playground tire swings, that he would go to school to learn architecture.[7]

That album was 1999's inescapable *Play*. You've heard it.

In the process of creating the album, Moby discovered *Sounds of the South*, a collection of early twentieth-century *a cappella* blues and gospel recordings from folk music historian Alan Lomax. Vocal samples of these earthy, spiritual field recordings became the emotional centerpiece of *Play*. Layered on top of velvety electronica, twinkly piano riffs, and looped hip-hop breakbeats, the innovative sound was hailed by critics but ignored by radio and MTV. So, as he had in the past, Moby poked convention in the eye and turned to Madison Avenue, famously licensing every one of the album's tracks for films, television commercials, and radio ads. The following year, in 2000, songs from *Play* showed up in everything from Nissan and American Express ads to Leonardo DiCaprio's movie *The Beach*. The eclectic album was everywhere, and without knowing it, half the world was grooving to Moby's new millennium beats. (He donated much of what he made from licensing to environmental and humanitarian charities.) Once the public discovered it, *Play* went on to sell more than 12 million copies. No one was more surprised than the artist himself.

His next release, *18*, played it safe. Following the winning formula of *Play*, it immediately achieved his previous success. It featured vintage gospel samples from New Jersey's Shining Light Gospel Choir, as well as new vocals from Angie Stone, MC Lyte, and Sinead O'Connor. Easily one of the most anticipated albums of the year, it rocketed up the charts upon release. After being introduced to the trials of album-to-album genre-hopping, Moby was less willing to experiment with *18*. Moby said the two albums were both motivated by "a desire to make compassionate records that meet a need in someone else's life ... I have records that I love, that come into my life and give me great joy and satisfaction. I want to make records like that."[8]

Ever the populist, he echoed that statement in *Interview* magazine: "I didn't sit down and think to myself, I want to make a record that can reach as many people as possible. I just wanted to make a record that was beautiful and compelling and interesting."[9]

THE RELIGIOUS MOBY

But back to Jesus. What of the shoutouts to the Son of God in his liner notes? What of his devotion to old spirituals and gospel music? What of his reputation as a clean-living Christian?

To Moby, it's just another label based on a sloppy mixture of truth and propaganda, on equal parts conviction and misunderstanding.

"It has to be made clear," he told *L.A. Weekly* in 1999. "I am not a born-again Christian. I am not a Christian by any stretch of the imagination. I am not anything. I don't want to define myself in any way. I don't see why I have to, and I don't see what purpose it serves. I'm not a raver, I'm not a techno kid, I'm not a Christian. I love techno music. I love Christ."[10]

That last declaration—"I love Christ"—has been something Moby's had to explain and explain since he was first embraced by the early house and techno communities, and even moreso once he entered the public consciousness of the Top 40 charts. He detailed his beliefs in-depth on a limited-edition promotional interview CD released in the U.K. in 1996. The question was, "Why does it say on your records 'thanks to Jesus Christ'?"

Moby's answer: "In my own strange way, I'm a Christian, in that I really love Christ, and I think that the wisdom of Christ is the highest, strongest wisdom I've ever encountered, and I think that his description of the human condition is about the best description or understanding of the human condition I've ever encountered. And although I try and live my life according to the teachings of Christ, a lot of times I fall short. I wouldn't necessarily consider myself a Christian in the conventional sense of the word, where I go to church or believe in cultural Christianity, but I really do love Christ and recognize him in whatever capacity as I can understand it as God."[11]

His path to faith is nearly as convoluted as the above description makes it sound. Though raised Presbyterian, Moby told Beliefnet.com his religious background had little or no early influence on him.[12] He admitted to *Rolling Stone* that his first introduction to Christianity was around the time he discovered masturbation: "When I was thirteen was when I first started [masturbating], and I felt so guilty that I thought I would take countermeasures." Those religious "countermeasures," he said, lasted no more than three months. The other pastime was not so quickly surrendered.[13]

A few years later, around the time he became a philosophy student at the University of Connecticut (he dropped out after a year), Moby stumbled into a deeper, less guilt-ridden faith. He lived on his own in a run-down area of Stamford, where the streets were lined with countless storefront churches "in the crappiest buildings with these hand-painted signs."[14] He would walk through the neighborhood on Sunday mornings and listen to the sounds of the gospel choirs radiating from the buildings. Moby described himself as too afraid to go in, but enthralled nonetheless.

That's when he ran headlong into Jesus Christ. "I had a friend who was a youth minister who talked me into reading the New Testament. I read it, and fell in love with Christ and the teachings of Christ, which then left me in the position of, well, how best to incorporate this into my life?"[15] Moby's first reaction was to become what he calls a "conventional conservative Christian"—attending a Congregational church, trying to convert people, reading the Bible. He did his best to conform to the image of what he thought a contemporary Christian ought to be, believing wholeheartedly that he and fellow disciples had cornered the market on truth. Their worldview was absolute; it was faithful and accurate. Everyone else was wrong.

That absolutism eventually faded. By the early nineties, Moby said he "started to see the world for what it is, which is a very complicated place." As much as he loved the person of Christ and was devoted to His teachings of humility, forgiveness, compassion, and peace, he decided he could no longer identify himself as a Christian, "because to call yourself a Christian implies a certainty that I don't have. I think that the world is too old and too complicated for me to say what is right about it and what is wrong. On an ontological level."[16]

What brought about the change? The metaphysics of existence aside, Moby said he dropped the label "Christian" because he didn't like what the term had come to stand for. Specifically it was a reaction to his cumulative perception of fundamentalist Christianity and the growing cultural and political voice of the conservative Religious Right in the 1990s. He came to distrust their black-and-white relationship with an increasingly gray world, compounded with their perceived tendency to turn Christ's moral teachings into heartless moralism. "On a very personal level, I hate the idea of a vindictive God," he told *LA Weekly*, "and I hate the idea of people being punished for their sins, because it's so hard just being human. If life is short and brutish and difficult, how dare the church make people feel bad? People feel bad enough as it is."[17]

Moby was particularly angered by the arrogance and hatred he saw among people who called themselves Christians but displayed few characteristics of the Christ he admired. "Christ said quite specifically, 'judge not lest you be judged.' I challenge the Christian right to work out their own salvation in fear and trembling and not worry about the supposed sins of others," he wrote in an essay from the *Animal Rights* liner notes. "Hate, violence, judgmental-ism, bigotry, homophobia, and misogyny are all ugly things, but for me they're particularly ugly and upsetting when they're attached to the name of Christ, whom I love."[18] More than anything, he became reluctant to be associated with a religious subculture to which he had grown strongly opposed.

Paul Raushenbush, a Beliefnet columnist and college and young adult minister at the Riverside Church in New York City, shares a few common acquaintances with Moby and once interviewed him. In his opinion, Moby is under the impression that calling oneself a Christian requires denying the validity of other beliefs. "I think he has come to the conclusion that people who call themselves 'Christians' allow no shadows of ambiguity, no room for doubt, no acceptance of the idea that Christianity might be a partial term implying a best effort understanding," Raushenbush said, "rather than a whole understanding of the meaning and purpose of life." As a pastor, he believes Moby's conclusion to be misguided—as is the absolute, doubt-free mentality the musician accurately associates with the conservative Christian subculture.[19]

Regardless, Moby has tenaciously held to his devotion to Jesus while remaining dismissive of Christianity and its flaws. He has no interest in Christian culture, no interest in attending church, no interest in the narrow-mindedness he perceives to be part and parcel of the religious aesthetic. But he still loves the teachings of Christ, and the image of Moby the Christian is fixed in the minds of dance fans, techno enthusiasts, and entertainment reporters across the industry. In fact, despite his misgivings, he still adheres to one of Christianity's central tenets: "Oh, I pray all the time," he told Beliefnet. "My prayers are pretty simple and I have to say that they are usually answered. A lot of times quite specifically too." And they're always qualified, he said, "by the idea of God's will be done and not mine."[20]

THE PHILOSOPHICAL MOBY

To say Moby has opinions is to say the ocean has water. Download an online interview, open up a CD jacket, thumb through a magazine, and you'll be treated to Moby's thoughts on countless causes, societal offenses, and a cornucopia of other subjects. Moby's a thinker, and he wants you to know what he's thinking.

On international politics: "As compassionate citizens we need to be adamantly intolerant of regimes that openly and intentionally victimize segments of their populations. Institutional racism, prejudice, homophobia, anti-Semitism, and hate of any kind, are, at the risk of sounding absolutist, always intolerable."[21]

On the aesthetics of vegetarianism: "Vegan food is nice to look at. Compare a plate with grains and fruits and vegetables to a plate with pigs' intestines, chicken legs, and chopped up cows' muscles. So that's pretty much why I'm a vegan."[22]

On the rights of animals: "Animals are sentient creatures with their own wills, and it seems wrong to force our will onto another creature just because we're able to."[23]

On alternative lifestyles: "When conservatives trot out their litany of evils—homosexuality, single-parent families, multiculturalism, etc., I'm always left asking 'why?' If people are happy being gay then what's wrong with that? It may be a lifestyle that's aesthetically different from what we've been brought up with, but so what?"[24]

Moby used to consider himself a Marxist. Moby has an honest appetite for porn and an appreciation for the flesh industry. In Moby's opinion, Creed sucks.

Moby will tell you what he thinks.

But to his credit, he has backed off from his most dogmatic statements in recent years. More than anything else, you'll now hear him espouse the virtues of ambiguity. He qualifies most statements now with a disclaimer: He's the first to admit to not having all the answers. In fact, he's on record as saying, if he had it to do over again, he'd be inclined to change the name of his first album *Everything Is Wrong* to *Everything Is Complicated.* The former title, it seems, was too inflexible. "As I get older, I just see the world as being a lot more ambiguous. When I was younger, I saw things in very black-and-white terms. I tended to be very arrogant and didactic—I don't see things that way anymore."[25]

Moby the Militant has matured into Moby the Impartial. Moby the Even-Handed. Moby the Neutral.

The universe is incomprehensibly huge and old, he has been fond of saying, and he's just a teeny white bald guy working from a flawed understanding of the way things work and three meager decades of existence. Who is he, then, to make assumptions about anything? To take seriously the limited perspective of any one spiritual tradition, or philosophical viewpoint, or outlook on God? His new, all-encompassing ideology has wrapped itself around the ideals of tolerance, combining them with a strangely satisfying acceptance of uncertainty. He has embraced this newly open-minded philosophy as thoroughly as he embraced the intolerance of his past.

"There is no way on this planet that any human being can be right and not wrong," he explained to Beliefnet. "When it comes to animal-rights activists dealing with people who own fur shops, rather than antagonize them, why not talk to them and learn from them? When pro-life and pro-choice people fight each other, why not get together and talk and discover your common things and learn about the opposite side? Because there's no position that's right—every position embodies elements that are right and wrong."[26]

THE REAL MOBY

There's a memorable story in ancient Celtic lore about the birth of Taliesin, the legendary Welsh bard. It is said that Taliesin was once a young peasant boy by the name of Gwion Bach. Given an important mystical task by the goddess Ceridwen, Gwion fails at it, and in doing so, unintentionally achieves knowledge of infinity. This infuriates the goddess, who immediately sets after the boy in hot pursuit. Gwion runs. At one point in his escape, he internally visualizes a rabbit scampering to safety. Suddenly and magically, he becomes a rabbit. To keep up, Ceridwen uses her supernatural powers to turn herself into a greyhound. Gwion takes a chance and, leaping boldly into the water, becomes a fish. Ceridwen remains on his trail, assuming the form of an otter. Gwion becomes a crow, then Ceridwen a hawk, matching her prey at each transformative step. Finally, she catches him and digs her talons into the crow's back. So Gwion changes one last time. He becomes a grain of wheat and falls through the clutching talons to the ground. Ceridwen responds by taking the form of a black hen. She pecks and scratches at the ground until, finally, she finds the grain of wheat. In an act of fury, she swallows the grain. It grows and grows in her stomach until, nine months later, a beautiful, talented baby is born. The goddess names him Taliesin.

At times it seems as if Moby, like the shape-shifting child Gwion, is constantly on the run from a society intent on attaching a label to him. Time after time, as the labels threaten to catch up with him, to trap him within a narrow musical and artistic definition, he changes his persona and slips away. The labels change with him and relentlessly follow. Moby lives in a labelmaking world. It keeps assigning him new identities because he keeps shattering the old ones.

An electronic music icon who plays live instruments all over his albums. A sold-out animal rights advocate who refuses to lend his famous name to the public protest. A vegan whose carnivorous friends don't concern him. A former Marxist who is comforted by the money he's made. A techno kid whose dance fans are mad at him, a thrash guitarist whose punk fans are annoyed with him, an ambient genius whose devotees think he's a sellout.

A self-described lover of Christ who can't stand the idea of Christianity.

So, who is he? Who is Moby? Which persona is the true Richard Melville Hall? The answer is as complicated as his discography: Maybe the identities are *all* true. Maybe he's all of them.

"A part of me is envious of people who can define themselves strictly and conveniently, but for myself, I just can't," he said. "My sense of identity is there, but it's sort of nebulous."[27]

To know the artist, you must understand his art. To get to know Moby, look closely at his music. *Everything Is Wrong* was a perfect blend of house and techno, *Animal Rights* a scandalous speedcore and punk guitar album with a final thirty minutes of gloomy in-strumentals. *The End of Everything*, under his Voodoo Child alias, was a light, ambient collection of electronica. *I Like to Score* fea-tured television and film soundtracks. *Play* and *18* layered archived blues and gospel voices over a textured hip-hop sound.

The real Moby is a musical schizo. He has musical multiple-person-ality disorder, and he won't apologize. "My approach to music is my approach to a lot of things—open," he says. "It's not intentional genre-hopping. It's just that I like *everything* ... Why pick when the world is so filled with interesting stuff? Why limit yourself?"[28]

He has applied that same approach to religion and ended up with a low-key Christ-centered spirituality that remains, as stated above, quite open. "I'm certainly not encouraging anyone to follow any one spiritual tradition," he has said in the past. Nor is he eager to tack any degree of certainty to his religious leanings. The most you'll get from him is this: "From my perspective, good spiritual practice involves humility and compassion. And hopefully a degree of lightheartedness ... You know human beings are f----ups. I find it really difficult to take ourselves too seriously when we are like a bunch of idiot puppies."[29]

And despite the militancy in his past—the attempts to convert people into Christians, or into animal rights activists, or vegans, or pacifists—Moby seems to have embraced humility and ambigu-ity more than anything else. He's got his beliefs, you're entitled to yours, and if they don't match, so be it.

1. Lawrence Ferber, "Hardboiled Wonderland: Moby's Electronic Overtures for Sentient Beings," *L.A. Weekly*, June 18-24, 1999.
2. Rex Rutkoski, "In Search of His Own Artistic 'Great Whale': The Many Sides of Moby," *The Inside Connection*, *http://www.insidecx.com/interviews/archive/moby.html*. Viewed Feb. 10, 2003.
3. Moby, "Moby Bio: In His Words," Moby-Online.com, *http://www.moby-online.com/bio/bio.html*. Viewed Feb. 13, 2003.
4. "Moby Bio: In His Words," Moby-Online.com.
5. Ken Switzer, "Moby," *EWire*, *http://www.ewirezine.com/music/moby/moby-1.html*. Viewed March 7, 2003.
6. That's why Moby seems to have supplied interviews to virtually anyone who has asked, from *GQ* to *Better Homes & Gardens*. As a result of the miserable U.K. press experience, Moby vowed to never complain about media coverage. He discovered the alternative to tons of interviews—an absolute lack of interest—to be devastating.
7. David Fricke, "Moby's Homemade Heaven," RollingStone.com, *http://www.rollingstone.com/news/newsarticle.asp?nid=15904&cf=1603*, Posted May 14, 2002.
8. Ibid.
9. Neil Strauss, "Moby," *Interview*, July 2000, 53.
10. Ferber, *L.A. Weekly*, June 18-24, 1999.
11. Audio interview, *Animal Rights* U.K. CD promo, 1996.
12. Paul Raushenbush, "A Talk with Moby," Beliefnet, *http://www.beliefnet.com/story/23/story_2346.html*. Viewed Feb. 27, 2003.
13. Mim Udovitch, "Q&A: Moby," *Rolling Stone*, March 2-9, 2000. 42.
14. Fricke, "Moby's Homemade Heaven," RollingStone.com.
15. Raushenbush, "A Talk with Moby," Beliefnet.
16. Ibid.
17. Ferber, *L.A. Weekly*, June 18-24, 1999.
18. Moby, untitled essay from the liner notes to *Animal Rights*, 1995.
19. Paul Raushenbush, Personal Interview, February 20, 2003.
20. Raushenbush, "A Talk with Moby," Beliefnet.
21. Moby, untitled essay from the liner notes to *Play*, 1999. The liner notes to Moby's albums, incidentally, don't contain printed lyrics but philosophical essays by the artist. An intellectual thinker and decent writer, he holds forth on a number of subjects, from animal rights to the treatment of prisoners to the benefits of vegetarianism. "These essays are not really related to the music," he wrote for *Play*. "So if you hate the essays you might still like the music, and if you like the essays you might hate the music. Who knows, maybe by some bizarre twist of fate you'll like them both."
22. Ibid.
23. Ibid.
24. Moby, untitled liner notes essay, *I Like to Score*, 1997.
25. Mike Bederka, "Moby Interview," Nada Mucho, *http://www.nadamucho.com/features/Mody062999.htm*. Viewed March 9, 2003.
26. Raushenbush, "A Talk with Moby," Beliefnet.
27. Ferber, *L.A. Weekly*, June 18-24, 1999.
28. Ibid.
29. Raushenbush, "A Talk with Moby," Beliefnet.

THE GOSPEL OF LOVE

By Steve Beard

The small 45-rpm record player had been catapulted through the air like a cannonball from the front door. The shattered fate of the turntable was soon joined by a stack of Jackie Wilson and James Brown records. Only moments before, eighteen-year-old Al Green was sneaking a listen to "A Woman, A Lover, A Friend." Of course, he had known that this kind of "devil music" was forbidden in the house. Nevertheless, he found himself singing along to Wilson's sultry ballad until the bedroom door flew open and his father stood tall above him. The next sound he heard was the long, cat-like screech of a needle scratching across his favorite record.

Shortly after his record player met its untimely demise, his father tossed his clothes in a cardboard box and threw him out of the house as his mother looked on in tears. "The day I came to him to ask forgiveness for my wicked ways and submit to the authority God had given him as head of the household would be the day I'd be welcomed back, like the prodigal son, beneath his roof," Green remembered. "But until that day, I would have to find out for myself the wages of my sin and the terrible price of my disobedience."[1]

Of course, the story of the prodigal son that Jesus told did not include Jackie Wilson or James Brown. Nor, did it feature a furious father or a record player smashed to bits. Nevertheless, as the story of Al Green unfolds, one can detect a connection.

When Elvis Costello was asked if he had ever had a religious experience, he responded: "No, but I have heard Al Green."[2] *Rolling Stone* has declared that Al Green is "the greatest popular singer of all time," describing his songs as "unsurpassed in their subtlety, grace, intimacy and invention."[3] In a recent issue of *GQ*, the number thirteen reason for you to leave a woman is if she "doesn't know the difference between Al Green and Al Jazeera"—a reference to the infamous Middle Eastern television network.[4]

Green rose to international fame with timeless hits such as "Let's Stay Together," "Call Me," "Take Me To The River," "I'm Still In Love With You," "Tired of Being Alone," and "Love and Happiness." His eclectic collection of covers included The Doors' "Light My Fire," the Beatles' "I Wanna Hold Your Hand," and the Bee Gees' "How Can You Mend A Broken Heart." In the early 1970s, he was the Prince of Love, the man with the trademark smile that made women swoon in near-riotous concerts as he tossed long stem red roses to adoring fans.

"Al Green seems bound to earth not by gravity, but rather by will—a commitment he's made—as if he's from another plane and is defined to us by where our life and his intersect, a realm illuminated by his voice," wrote historian Robert Gordon.[5] That voice scored him more than fifteen top ten singles. In just a handful of years, Green had sold 35 million albums worldwide, eight gold singles, and six gold albums.

Like many great artists before and after him, Green wrestled with the sacred and the profane, the flesh and the spirit, the holy and the hedonistic. He comes from a lineage of other phenomenal black artists such as Sam Cooke, Marvin Gaye, and Aretha Franklin who grew up in the church, cutting their teeth on hymns and spirituals. "Anybody can tell you that all the great soul singers learned their best licks in the choir loft, that the church is the mother of R&B and the grandmother of rock 'n' roll," Green said. "But no one can tell you the pain of having the choice between lifting up your voice for God or taking a bow for your third encore. That's something you have to experience for yourself."[6]

While growing up in Arkansas, the family attended two nearby churches—The Church of the Living God, known for its dignity and decorum, and Taylor's Chapel, a "certified, spirit-drenched, twenty-four-hour-a-day Pentecostal salvation station," as Green described it. "You were sure the roof was going to lift off and the heavenly host descend to see what all the commotion was about," he recalled.[7]

"I never did develop a preference for one church over the other," he said. "To me, shouting at the top of your lungs while hammering on a tambourine or whispering your prayers as the organ softly played were just two different ways of saying the same thing: *We're all down here, Lord, doing the best we can.*"[8] The church has always played an influential role within the African-American community. "Church is so important for black people because it's the only place we had to go when we couldn't go no place else," he said. "Couldn't go to the bar—wasn't allowed. Couldn't go to the hotel because we weren't able to rent a room. Couldn't go to the restaurant because we weren't allowed to be seated. So we went to church."[9]

Robert and Cora Greene (Al later dropped the "e" from his last name) supported ten children as sharecroppers. Robert had visions of his family travelling on the gospel music circuit, with his boys singing for the Lord. He wanted something better for his clan and hoped that their voices would pull them out of their dependence on the back-breaking, paltry-paying farm work they were doing. When the family moved to Michigan in search of an improved life, the boys began to get invitations to sing in churches. Their father drove them to nearby states for concerts hoping that their success would lift the fortunes of the family.

When they were not out singing, the Greenes could be found on Sunday mornings at Mother Bate's House of Prayer. She made a tremendous impression on the mind of a young Al. "I learned more of what true faith is all about just by watching Mother Bates," he said. "There was no derelict drunkard so lost he didn't deserve a good meal; no ratty and worn-out streetwalker too forlorn to reach with a loving touch; no chip on the shoulder of a tough kid that wouldn't melt at her words of love or the promise of her prayers."[10]

While Green loved church and singing gospel, he also had an ear for the pop sound that was being played on the radio. "I could appreciate Elvis for that smooth-as-silk delivery and the way he could moan and croon and hiccup his way through a song...," Green said. "I liked Fats Domino for that rolling barrelhouse style that sounded like it was coming up out of the floorboards, and I always got a kick out of Little Richard, shrieking and wailing like he'd stuck his finger in a light socket. And naturally, I loved Otis Redding and Sam Cooke for the way they could wring longing and loneliness out of every last note."[11]

Green's father knew the siren song of the devil—all too well, perhaps. As a young boy, Green remembered his father saying, "Now, don't tell your mama," as he would slip off into some seedy juke joint by the side of the road, leaving the boy to sit in the car while his father listened to the down-and-dirty blues. "Daddy wasn't about to let me loose to scorch my ears with the sound of hell's own house band," remembered Green. "In the days since his secret—and not-so-secret—visits to the local honky-tonk, daddy had gotten steadily more strict and set in his ways. And to his way of thinking, there was God's music and the devil's music, nothing in between and no two ways about it."[12]

That clash culminated on that fateful day when the boy was thrown from his father's house. Like the record player smashed on the sidewalk, dreams of the family travelling on the gospel music highway were irreparably destroyed.

PIMPIN' IN THE DARKNESS

Out from under the roof of his father, Green was free to pursue his own vision of a singing career with a group who enjoyed local success. Music was not the only thing he began to experiment with out on his own. At the age of twenty, he fell in love with a beautiful woman named Juanita—a prostitute ten years his senior. Their relationship "took on every kind of variation you could imagine: from mother and son, to father and daughter, to pimp and whore," he recalled. "At any given time, I was her lover, her 'pretty little boy,' and her confessor. In the same way, she would play the role of the daughter, the breadwinner, or the hardworking mother who only wanted to have her feet rubbed at the end of a busy day."[13]

Green energetically plunged into the darkside of the underbelly of Grand Rapids, Michigan. "My family, the church and most of the time even the light of day became a memory as she and I prowled the streets after dark, working the clubs and dark alleys where Juanita plied her trade," he wrote in his autobiography *Take Me To The River*. "I could tell you how to run a profitable three-card monte scam or how to load a pair of dice so that no one would ever catch on ... I could tell you the going price for a bag of weed just by smelling it or how your cocaine had been cut with a taste on the tip of my pinkie," he remembered. "I knew the best techniques for snorting, skin-popping, and mainlining, could show you how to raise a vein and keep your kit clean. And if you couldn't afford the good stuff, I knew every cheap high under the sun, from rug lacquer to airplane glue, nutmeg to cigarettes soaked in formaldehyde."[14]

He was also a quick study of his lover's clientele. "I could tell you the sexual preference of each regular customer, which prosperous white businessman liked to dress up in women's underwear and which one liked to be tied up while Juanita talked sass and dropped cigarette ashes on his head," he stated matter of factly. "The simple truth was, in that first year with Juanita, I learned more about the dark and depraved side of the human animal than I care to pass along. Those are memories that have a left a scar on my soul, one I'd rather keep to myself."[15]

Women would always play a disproportionately important role in Al Green's life. They loved him, and he loved them. "In my mind, Juanita will always occupy a place in my life directly opposite from, but equally important to Mother Bates," he observed. "They are like two magnetic poles, forces that kept me in balance between them, the one calling me to the purity of the faith, the other to the pleasures of the flesh. I make no judgment, nor do I cast any condemnation. As Mother Bates was born to her work, so was Juanita, and if circumstances had been a little different for either one of them, they might have found themselves in switched places." Looking back on this time in his life, he wrote: "I loved Juanita, as purely and simply as I ever loved Mother Bates, and I thank God for the day He brought her into my life."[16]

SOUL MATES

Al Green and his band, the Soul Mates, experienced their first R&B hit with "Back Up Train" in early 1968 (the same year that Otis Redding scored with "Dock of the Bay"). It was playing on the radio throughout the Great Lakes region that served as the band's homebase. The song even landed them a coveted spot at the Apollo Theater in Harlem. "For a black entertainer, there *was* no more legendary venue, and you can throw Carnegie Hall, the Royal Albert Hall, and any other hall you might care to name onto that list," he said. "It was Mecca, Jerusalem, and the Promised Land all rolled into one, for generations of great stars from the Golden Age of Jazz right down to today, when any hip-hopper or rapper on his way up has got to make a scheduled stop on that fabled stage."[17] The notoriously hard-to-please crowd loved them, calling the Soul Mates back for an unprecedented nine encores.

Despite that magical evening, the Soul Mates slowly began to grow apart and Green went out on his own, touring the "chitlin' circuit"—a group of small, dive-like clubs—off the notoriety of "Back Up Train." Spinning his wheels off the fumes of one hit, a disheveled Green found himself in a Midland, Texas, roadhouse singing as the warm-up act for a successful producer and trumpeter named Willie Mitchell who was touring off the strength of his instrumental hit "Soul Serenade."

Mitchell was a smooth operator and a class act with a thin moustache hugging his upper lip. He nursed his drink at the bar as he heard Green warm-up and thought to himself, "This guy has got the style, he got the sound to really be something." He grabbed a phone and called up the owner of Hi Records, Joe Cuoghi, and said, "I found a singer down here, and I want to bring him back to Memphis."

Mitchell had a reputation for discovering artists—being a fixture in the Memphis music scene and having worked with legends B.B. King and Isaac Hayes. He kept an ear open to find new talent for record companies such as Sun, Stax, and Chips. "Why don't you come on back to Memphis with me?" Mitchell asked. "You can be a star." Al asked how long that would take and Mitchell told him about a year and a half. "I really can't wait that long," he replied.

At the end of the evening, both acts got stiffed by the owner. Out of money, and with no way to get back to Michigan, Green asked Mitchell if he could hitch a ride in his eight-passenger van in order to at least get a little closer to home. Green sat on the hump as they made the long trek to Memphis. As they drove through the night, Green said, "You really think I could be a star?" Mitchell assured him that it was possible with hard work and determination.

In a fit of presumption, bravado, or providence, Green asked if he could get an advanced loan in order to pay off some debts back in Michigan. "I could come to Memphis, and we could really do it," said Green. Despite the fact that Mitchell had only met the singer for the first time the night before, he agreed. Once they got to Memphis, Mitchell gave him $1,500 without a contract (the loan was made possible by Cuoghi of Hi Records—the smartest investment ever made). Green was supposed to have returned to Memphis the following week but he never showed up. Mitchell forgot about him, being consumed with his other projects. "I was at home one morning about six o'clock, and somebody hit on my door—this is almost two months later," remembered Mitchell. He was having his house painted and thought that the workers had arrived early. "Why y'all come to paint so early?" The man at the door said, "Don't you remember me? I'm Al Green."[18]

That chance meeting in a Texas roadhouse ended up becoming one of the most fruitful collaborations in musical history. Al Green had watched the Soul Mates slip through his fingers but in the process discovered a soul man who would take him to the top. Based out of Royal Recording Studio, Al would become the mouthpiece that would shape soul music with the legendary Hi Rhythm Section made up of Al Jackson, Howard Grimes, and the Hodges brothers—Teenie, Charles, and Leroy—under the directorial genius of Mitchell.

In his magisterial book *Sweet Soul Music*, Peter Guralnick described the collaboration as "a muted string section, soft sophisticated melody with a gospel twist...and the unique coloration of Al Green's voice(s), given free rein for the first time in all their fragile intertwined glory, wherein falsetto interpolations meet the last refined tendrils of religious ecstasy."[19] All of that is an elegant way to say something beautiful emerged.

"It's the laziness of the rhythm," Mitchell remarked. "You hear those old lazy horns half a beat behind the music, and you think they're gonna miss it, and all of a sudden, just so lazy, they come in and start to sway with it. It's like kind of shucking you, putting you on."[20]

Mitchell told Green, "We got to soften you up some. You got to whisper. You got to cut the lighter music. The melody has got to be good. You got to sing it soft. If we can get the dynamic bottom on it and make some sense with pretty changes, then we going to be there." Incredulously, Green responded, "Man, I can't sing that way. That's too soft. That ain't gonna sound like no man singing."[21] They bickered about the advice but "Let's Stay Together" convinced Green that Mitchell knew what he was talking about. Although Green was skeptical of the direction of the song, it was gold in two weeks, knocking Don McLean's "American Pie" from its reign at number one.

"Slow it down," Mitchell would say. "Soften it up. *Feel* what you're singing." He would have the rhythm section encircle him and say, "See, let *them* be gritty. You be smooth. Remember, Al. It's silky on top. Rough on the bottom."[22]

Guralnick said that a gospel singer is "often described as 'worrying' the audience, teasing it, working the crowd until it is on the verge of exploding, until strong men faint and women start speaking in tongues. This is commonly referred to as 'house wrecking.'"[23] In the studio, Green perfected the fine art of wreckin' the house.

His silky smooth voice was coupled with stage charisma, sex appeal, and undeniable charm. In 1972, he was *Rolling Stone*'s rock star of the year. In 1973, *Billboard*, *Cashbox*, and *Record World* unanimously named Green the top vocalist based on the success of his singles. He dressed the part and waved the long stem roses like a magic wand. Green provocatively pranced about in feathers, rabbit fur coats, brightly colored paisley prints, gold chains, pinky rings, and the highest pair of platform shoes money could buy.

"They say that clothes make the man, but I say God made the man," Green said. "He just left the decorating up to us."[24]

He was the consummate ladies' man. His voice was a liquid calling card, wooing the listener into a sensuous and lush boudoir of his own creation. "Al Green was a dream to them, a voice they heard on the radio, singing about all the romance and the passion that was missing from their own lives," he said. "I was nothing more than the sum of my songs, those three-minute pop tunes that could make them feel special by just closing their eyes and pretending it was them—and them alone—I was singing to. They were as hungry for love as I was—and just as ignorant about where to find it."[25]

SCREAMIN' HALLELUJAH!

At the height of his fame, Green was playing the Cow Palace in San Francisco, sharing the bill with Smokey Robinson in the summer of 1973. He flew to Anaheim, California, on a plane sent by Disney for his next show. When he got to the hotel, he told his girlfriend that he was tired and headed off to bed. "I'll see you in the morning," he said as he retreated to his room in the suite.

Shortly after four in the morning, everything changed. "I couldn't have been asleep more than a hour or two when I was suddenly awakened by the sound of shouting," he said. "I sat bolt upright in bed, frightened that some crazy fan had broken into the room." He then realized that the commotion he was hearing was coming from his own mouth. "And while the words I shouted were of no earthly tongue, I immediately recognized what they meant. I was praising God, rejoicing in the great and glorious gift of salvation through His son, Jesus Christ, and lifting my voice to heaven with the language of angels to proclaim His majesty on high."[26]

He laughed. He cried. He tried to cover his mouth with a rolled up towel. "I was knocking on doors of the hotel, telling complete strangers I'd been born again," Green said. "Some lady slammed the door in my face, I went to the next door and said, 'I been born again!' They called security."[27]

The Apostle Paul was accosted and converted by Jesus on the Road to Damascus, Al Green was made righteous off Interstate 5 near Disneyland. Moses had his encounter with God at Mt. Sinai. Al Green came face to face with Yahweh under the shadow of the Matterhorn.

Although he was alone in his room, he responded to a voice that was distinct and piercing: "Are you ashamed of Me?" It rocked him to his core. "Lord, no!" Green shouted. "No!" he screamed again. That is when his girlfriend began pounding on his door asking him if he was alright. He flung open the door and shouted, "I am not ashamed of the Lord Jesus Christ! I am not ashamed of His Gospel!"

Of course, this was not exactly what one would expect as the aftereffects of an evening's performance at the Cow Palace and a little champagne on the plane. "Whatever it was that I knew of God and His love up until that moment—all the sermons I'd heard preached and all the gospel songs I'd sung and all the times I seen folks weeping and wailing as they made their way to lay down their lives at the altar of Mother Bates's revival tent—all that faded into insignificance," he remembered. "I was in the middle of a personal encounter, one on one with my Creator and now, at last, I understood what all the words and all the songs and all the tears had really meant."[28]

Green distinctly recalled God telling him, "Whatever it is, you honor me. You hold up the Light. You be a light." When his father was awakened by all the commotion (they had since reconciled and he was working and travelling with his son), Al thrust his hands under his father's nose. "Look, Daddy! Look at my hands! And my feet, Daddy."

"What is it, son?" the elder Greene asked. "What's wrong with your hands and feet?" "Can't you see?" Green answered, the tears pouring from his eyes. "They're brand-new! All of me is brand-new!"[29]

WHAT NOW?

Conversion or not, Al Green had obligations—contracts to fulfill, records to make, and a staff to support. This was hardly a convenient time to "get saved." He returned to the road, trying to reconcile what had taken place and how it fit into his career. He knew he wanted to live for God, he just didn't know how. "I'd be up in front of a sold-out crowd, singing 'Let's Stay Together' or 'For the Good Times,' and suddenly, right in the middle of the number, I'd break out in a long and heartfelt passage of Scripture. The audience would kind of rock back all at the same time, like they were bowled over by a shock."[30] You can imagine. It happened when Bob Dylan sang gospel and when Cat Stevens abandoned his career to follow Islam. For Green's fans, it was stunning.

It should be noted that even when he was posing for albums barechested, his spiritual longings tried to find life in his music. "God Is Standing By" is found on his 1971 *Al Green Gets Next To You*, "My

God Is Real" is on the 1972 *Livin' For You*, and "Jesus Is Waiting" is on the 1973 *Call Me*.

"My spiritual beliefs were as much a part of the records I made in the '70s as they are a part of what I'm doing now," he told the *Los Angeles Times* in 1989. "My audience today isn't as big as it was during the '70s, but the concentration is heavier. It's like the difference between regular and premium gas—you get better mileage with gospel. 'Baby come shake your thing, let's shake our thing together'—that's great fun, but with gospel you're talking about something with substance that means something to people who already shook their thing and left that behind."[31]

Green was singing about love and happiness, but there was a war going on inside—a battle for the substance of his soul. "When that siren song of worldly fame and fortune calls, it's not just temptation we have to wrestle with," he said. "It's that nagging voice in the back of our brains, telling us we've betrayed our calling and commission. Sam Cooke, Aretha Franklin, James Brown, Marvin Gaye—the list goes on and on, each one of them facing that dark night of the soul when they must make that choice between the things of God and the lures of the devil."[32]

Al Green knew the taste of fame, he rode in the chauffeur-driven Rolls Royce of success. Looking back on it now, he said, "You know you're in trouble the first time you step out onto a stage with the light shining down and the audience all hushed and ready and willing to believe anything you tell them. That's the moment when the devil steps forward, pulls out that parchment scroll and quill pen, and points to the dotted line."[33]

For all the material benefits of fame, he also experienced the loneliness of stardom, trying to drown it out with his many female friends—some of them were wonderful companions and confidants. Others were not. A year after his dramatic conversion, Green experienced one of the most horrific and bizarre tragedies at the hands of one very disturbed admirer. He had grown attracted to Mary Woodson from the first time that they met. She had prophetic premonitions about Al's life—telling him that he would become a preacher and have a church. "You're going to preach wonderful sermons that will turn the hearts of many," she would tell him. "When you preach in your church, will you save a seat up front for me?" she would ask.

On the evening of October 18, 1974, she was one of the guests in his twenty-one-room mansion. As he was returning from showing another female friend to a guest room he walked past the kitchen and saw Mary boiling water. "Al, honey, have you ever thought of getting married?" she asked. "Married? Maybe we should talk about this in the morning, baby."

"You know Al, I would never do anything to hurt you," she said. The conversation was becoming stranger by the minute. With that, he excused himself to draw a bath. He was washing his face, when all of a sudden he felt this "excruciating pain, and water or something flies all over the place," he said. "In the next second, my world exploded into a thousand splatters of pure agony. Woodson had added grits to the water, making a thick, boiling hot paste. With all her strength, she hurled it at me, splashing the bathroom walls and scorching my naked back. The pain was so intense that I wasn't sure what was happening for a moment before I heard screaming." The screaming was his own.

Moments later a shot rang out while Green was being attended to by the other houseguest and his bodyguard. Woodson had ended her own life in the next room with a .38 caliber revolver.[34]

Understandably, Green took several months off to recuperate from the third-degree burns on his back that required skin graft surgeries. He prayed, read his Bible, and went back to the studio. He was not off the charts for long. *Al Green is Love* was released in 1975 and the song "L-O-V-E" went straight to the top. The success was there but the vibe was not the same. The times were changing and disco was all the rage. Soul music was losing ground to the beat of Studio 54. The world may have been sucked into the *Saturday Night Fever*, but Al Green was being beckoned to Sunday morning fervor.

"I ran for three years. I went away," he told *Rolling Stone*. "I did me some fasting and praying. I rented a cabin next to a stream. No phone, no TV, no Coca-Cola. I didn't eat for forty days. 'Lord, what are you trying to do to me?' And then I bought me a church, and I started the ministry, in 1976."[35] Of course, he is referring to the Full Gospel Tabernacle in Memphis.

In 1977, Green released *Belle*. The title track laid the foundation with the lyrics: *It's you that I want/ But Him that I need.* Writing in *Rolling Stone*, noted music critic Marcus Greil observed that Green "joins a long line of rock & roll want/need oppositionists—from Bob Dylan with 'Memphis Blues Again' to the Rolling Stones with 'You Can't Always Get What You Want,' to name only the best. He leaves them behind in his attempt to resolve the contradiction: Green tries to get Belle to accept Jesus, too." Greil fawns over the song "All n All," saying that it "carries a sense of liberation and purpose deep enough to make the sinner envy the saved." He also makes a key observation regarding Green's subtlety in mixing his newly expressed faith and his music. "Its subject matter—God's grace, and how good it (It?) feels—isn't pushed; there's no ad for Green's ministry on the back cover."[36]

For the next several years, Green preached in Memphis on Sundays and toured the country throughout the week. In 1979, he accidentally fell off a stage in Cincinnati and barely avoided serious injury. Green interpreted the horrific incident as a sign from God. "I wasn't moving toward God fast enough. The fall was God's way of saying I had to hurry up."[37] From that point on, he devoted his singing to gospel music and turning his back on the songs that had made him rich and famous. His 1981 album *The Lord Will Make A Way* was a demarcation point for his turn to strictly sanctified recordings. "This is a good album by secular or sacred standards," wrote Carol Flake in the *Village Voice*. "Which gives me the chance to say that I'm tired of critics complaining that when an artist 'gets religion,' it's curtains for his creativity. When Al Green goes to the river as preacher rather than lover, in search for some imperishable bliss, when he goes to the backwaters of gospel rather than mainstream R&B, I say amen."[38]

One should not be surprised. His voice is one of the most powerful wooing forces on the planet, whether he is drawing a woman into an embrace of love or beckoning the Almighty through praise and worship. "I took what I learned from the rock 'n' roll: the ingenuity, the class, the charisma, the steps, the movement, the hesitation," he observed. "You take all of this that you learn in pop, rhythm & blues, and you use it to your best advantage. But it doesn't give you the fire. You can't create the charisma for fire. Either you have the fire or you don't have the fire, the spiritual fire."[39] Make no mistake about it, The Reverend Green had the fire and he has landed eight Grammy awards for his gospel music to prove it.

For eight years, Green sang only gospel until he had a conversation with God while praying and fasting in the mountains of Trinidad. He said God told him, "I gave you the songs. Those are your songs. I gave them to you in your own heart," Green recalled. "You wrote the music. I gave it to you. Use those songs, sing your songs. People are going to disagree with you—they disagree with me. But while you're singing it what I called you for is to drop a little seed over their head."[40]

In addition to his gospel recordings, Green has occasionally popped up on the radar screen since that time with a top ten duet with Annie Lennox of the Eurythmics performing "Put A Little Love in Your Heart" for the 1988 movie *Scrooged*. In 1994, he won a Grammy for his duet with alt-country singer Lyle Lovett performing "Funny How Time Slips Away" by Willie Nelson. During that same year, "Let's Stay Together" was featured in Quentin Tarantino's *Pulp Fiction* (a large poster from the film actually hangs in Green's private music studio). He was inducted into the Rock and Roll Hall of Fame the following year. In 1999, his version of "How Can You Mend a Broken Heart" was featured on the romantic-comedy *Notting Hill* soundtrack and he landed a recurring role that same year in a handful of *Ally McBeal* episodes. "Let's Stay Together" reemerged once again on the soundtrack of the 2003 comedy *How to Lose A Guy in 10 Days*.

Admittedly, straddling two worlds is not easy—as Green is the first to admit. "I could be up onstage, ready to get funky, when the preacher suddenly arrives. Or I could be in the church, primed for the Holy Ghost, when the soul man shows up," he confessed. "I could be trying to go about my daily routine and the heavens will open wide and reveal the hidden things of God. Or I'll be seeking His face with every fiber of my being and all I'll be seeing in my mind's eye is that woman who happened to pass by while I was waiting for a red light. There's been times I've tried my best to explain some simple thing and find myself talking in tongues and other times when all I want to do is praise God and find myself singing some old blues song instead."[41]

The soul man still puts on the pizzazz with roughly twenty concerts per year in mainstream venues. Resplendent in his white suit, Ray Ban sunglasses, and loaded with long stem roses like a florist, he still has the magic to commandeer the human heart, making it pulse in romance or worship—our very own funky St. Valentine. "Now I am comfortable mixing everything up, and my audience has responded favorably," he said. "When I finished a short prayer at this gig ... people stood up and cheered. That told me that I could give audiences a little bit of the Reverend and they'd likely rejoice."[42] He sings *Amazing Grace* in casino showrooms in Las Vegas and Lake Tahoe knowing that many of his admirers hunger for redemption just as he once had.

"I had a crowd of people tonight who ... have a house, more cars than they can drive and a little bit more money than they can spend," he told the *Daily Telegraph* after a 1999 concert in England. "I can understand that. But I had some people there who raised their hand when I did the sinner's prayer. So that's good, because if it's just for one person, it's worth coming. The angels rejoice in heaven for the repenting of one soul."[43]

That is what lures him to the casinos and that is what keeps him in the pulpit. He is an undeniable soul man.

THE MEMPHIS FIRE

Memphis is to popular music what Kitty Hawk, North Carolina, is to aviation. It is the cradle of the world-shaping beat of soul and rock 'n' roll, the distillery of black and white musical moonshine. Elvis, Johnny Cash, Jerry Lee Lewis, and Carl Perkins revolution-ized American culture in the scrappy Sun Studio. Across town, Otis Redding, Carla Thomas, and Booker T. and the MG's first recorded at Stax/Volt records. The city is also the site of two of the most profound tragedies in our nation's pop culture—the murder of the Reverend Martin Luther King Jr. in 1968 and death of the king of rock 'n' roll nine years later. It is a city that knows triumph and tears.

On the legendary Beale Street, B.B. King occasionally holds court at his restaurant, while Isaac Hayes fronts his nightclub a few blocks away. Adoring fans fly into the city from all over the globe to visit Graceland and pay homage to the memory of Elvis. Many of them slide into the pews of the Full Gospel Tabernacle to hear the Reverend Al Green on Sunday mornings.

The unassuming geodesic sanctuary is tucked in on the left side of a quiet residential road, a few miles south of Graceland off Elvis Presley Boulevard. It has played host to a myriad of music fans who make it a part of their Memphis pilgrimage. They stick out like sore thumbs, showing up promptly at 11 A.M. for a service that will not start for another half-hour. One Sunday, they appear from Ireland, Arkansas, Nebraska, Minnesota, North Carolina, and England. A handful of students even show up from the nearby Rhodes College for a religious studies course. When I asked how much they knew about Al Green, one said, "'Love and Happiness,' man."

The visitors are greeted warmly. After all these years, the congregation has become very familiar with the novelty factor involved with having a musical icon behind the pulpit. Nevertheless, they are here to get down with God, not impress the guests (for example, there are none of Green's *Greatest Hits* collections sold in the church lobby). The choir marches in and the B-3 Hammond organ starts to crank up the funk, while the electric guitar starts to wail (one imagines this is what the psalmist had in mind if he would have had electric instruments instead of a harp).

Reverend Al walks around the sanctuary fiddling with his lapel microphone, gently patting visitors on the shoulder as he glides to the back of the sanctuary to adjust his own sound at the mixing board.

Back at the pulpit, Reverend Al is feeling the "unction of the Holy Ghost," as he calls it. He starts to bob and weave like a boxer as he delivers his sermon on faith. "Hold on, God is coming!" he shouts. "Help is on the way," he purrs. When he calls for the assembly to give a wave offering by lifting our arms, you can see the nervousness rise in the visitors. Awkwardly, we wave our arms in the air. Who is going to refuse Reverend Al? "Thank you, Jesus! Thank you, Jesus! Stop looking at Al Green," he says. "Al Green himself came to worship God. He's been soooo good to me," he starts to sing as the musicians key up the volume.

When he starts singing "One Day at a Time, Sweet Jesus," you know you have been to church. "You are not here by accident," he says. "I am the same person you heard sing all those songs, but I am not the same person," he testifies. "I couldn't preach for twenty-five years if something didn't happen to me." Speaking to the visitors with a winsome grin, he says, "Come and see Al, but Al doesn't hold the key to your salvation. I can sing 'Love and Happiness' four times and I still will not hold your salvation." I grin, wondering if the college student caught the remark.

The Reverend closes out the eleven o'clock service at 1:25 P.M. with a soul-felt version of "Gonna Sit Down on the Banks of the River" by the blues legend the Reverend Gary Davis. He leaves us at the banks, and the decision is ours. Shall we jump in or walk away? You can tell what Green has done. You can see it in his eyes, in his smile, in the intonations of his honey-like voice. Otis Redding died in a plane crash at twenty-six, Sam Cooke was shot at thirty-three, Jackie Wilson's career was over at forty-one, and Marvin Gaye was killed by his father at age forty-four. Al Green is alive—and he is grateful. Somebody shout Amen!

Every Sunday that Reverend Al preaches to his congregation he sees two enormous folk-art style murals on the back wall of his sanctuary. On the left, he sees the portrayal of what theologians call "the rapture" during the second coming. Cars and trucks are overturned on a highway and an airplane crashes into the top of a building while the souls of the departed cruise through the sky, launching toward Jesus. On the right, he sees a peaceful, African-looking Jesus striding on water toward him.
All at once, he is reminded of urgency and tranquility—twin messages for the preacher. It is one thing to sing about love and hap-

piness, it is an entirely different enterprise to experience it. "The greatest thing that ever happened to me, to Al Green, the little boy from Arkansas," he once told *Esquire* magazine, "was that amidst all the doubts and speculation, I found peace."[44] As he grabs hold of the pulpit, festooned in his preaching robe, you can see it on his face. He has left the long stem roses at the river's edge and taken a dive. He looks up at us with a grin and seems to say, "Hop in. The water's fine."

1. Al Green with Davin Seay, *Take Me To The River*, (New York: HarperEntertainment, 2000) 96.
2. Caspar Llewellyn Smith, "Preacher with the Voice of an Angel," *Daily Telegraph*, February 7, 1999.
3. Scott Spencer, "Al Green's Gotta Serve Somebody," *Rolling Stone*, September 4, 2000.
4. "25 Reasons Why You'd Never Leave Her ... And 25 Reasons Why You Would," *GQ*, February 2003.
5. Al Green, *Al Green Anthology*, The Right Stuff/Hi Records, liner notes.
6. Al Green with Davin Seay, *Take Me To The River*, (New York: HarperEntertainment, 2000) 6.
7. Ibid., 7.
8. Ibid., 8.
9. Al Green, "What I've Learned," *Esquire*, November 2001.
10. Al Green with Davin Seay, *Take Me To The River*, (New York: HarperEntertainment, 2000) 76.
11. Ibid., 24.
12. Ibid., 71.
13. Ibid., 130.
14. Ibid., 136-137.
15. Ibid., 137.
16. Ibid., 127-128.
17. Ibid., 169.
18. There are various versions of this story. Al Green's perspective can be read in *Take Me to the River* (195-213, 225-230). Willie Mitchell's memory of events can be found in *Sweet Soul Music* (303-307). There are other perspectives that can be read in the liner notes to the *Al Green Anthology*—a superb four-disc collection produced by Robert Gordon.
19. Peter Guralnick, *Sweet Soul Music*, (Boston: Back Bay Books, 1999), 305-306.
20. Ibid., 302.
21. Ibid., 306.
22. Al Green with Davin Seay, *Take Me To The River*, (New York: HarperEntertainment, 2000) 239.
23. Peter Guralnick, *Sweet Soul Music*, (Boston: Back Bay Books, 1999), 8.
24. Al Green with Davin Seay, *Take Me To The River*, (New York: HarperEntertainment, 2000) 108.
25. Ibid., 276.
26. Ibid., 293.
27. Al Green, "What I've Learned," *Esquire*, November 2001.
28. Al Green with Davin Seay, *Take Me To The River*, (New York: HarperEntertainment, 2000) 295-296.
29. Ibid., 296.
30. Ibid., 304.
31. Kristine McKenna, "Al Green: the Prince of Love," *L.A. Times*, July 30 1989.
32. Al Green with Davin Seay, *Take Me To The River*, (New York: HarperEntertainment, 2000) 90.
33. Ibid., 275.
34. Al Green with Davin Seay, *Take Me To The River*, (New York: HarperEntertainment, 2000) 310-319. Despite her premonitions about him entering the ministry, there were many things that Mary Woodson never told Al Green—namely, that she was married and the mother of three children in Madison, New Jersey. As an endnote to a tragic episode in Al Green's life, after his church had been founded, he placed a name plate on one of the pews near the front just as she had requested.
35. Scott Spencer, "Al Green's Gotta Serve Somebody," *Rolling Stone*, September 4, 2000.
36. Greil Marcus, "The Belle Album," *Rolling Stone*, February 23, 1978.
37. Bill Barol with Vern E. Smith, "In the Name of the Lord," *Newsweek*, January 20, 1986.
38. Carol Flake, "Green Pastures," *Village Voice*, February 4, 1981.
39. From the movie *The Gospel According to Al Green* (a 1988 film documentary directed by Robert Mugge). This quote can be heard on the *Al Green Anthology*, disc three.

40. Q&A with Al Green, VH1, *http://www.vh1.com/shows/events/say_it_loud/algreen.jhtml*.
41. Al Green with Davin Seay, *Take Me To The River*, (New York: HarperEntertainment, 2000) 3.
42. John Roos, "The Reverend's Own Soulful Blend of Gospel and Romance," *L.A. Times*, September 3, 1999.
43. Caspar Llewellyn Smith, "Preacher with the Voice of an Angel," *Daily Telegraph*, February 7, 1999.
44. Al Green, "What I've Learned," *Esquire*, November 2001.

WYCLEF JEAN

THE PREACHER'S SON

By Chad Bonham

The story of Wyclef Jean would have been perfect for the Old Testament. The pop icon is part progenitor, part poet, and part prophet—kind of like Abraham, David, and Isaiah all rolled up into one nappy-headed Haitian prodigy. Take for instance Jean's role as the forefather of post-modern hip-hop, the first producer/artist to legitimately integrate rap with every other conceivable genre of music. The father of many nations if you will. As a poet, his words cut through to a multitude of cultural proclivities, and with songs like "Apocalypse," Jean displayed revelatory foresight unlike any of his peers.

And much like those BC predecessors, Jean too is a man of many contradictions. On one hand, the self-proclaimed "spiritualist" incorporates biblical thought into the vast majority of his songs.[1] He's a humanitarian and a preacher of peace who celebrates diversity. By most rock star standards, Jean is a minimalist and realizes that earthly riches are temporary. On the other hand, Jean has dubbed himself "the biggest sinner."[2] His struggles with infidelity are well documented, and his late-night parties (complete with government officials and high-dollar strippers) are the stuff of legends. So how does a preacher's son with a wild side reconcile such an extreme dual nature? If the subject in question is Wyclef Jean, he does so with no apology, but instead with a rare humility that originated from his modest beginnings.

TWO EXTREMES

Just mentioning the word "Haiti" conjures up a vivid array of images. It is one of the poorest nations in the world, despite its rich natural resources and inspiring beauty. Thousands of Haitians have fled the country seeking to escape poverty. These refugees have ended up in Miami, New Orleans, New York, and other large U.S. cities. Many of these "boat people" literally died in an effort to reach their so-called "Promised Land."

But in a word, to most people, Haiti means "voodoo," the national religion that over 60 percent of its people practice. It was in that country's notorious environment, in the town of La Plaine, that Wyclef Jean was born on October 17, 1972, and lived until the age of nine. Even further back in the musical phenom's history was a Cuban great grandfather. But most people tend to get hung up on the Haitian thing and more specifically on the fact that his grandfather was actually a voodoo priest. Jean's first encounter with music came at the age of three when he played African drums at a voodoo "Rah Rah" ceremony.[3] Still, he denied the religion as having any impact on his life. "I don't practice voodoo," Jean told *Kompa* magazine. "You know how some people are. You say you're Haitian and they automatically associate you with voodoo like we don't believe in God."[4] Jean's off-the-cuff remark may seem odd to anyone who truly understands the religion. Voodoo actually believes in a supreme, God-like being, and in fact, many Americans who follow its tenets have integrated certain Christian traditions into their own, such as a reverence for Jesus Christ.

Adding to the mysterious dichotomy is the major generation shift that took place when Jean's father Gesner Jean became a Christian. He would later become the pastor of Nazarene churches in both Brooklyn, New York, and Newark, New Jersey. Jean was a bona fide preacher's kid and "grew up believing in God." The Christian influence also crossed over into the experience of his cousin Praka-zrel "Pras" Michel, whose father was also a high-ranking church official. Jean and Pras would later become two-thirds of the hip-hop group known as The Fugees, named as such in an effort to pay proud tribute to the thousands of Haitian refugees seeking a better life in the United States. As Jean said himself, "I'm 100 percent Haitian ... I'm proud to be Haitian ... I represent Haiti in everything that I do ... I was Haitian first. Haiti till I die!"[5] His devotion to this storied heritage would prove true even as a world famous artist.

COMING TO AMERICA

In 1981, a nine-year-old Jean and his family took the courageous leap from their impoverished homeland to a supposed utopia. But for Jean, the Marlboro Projects in Brooklyn didn't exactly live up to his lofty expectations. He had hoped to find money falling from the sky. Jean quickly learned that a love for the simple things, such as fresh milk and new shoes, would suffice just the same. And even when he acquired great wealth as a recording artist, he never lost sight of the past. "I know that the nice shines I have on is going to pass," Jean told Launch.com.[6] Oddly enough, it was both his Christian father and voodoo-practicing grandfather who handed down similar philosophies on materialism. Jean credited his dad with teaching him, "You can have everything but if you don't have no spirituality and no culture, money doesn't equal respect and culture."[7]

The money issue never really was a problem to begin with, but for Jean, showing respect to his parents while at the same time experiencing New York culture was next to impossible. He quite

literally played church as a child and throughout his teenage years.
Jean and his brothers and sisters fulfilled their father's dream by
providing the music for his ministry. But according to an interview
with Launch.com, he "sort of like drifted" and "wasn't having any
of that (church) stuff at all."[8] Jean admitted that the double life
he led was responsible for this rebellion. One moment he was in
church, the next he was running the streets learning the ways
of hip-hop (an art form that actually helped the Creole-speaking
youngster learn to speak English). "I couldn't look at my dad and
say I wanted to be a rapper," Jean said. "That just wouldn't fly well
in the environment I was living in."[9]

In contrast, Jean's father wanted him to attend theology school and
become a minister. His refusal ultimately resulted in an expulsion
from the house. The two would reconcile just a few weeks later,
but it would be several years before Gesner Jean would finally
comes to terms with his son's career choice. "I told him I was a
minister through music," Jean said to placate his father.[10] It was a
hard pill to swallow for the conservative preacher, who believed
music that wasn't about God was of the devil. Ironically, his son
would spend the next several years writing a great deal of music
that was inspired by the biblical teachings he learned from his
father.

THE REBIRTH OF HIP-HOP

By 1993, Jean's musical career was on the launch pad and just a
few short years from its astronomical takeoff. He and Pras met up
with a fourteen-year old singer and actress named Lauryn Hill. It
was Hill who would first attract the spotlight with her co-starring
role in *Sister Act 2*. The music industry saw a star in the making,
but Hill's commitment to her friends would take preeminence.
Jean, Pras, and Hill formed Tranzlator Crew and signed on with
a production company to record a demo. The group eventually

signed with Ruffhouse Records but first had to change their name due to the fact that a rock band had already claimed the moniker. The trio settled on The Fugees and released the 1994 debut *blunted on Reality* [sic], an album title that had many misinterpreting the group as a purveyor of marijuana use. All three members flatly denied the accusations, saying instead the album was meant to make the exact opposite statement.[11]

The debut was a mild success, but clearly, The Fugees were a force to reckon with. This would become clear with the 1996 release of *The Score*, an album that is now referred to as one of the greatest hip-hop recordings of all time. In an apparent attempt to communicate with a hardcore hip-hop audience, The Fugees opted to speak in a harsh and colorful language. In one breath, the trio would pay homage to God just before exhaling with an array of profanities. Strangely, their use of such verbiage did not come off nearly as gratuitous as their "gangsta rap" counterparts and sometimes actually helped drive a poignant thought home. But still, the blatant hypocrisy was there for the world to see, and ultimately, it glazed over to the tune of 11 million sold copies of *The Score*. Not only was the album a commercial success, critics also raved over the groundbreaking new sound of hip-hop. The music community also chimed in with their approval, handing The Fugees a pair of Grammy Awards (including Best Rap Album) for their efforts.

The Score was both musically different from the current hip-hop trends, as well as miles apart from the day's popular lyrics that consistently painted a picture of the violent streets and a general disrespect towards women. This was a fact that The Fugees themselves pointed out throughout the record. On the hit radio single "Ready or Not," Hill charged that other rap acts were "imitating Al Capone." Instead, they prided themselves on a quick-witted intellect with a heavy emphasis on metaphorical lyricism. The Fugees addressed gang violence, but not in the traditional way. Their stark portrayal of life on the streets managed to come off more like a highbrow documentary and not like an R-rated action movie. *The Score* also addressed thoughtful issues such as social and political injustice and the complexity of relationships. Jean and the gang managed to have some fun, too, with the biographical "Fu-gee-la" and the popular remake of Roberta Flack's "Killing Me Softly With His Song."

But most of *The Score* contained a range of deep-seeded messages. Within that context, biblical sayings and themes popped up on a regular basis. Considering the church backgrounds of all three members, it was no surprise. On the aforementioned "Ready or Not," Jean referred to himself as "a born again hooligan only to be king again." A year later, he would appear to recant the lyric saying, "I am not a Christian. I am a spiritualist."[12] On the song "Zealots," the Fugees took aim at any rappers who might challenge their self-proclaimed hip-hop supremacy. Jean depicted a metaphorical battle in which "another MC lose his life tonight, lord." His pled with his victim to "pray to Jesus Christ" for a presumed eleventh-hour salvation experience. In one of the album's strongest statements, "The Beast" used a bold analogy from the book of Revelation in an effort to take corrupt police officers to task. "Things are getting serious Kumbaya," Jean rapped. "On a mountain Satan offered me Manhattan help me Jah Jah." The rhyme implied the existence of a natural temptation for law enforcement agents to use their authority for evil, not for good.

This early in the group's career, no one could tell whether this biblical imagery was coming from deep within their souls or if it was simply a product of their collective environments. Solo projects would soon show Jean and Hill in particular to be even more spiritually aware, although Jean would maintain a lukewarm commitment in comparison to his female counterpart. Nonetheless, the influence of his church upbringing would prove too strong to ignore.

CARIBBEAN CRUISE

The Fugees were still riding high from the multi-platinum success of *The Score* when Jean began working on his first solo project. *The Carnival* received nearly as much critical acclaim as his previous work with Pras and Hill. Not surprising was their heavy involvement in the project as co-executive producers and guest performers as part of the featured "Refugee Allstars." Other "Allstars" on the project included Melky Sedeck (consisting of Jean's brother and sister), Celia Cruz, Funkmaster Flex, DJ Skribble, John Forte, the Neville Brothers, and Rugged Out Come.

As if *The Score* hadn't provided enough diversity on its own, Jean made it his personal mission to push hip-hop to greater heights. He did so by pulling up a healthy handful of his Caribbean roots and mixing them with a potpourri of the American music that surrounded him during his youth. Jean also incorporated elements of Latin folk ("Gunpowder"), disco ("We Trying To Stay Alive"), doo-wop featuring the Neville Brothers ("Mona Lisa"), reggae ("Jaspora"), salsa ("Guantanamera"), smooth jazz ("Bubblegoose"), and classical ("Gone Till November").

He made sure to pay special attention to his Haitian homeland with four songs that used the Creole language ("Sang Fezi," "Jaspora," "Yele,'" and "Carnival"). What most marketing gurus would label a bad idea did nothing to hurt the album's sales, and if anything added even more credibility to Jean as the eclectic artist people already knew him to be. Some critics were wary of the album's sporadic nature. Chris Morris of Launch.com decided to "chalk this one up as a strong but decidedly mixed affair."[13] Most praised its groundbreaking flair. Ed Morales of *Rolling Stone* rhetorically asked about Jean, "If that isn't an original hip-hop voice, what is?"[14]

Not to be lost in the diversity of style was the strong sense of social conscience. Violence was of particular interest to Jean throughout much of *The Carnival*. Obviously impacted by his surroundings growing up in Brooklyn and Jersey, the stark nature of gang and drug-related death somehow managed to slip in and out of the thick production and heavy beats. "Bubblegoose" contended that bad things happen to the innocent bystander. "Street Jeopardy" took a shot at "gangsta rappers" making a financial killing off of violent lyrics. "Gunpowder" offered up the album's most sobering plea for peace. Jean also looked at sexual politics with songs like the uncomfortably transparent "To All The Girls." In a pseudo-parody of Willie Nelson and Julio Iglesia's "To All The Girls I Loved Before," Jean instead addressed his open letter "to all the girls I cheated on before." Months later, it would be revealed that one of those unfortunate victims was Jean's own wife and the "other woman" was none other than Fugees bandmate Lauryn Hill. Jean confirmed this allegation in an interview with *Kompa Magazine*.[15]

To occasionally lighten the load, Jean blended in a continuing story line that revolved around a trial in which both his personal character and musical prowess were being judged. There were some fun moments as well helping reflect the album title. The final three tracks ("Jaspora," "Yele,'" and "Carnival") were performed in Creole and lent themselves to an all-night fiesta on a Caribbean cruise. "We Trying to Stay Alive" featured samples from the Bee Gees classic "Stayin' Alive" and would provide the nightclubs with one of the year's most requested dance tunes.

But amid the social commentary and straight-up party elements of *The Carnival*, Jean's church upbringing made the subtlest of intrusions, much like his previous work with The Fugees. In "Apocalypse," the opening track, Jean proclaimed, *Cloud's getting darker/ Sun's getting nearer/ I'll turn an atheist into a God-fearing believer*. The references were mostly jumbled and even nonsensical at times. The alarmist tone of "Year of the Dragon" warned, *666 watch your back don't get caught in the rapture/ Yo AIDS, Moses the plague watch your back/ Pharoah let my people go/ Yo watch your back/ Last days, last days/ Nobody's protected.*

For a songwriter who skipped out on the chance to pursue theology, Jean continued to display a consistent sense of spirituality that dated back to his work with The Fugees. The offbeat placement of such biblical tones may have been a result of not attending Bible school as his father had hoped and could also have indicated attention deficit issues throughout his church years. For Jean, the explanation was simple enough. "I was brought up with biblical terms all of my life," he told fans during a 1997 MTV.com chat.[16] But other songs pointed to deeper conflicts. "Gunpowder," a stark portrayal of life on the mean streets of Brooklyn, begged the question, *I wanna know why Christians pray for a new day/ But it's still the same way?* Jean's challenging of the power of prayer was unmistakable. His diatribe may have been directed toward his own father as he continued by saying, *But the preacher man told me good things come to those who wait/ Do good things come to those who wait?*

Jean's explicit beliefs may have remained vague throughout *The Carnival*, but certain basic truths did shine through. The reggae-flavored "Sang Fezi" donned Creole language verses, but its chorus (sung by Hill) promoted the biblical principle of corruptible riches. Jean's words exhorted listeners to "keep your head to the sky." And in the tradition of Apostle Paul, the song served as a reminder, "The path we refuse is the path we should choose." The concept of walking the less-traveled "straight and narrow" would prove to be one of Jean's most constant challenges.

THE NEW QUINCY JONES

The following year saw fellow Fugees members Lauryn Hill and Pras also release albums. Hill would make the biggest splash of the three with her critically acclaimed project *The Miseducation of Lauryn Hill.* For reasons that still have not been fully disclosed, The Fugees have to date not reformed to work on a follow-up to *The Score.* Some have cited the tension that followed Jean and Hill's ending of their illicit love affair while others have speculated that jealousy between the three may have been the root cause. Conventional wisdom would point to the fact that each member had simply taken their careers in much different directions.

In the meantime, Jean was content to pursue his other love: producing. When Jean claims to be "the hip-hop Quincy Jones of today," he's being more truthful than arrogant.[17] In fact, if asked which he enjoyed more, making solo records or producing other artists' records, he might not be able to give a definitive answer. Jean's résumé as a highly sought-after producer or re-mix specialist is as lengthy as it is impressive. In addition to producing his own records and most of The Fugees' material, he has also worked with Canibus, Destiny's Child, Mick Jagger, Sinead O'Connor, Bono, Michael Jackson, Tevin Campbell, Gloria Estefan, and Rita Marley, just to name a few. The infectious chart-topping melody of "Maria Maria" performed with Carlos Santana has provided his most successful pairing to date, but his work with Bono was arguably the most rewarding. In July of 1998, the two collaborated on the song "New Day" which was recorded to benefit Net Aid, a United Nations organization aimed at helping the poorest nations of the world, and the refugee-aiding Wyclef Jean Foundation.[18] Its positive vibe was typical of both artists' philosophies, encouraging the downtrodden to *look towards the sun/ Even when the darkness shall come.*

Jean's ability to sniff out other talent eventually garnered attention from one of the music industry's most well respected record moguls. In September of 2000, Arista's Clive Davis signed a joint venture deal with Jean that created Clef Records, a sister label to J Records. The younger executive was placed in charge of signing and producing new artists. "Wyclef is one of the premier creative talents of our time," Davis told *Business Wire* magazine. "He is also one of the few artists who can be a great entrepreneur as well, sensing the cutting edge and the outer frontiers of music and knowing which discovery can become a lasting star."[19] For Jean, it was a greater opportunity to fulfill a lifelong dream of helping others fulfill theirs as well.

SELF-MADE MONIKERS

By early 2000, the ever-restless Jean was working on his sophomore solo project. As much as he loved collaborating with other artists on their projects and producing up-and-coming acts, he had an equally strong desire to share his unique message of peace and diversity to the music world. Jean had produced and performed much of 1999's *Life: Music Inspired by the Motion Picture*, a film that featured Eddie Murphy and Martin Lawrence. Both the movie and the album were moderate successes, but that effort could never replace the music that made up his uniquely personal and enigmatic score.

On the horizon was a project that was originally called *The Preacher's Son: Two Sides To A Book - Sodom and Gomorrah*. The cumbersome title would later be changed to simply *The Ecleftic: 2 Sides II a Book*. After receiving a Grammy nomination for his previous effort, the sophomore release would not be received as kindly by critics. One review referred to the offering as "a sprawling mess."[20] Evelyn McDonnell of *Interview Magazine* pointed out Jean's distracting tendency to meander between genres, but felt compelled to give him props as "one of the last real auteurs."[21]

The Ecleftic's content maintained a certain duality, displaying the past history that has revealed Jean as a conflicted soul. If *Carnival* was a subtle hint of the artist's issues with his religious upbringing, then in sharp contrast, *The Ecleftic* was a lyrical slap to the face.

All of its biblical references came amid Jean's predictable attack on social injustice, violence, and stereotypes. The song "Diallo," for instance, referred to the true story of an unarmed New York man who was shot forty-one times by the police. *Even though I walk through the valley of the shadow of death/ I fear no evil for thou art with me thou ride with me*, Jean sang. In the next line, he referred to "Jah Rastafari" with his "knotty dreads," continuing the confused spiritual metaphor. According to Jean, "Thug Angel" contained a concurrent theme. When describing the song, he quoted a portion of Psalm 23: "Thug Angel basically means that the Lord is my shepherd, and I shall not fear."[22]

The rest of *The Ecleftic* dealt with relationships and personal experiences. "Where Fugees At?" was a thinly veiled jab at his AWOL companions Pras and Hill. Both had also recorded solo projects since *The Score*, but to that point had done a poor job of keeping in touch. *Ya'll flip like Pharisees and charge me with blasphemy*, Jean wrote as he pointed out their presumed hypocrisy. In an effort to remind them of their not-so-distant past, he pointed out, *Success don't come overnight/ I was in Noah's Ark for forty days and forty nights.*

Jean let his more heated feud with former protégé Canibus play out through the song "However You Want It." The premise was a nightmare loaded with violent imagery. Strangely enough, for a man who preached peace so effectively, Jean showed an uncanny affixation with guns. *I found myself loadin' magazines after magazines*, he described. *Ski mask on my face, gun on my waist.* Just one year earlier, between solo projects, Jean and Canibus were still on friendly terms. While helping the younger hip-hop star promote his debut album, Jean had an alleged run-in with Jesse Washington, editor of *Blaze* magazine. Jean was accused of aiming a gun at Washington, threatening to shoot him if he ran a negative review. The incident was written off and charges were never officially filed. "I don't preach violence, and anyone who knows me knows that

I carry a guitar, not a gun," Jean defended himself in a prepared statement. "I attack with my pen, not a pistol. I'm all about making music. The editor of *Blaze* is all about selling magazines."[23]

In addition to *The Ecleftic*'s strange lyrical bedfellows came the odd reference to his father in the song "Low Income." While Jean had always been frank about the strict nature of his upbringing, he rarely spoke negatively about his father. However, in this instance, one line stood alone: *At 17 I left the house/ 'Cause my father was a minister/ And I didn't want the Marvin route.* The logical implication was that Jean left home at a young age due to a fear of his father. The song was talking about Marvin Gaye who was shot and killed by his own father, but that was an extreme reality even to Jean's strict household, in which he claimed his father "smacked me up 'til I was 20."[24]

The two sides to Jean's book appear most contradictory on the songs that portray his wild side, a side he says developed from life on the streets, making him the typical preacher's kid. In "Something About Mary," he speaks against LSD, ecstasy, cocaine, and pills, but manifests an affable longing for a "kiss from Ms. Mary." Jean hinted that his earliest affiliation with marijuana came from watching his grandfather smoke the mind-altering drug. While the song led one to believe that Jean was a proponent of marijuana, he had previously denied actively using it.

The song "Perfect Gentleman," discusses one of Jean's undisputed vices—strippers. His escapades have been well documented, and by his own admission, sexual temptations were the cause of much sorrow. *Twenty grand, know it's a sin*, he candidly sang. But Jean doesn't take kindly to those who might lob self-righteous accusations. "He without sin cast the first stone," Jean challenged. No one can be sure if his harsh retort was legitimately aimed back at those he deemed hypocrites or instead just a deflection of his own guilt. Future statements would tend to point toward the latter.

In an AOL chat that Jean participated in just six weeks after *The Ecleftic*'s release, he showed signs that the two sides of his life didn't leave him in the most confident state of spiritual being. "I believe that we all are sinners." Jean said. "I always refer to God, hoping that He's forgiving me for all the sins I'm committing on Earth."[25] Nearly two years later, he admitted that his lifestyle choices had caused more pain than pleasure. "I'm definitely more mature," he told Launch.com. "But I was actin' a fool ... If you value your life, you're not gonna be doing that type of thing."[26] Thankfully for Jean, the ill-advised escapades did not cost him his longtime marriage. Despite his mistakes, he has always maintained a high level of respect for the importance of family.

WYCLEF UNMASKED

As Jean was working on his third solo project, *Masquerade*, something much more important was taking place in his life. He and his father Gesnar Jean were repairing the slight breach in their shaky relationship. Yes, they had reconciled shortly after Wyclef left home to pursue his music career, but Gesnar had never quite accepted his son's decision and in fact had declined to watch one of Jean's performances. But the two were growing closer as the elder's aging softened the rigid nature. Jean and Gesnar began taking trips around the country and even to other parts of the world. The father finally tore down the last pieces of the wall built between them and attended a highly publicized concert at Carnegie Hall. "I didn't even think he was going to show up." Jean would later admit. "When I got on the stage and I looked at the balcony and I saw this man with the beard and stuff ... It was the coolest thing."[27]

Jean's joyous moment was short lived. Just eight days before the infamous September 11 attacks on New York, Washington D.C., and Pennsylvania, a sixty-year-old Gesnar Jean was killed in a freak accident in which he was crushed to death between a car and his garage door.[28] The tragedy of his father's death understandably put a damper on the recording process. But instead of wallowing in his grief, Jean decided to use music to cope with the pain. "I *had* to make this album," Jean told Launch.com. "It was my therapy after losing my dad. If I didn't have music, I'd probably be strung-out somewhere."[29]

The most direct result of Jean's recovery was a touching tribute aptly titled "Daddy." In the hip-hop ballad, the speaker took solace in the fact that his father was "knockin' on heaven's door." Jean waxed nostalgic and showed a new appreciation for the Christian values that he had resisted throughout much of his young life. The song speculated as to what his father might say to him now. Jean imagined it might be a passage from Psalm 23. He also pined for the future when he supposed he might see his father "at the resurrection."

But the tribute to his father didn't stop there. *Masquerade* would turn out to be Jean's most spiritual album to date. "Peace God" set the tone with its worshipful and prayerful attitude. The song gave thanks to God while asking for protection and peace. Jean acknowledged that the Almighty gave him "the voice to speak," made mention of Christ's crucifixion, and encouraged listeners to "stay pure in the city of sin." Jean was also publicly contemplating his beliefs more than ever before. Clearly, the death of his father was having a major impact on his spirit. He openly displayed a hope that one day the two would reunite in heaven. It was a hope clouded by his doubt and confusion over the after life. "You never really know how you come to the earth," Jean said. "It's really a mystery, and when you leave, it's sort of a mystery too."[30]

Despite the album's inspirational nature, it did contain the occasional misstep. Songs such as the remake of "What's Up Pussycat" (which featured the original artist Tom Jones) and the unflattering attempt at Bob Dylan's "Knockin' On Heaven's Door" were easy targets for music critics. Much like *The Ecleftic*, they found themselves scratching their heads and asking the real Wyclef Jean to please stand up. Reviewer Bill Campbell called him "an enigma" and "not necessarily in a good way."[31] Robert Christgau of *Rolling Stone* suggested that *Masquerade* was "short on the sane, humane pleasures so plentiful on the first two (albums)."[32] Most writers recognized his genius but were left unable to give an enthusiastic "thumbs up." Much like Jean's entire solo career, his third album garnered a mixed bag of reactions. It was not unlike the hodgepodge that had become of his spiritualistic leanings as well.

TWO SIDES TO A 'CLEF

To place Jean on the same pedestal alongside the Bible's Old Testament heroes would be a gross overstatement. It would not, however, be a stretch to say he exudes many of the same qualities that make those same heroes a study in human behavior. Jean has lived most of his life dancing precariously on the high wire that separates spiritualism and secularism. Not one to take a definitive stance either way, his fence-straddling ways can only last so long. Critics have detected the contradictions, arguing that Jean's need to both sermonize and "keep it real" often causes a lyrical train wreck. Writer Don Leroy noted that one of his weaknesses was a "quest to become Bob Marley's spiritual heir-apparent"—a quest Leroy believes to be "a futile chase."[33] Jeff Lorez referred to Jean as "a paradox: a hip-hop renegade who happens to be the son of a preacher, a married man and who's also a playboy."[34]

An older and wiser Jean claims to have drifted from his wild days. Certainly the death of his beloved preaching father has played a factor, as evidenced in the title of his fourth solo album, *Preacher's Son*. Yet the spiritual duality still remains. He recognizes that "creativity comes basically from God,"[35] and songs such as "Peace God" make bold reference to the putting away of idols and an

appreciation for the "the blood shed" by Christ. His involvement
with the 1998 Tibetan Freedom Concert raised eyebrows to the
contrary. "Peace of mind, any form, is important," he told the
Washington Post.[36] But at the end of the day, only Jean and God
know just where this musically and spiritually "ecleftic" artist is
headed. If his previous work is any indication, at the very least, the
soundtrack will be an intriguing delight to the ears.

1. Wyclef Jean live chat with MTV.com, June 23, 1997.
2. Wyclef Jean live chat with America Online, August 24, 2000.
3. Ibid.
4. Fred Fabien, "Interview With Wyclef Jean," *Kompa*, October-November 2000.
5. Ibid.
6. Billy Johnson Jr., "The Carnival Barker Speaks," Launch.com, March 1, 1999.
7. Ital-K, "Interview With Wyclef Jean," Afiwi.com, May 5, 2002.
8. Dave DiMartino, "Carnivals and Masquerades," Launch.com, September 30, 2002.
9. Ibid.
10. Jeff Lorez, "Clef Unmasked," Launch.com, May 28, 2002.
11. "Artists A-Z: The Fugees," VH1.com.
12. Wyclef Jean live chat with MTV.com, June 23, 1997.
13. Chris Morris, "Review of *The Carnival*," Launch.com, June 24, 1997.
14. Ed Morales, "Review of *The Carnival*," *Rolling Stone*, July 1997.
15. Fred Fabien, "Interview With Wyclef Jean," Kompa, October-November 2000.
16. Wyclef Jean live chat with MTV.com, June 23, 1997.
17. Billy Johnson Jr., "The Carnival Barker Speaks," Launch.com, March 1, 1999.
18. Richard Skanse, "Wyclef Records Charity Single with Bono," *Rolling Stone*, July 12, 1999.
19. Entertainment Editors, "Wyclef Jean Launches Own Label," *Business Wire*, September 21, 2000.
20. "Artists A-Z: Wyclef Jean," VH1.com.
21. Evelyn McDonnell, "Review of The Ecleftic," *Interview*, July 2000.
22. Wyclef Jean live chat with America Online, August 24, 2000.
23. Anni Layne and Ari Bendersky, "A Carnival of Sorts," *Rolling Stone*, August 14, 1998.
24. Jeff Lorez, "Clef Unmasked," Launch.com, May 28, 2002.
25. Wyclef Jean live chat with America Online, August 24, 2000.
26. Jeff Lorez, "Clef Unmasked," Launch.com, May 28, 2002.
27. Dave DiMartino, "Carnivals and Masquerades," Launch.com, September 30, 2002.
28. Andrew Dansby, "Wyclef's Father Killed," Rollingstone.com, September 5, 2001.
29. Jeff Lorez, "Clef Unmasked," Launch.com, May 28, 2002.
30. Dave DiMartino, "Carnivals and Masquerades," Launch.com, September 30, 2002.
31. Bill Campbell, "Review of Masquerade," Ink19.com, July 2002.
32. Robert Christgau, "Review of Masquerade," *Rolling Stone*, July 4, 2002.
33. Dan Leroy, "Review of Masquerade," Launch.com, June 27, 2002.
34. Jeff Lorez, "Clef Unmasked," Launch.com, May 28, 2002.
35. Wyclef Jean live chat with America Online, August 24, 2000.
36. Mark Fisher, "Tibetan Freedom Concert," *The Washington Post*, June 7, 1998.

RUNNING FROM RELIGION

By Chad Bonham

In 1993, author Bob Briner wrote a revolutionary book called
Roaring Lambs, which called for the Church to reevaluate its
involvement with the liberal arts. Briner was especially harsh on
the Christian music industry and its inability to make an impact on
the mainstream.[1] As Briner was losing his battle with cancer (he
passed away in 1999), a curious phenomenon was taking place—
one that may have caused even the original "roaring lamb" to raise
his eyebrows in wonder.

While artists like Sixpence None The Richer, Amy Grant, Jars of
Clay, and Kirk Franklin were busy "crossing over" from the Christian market into the mainstream music scene, there was a band
that on the surface bore a peculiar resemblance to the others. A
closer look would reveal many disparaging facts, but still the imagination was led to run wild as the overnight success of Creed drew
questions from multiple fronts. How does one explain the multi-
platinum album sales of a band that writes so much music from
a biblical perspective? More specifically, what does one make of
Creed's charismatic yet brooding frontman Scott Stapp, the band's
lyricist and source of spiritual inspiration?

Creed's story is made even more fascinating by the lack of comparisons that can be drawn between them and U2, the band that they themselves hold in the highest of esteem. U2 sported three known Christians, while Creed housed a disgruntled former church attendee. The members of U2 outgrew their much-beloved Christian fellowship in the name of rock 'n' roll. Stapp sought out stardom while running from a life of faith he admittedly has never quite understood. U2 embraced its beliefs from the start, making no apologies to the politically correct naysayers. Creed has never publicly espoused any religion, but in a strange twist of fate, the band (and more specifically Stapp) has gained great notoriety and fame in large part due to the positive spin it put on what had become a negative segment of music. It would be Stapp's infatuation with his spiritual upbringing that would arguably resonate most with the masses.

HOW TO RAISE A ROCK STAR

Much has been made about Stapp's childhood—and for good reason. It was those formidable years growing up in Central Florida that spurred him to achieve greatness. Stapp was born Anthony Scott Flippen on August 8, 1973, in Orlando, Fla. Two events would take place in his life by age ten that would irrevocably stamp his future. The first happened when Stapp was just five years old. His biological father left the family, leaving mother Lynda to fend for three young children. For the most part, the load was too heavy for the single mother to bear. Stapp spent many months at a time with his great-aunt and great-uncle in North Carolina on a Cherokee Indian reservation. At the time, he thought they were his grandparents.

Stapp's next life-changing experience took place five years later, when his mother remarried, and a new man of the house filled a long-standing void. His name was Steven Stapp, a dentist and perhaps more importantly a staunchly religious man who was actively involved in the Assemblies of God. The family would soon follow his lead, attending their local church any time its doors were open. At first glance, the situation couldn't be more perfect. Three young children now had a complete set of parents to raise them. But for Stapp, a life that already included regular church attendance intensified. Most noticeably was the area of discipline.

The stories of Stapp's punishment have become legendary, some of which included writing lengthy passages from the Psalms and Proverbs. Even before his step-dad came into the picture, Stapp's mother set the tone by forbidding any rock music from entering the home. Furthering the problem was Stapp's difficulty understanding certain aspects of Pentecostalism, in particular the common practice of "speaking in tongues." He also wrestled with the question of exclusivity and wondered if this was the only true religion. Music was also an issue. The Stapps forbade their children to listen to rock music, even Christian rock. The only exception was U2's *The Joshua Tree*, an album that Stapp would later credit with changing his life. The struggle is one that many children of the evangelical movement face at one point in their lives. Preacher's kids have notoriously been much maligned for their behavior issues, but with Stapp, the confusion about the purpose of having faith in God ran much deeper. It would become all too clear that his straying from the flock was more than just petty teenage rebellion.

By the age of 17, Stapp had reached the end of his rope. Deciding he no longer needed his parents' support, Stapp left home in an effort to find his own way. He moved in with a friend's family and eventually graduated from a prep school. His first foray into higher education was disastrous. At Lee College (a Christian school in Cleveland, Tennessee), he was expelled after admitting to using alcohol, marijuana, and a host of other illicit drugs. Stapp headed back to his home state and enrolled at Florida State University, partly due to the fact that his hero, Jim Morrison of The Doors, spent time in Tallahassee. It was there that the early makings of Creed started to fall into place. Stapp first met Mark Tremonti, then meeting Scott Phillips shortly followed. Brian Mitchell (who is no longer with the band) was the last to join the band that was first known as Naked Toddler. They played the local bar scene mostly as a cover band, but Stapp had a strong desire to write his own music, a desire that would soon impact millions.

BREAKING FREE

Once Stapp, Tremonti, Phillips, and Marshall were ready to take the next step, they had a paltry six thousand dollars to record a full-length demo. By now, the band had changed its name to Creed and was established as one of the more popular nightclub acts. The foursome created Blue Collar Records in preparation for the regional release of its first project, but when Tallahassee station WXSR got hold of the album's title track, "My Own Prison," the buzz quickly spread, and national independent labels started to show interest. One small company in particular decided to take a chance on this relatively unknown band. Until that moment, Wind-up Records had existed as an upstart label looking to find its place in a crowded market. Creed would shortly take Wind-up from obscurity to the top of the heap.

The Cinderella story didn't come without a few bumps in the road. Music critics were quick to call Creed a cheap Pearl Jam knock-off—and five years behind the times at that. Stapp himself was criticized for grandstanding, playing the role of the rock 'n' roll poser. Most tried to write him off as an Eddie Vedder impersonator. In one particularly harsh review, Rob O'Connor compared Stapp's vocals to those of classic rock band Nazareth by describing them as "a rabid dog in desperate need of a leg to chew on."[2] MTV wasn't terribly hip to the band at first either. But the music industry took a much different approach. Record labels saw the huge phenomenon of Creed's overnight success for what it was and began scouring the country for more of these neo-grunge/hard rock hybrids. The late nineties would produce other bands like 3 Doors Down, Days of the New, Nickelback, and Puddle of Mudd.

More puzzling than Creed's rise to fame in a post-grunge musical world was the band's overtly spiritual lyrics. During the late nineties, bashing organized religion was becoming an art form with the success of such bands as Marilyn Manson, Nine Inch Nails, A Perfect Circle, and Slipknot. How could this multi-platinum selling and overnight success resist the temptation to engage in typical rock 'n' roll debauchery and instead extol Christian virtues? Their philosophy flew in the face of an entire industry. "There is no rule that says if you're a rock star you have to have sex with as many groupies as you can," Stapp told *People* magazine. "There is no rule number two that says take as much drugs as you can so you can die at 27."[3] His latter comment was in reference to the premature death of the Doors' legendary front man Jim Morrison, a rock star that Stapp has often cited as one of his musical heroes.

While anti-everything records were selling by the millions, a new breed of rock music was about to dispel the myth that positive lyrics couldn't sell. Even before P.O.D. and Linkin Park proved that hard rock did not require violence and profanity, Creed burst onto the scene with a strange kind of angst. This outpouring was much different from Nirvana's tortured bemoaning. Instead of just crying out, Creed added a new element—a call for change. As the writer of all Creed lyrics, Stapp's pattern of deeply felt themes was easy to detect. Most of his songs were based on the human condition and primarily, issues dealt with internally. Pride, hatred, self-worth, inner-peace, and fear were just a few of the heavy topics addressed throughout *My Own Prison*.

These deep issues were usually manifested in the form of theoretical questions. The song "Torn" appeared to ponder the complexities of the Church. *Peace is what they tell me*, Stapp wrote. *Love, am I unholy/ Lies are what they tell me/ Despise you that control me.* In "In America," he continued to paint a less-than-glimmering picture: *Church bell's ringing/ Pass the plate around/ The choir is singing/ As their leader falls to the ground.* Stapp wasn't just singling out organized religion but declining moral values in general. Mentions of abortion, greed, and a blurred line between right and wrong showed his disdain for the ills of American society. The entire project (and particularly the song "Pity For a Dime") found Stapp openly admitting that these were all "signs of losing my faith."

Encouraging "signs" that Stapp hadn't completely written off his Christian past came in such songs as "What's This Life For" where he acknowledged, *We all live/ Under the reign of one king.* And while the title of the song "Unforgiven" may have led listeners to believe that Stapp was unsure of his own salvation, the lyrics actually made a strong statement of faith: *Step inside the light and see the fear of God burn inside of me*, he wrote. *The gold was put to flame/ To kill, to burn, to mold its purity.*

The starkest biblical reference, however, came from the album's title track and first breakaway hit single. It was the oddly sublime nature of "My Own Prison" that would put Creed on the map. The slow-building acoustic (then suddenly electric) tune described a courtroom setting in which the singer was on trial, not for a crime per se, but rather "my own sin." It was a stark reversal of philosophy from the normal rock mantras in which sin is worn as a badge of honor. Stapp took the imagery even further as the song continued to paint a picture of the struggle between forgiveness and guilt: *I hear a thunder in the distance/ See a vision of a cross/ I feel the pain that was given/ On that sad day of loss.* "My Own Prison" in essence described a feeling of remorse for Christ's crucifixion, a feeling that Stapp seemingly could not quite reconcile. According to Stapp, the song helped him realize he had to "move forward" and "make better decisions."[4]

Instead of being turned off by the song's overt lyrics, throngs of fans (to the tune of five million records sold) were mesmerized by this new approach. Creed had struck a chord; apparently Stapp was not the only tormented soul seeking truth. About two years later, Stapp would make a candid revelation about the song. "The message of salvation is in 'My Own Prison' and I didn't think about it until after it was done." Stapp said. "How many people who would never have stepped into a church hear 'My Own Prison' every day?"[5] Even though he was not attempting to reach people with the Gospel message of Jesus, Stapp understood the impact he was unwittingly having on the band's fans.

WATCHFUL EYES

Despite the fact that boy bands (i.e., *Nsync and the Backstreet Boys) and female pop singers (i.e., Britney Spears and Christina Aguilera) were all the rage during the late nineties, Creed was forging ahead with its unapologetic posturing rock sound. But what made this phenomenon different was the intense scrutiny from the Christian community that quickly followed. In fact, some argued that the confusion over Creed's spiritual intentions caused a multitude of believers to give initial support to the band's plight.

A closer look, however, revealed that there was more to Creed than the "Christian rock" label that the mainstream media had haphazardly placed on them. If discriminate ears failed to hear the recurring hints of doubt in Stapp's lyrics, then the use of "God d---" in the song "What's This Life For" provided the starkest wake up call. In an odd twist, the band actually addressed the use of the phrase through its website. Rock bands aren't generally known to apologize for much of anything, much less for swearing, so the message

Stapp personally wrote to the band's faithful fans was particularly telling. "There was never an intention of cursing God," Stapp explained. "My heart has no conviction for the use of this word because I feel God understood my situation."[6] Stapp had written the song out of a sense of desperation and personal tragedy caused by the suicide of two close friends. His frustration throughout the song was palatable. Yet even more surreal than Stapp's need to defend his choice of words was his seemingly evangelistic rationalization. Added Stapp, "it is a cry to the lost, put in a way that they could understand."[7]

While many were quick to write Creed off as another spiritually confused band, a large segment of the Christian media were intrigued and in fact took on the challenge of trying to establish a root cause behind Stapp's semi-cryptic message. Editorial writer Bill Carl used Creed as the centerpiece for his questioning of what exactly constitutes Christian music. "Does a song, a band, a television show, a movie, or a painting have to be stamped 'Christian' and sprinkled with 'Jesus,' 'God Loves You,' and 'Get Saved' to be worthy of my attention?" he asked. "Is the truth invalidated by a glass of 'Bud' and a smoking cigarette?"[8]

Thanks to Creed's refusal to facilitate any requests from the Christian media, writers and columnists were simply left with conjecture. There was one exception to that staunchly followed rule. In the only known interview with a Christian publication, Stapp spent time talking with Tim Bisgano and pastor and author Chris Seay. Throughout the conversation, Stapp revealed many of the deep issues that have led him to continually question where he stands on the topic of faith and Christianity. "I became disillusioned by a lot of things that happened to me by Christian people," he said. "I wanted to get away and try to figure out things on my own, through my own study and my own search, and I'm still there. I haven't come to any resolutions."[9]

Ultimately, Christians seemed to become disenchanted over Stapp's constant questioning of his own faith and his intensified criticisms of the Church. Hearing such honest critiques was deemed too uncomfortable a listening experience. But did Stapp's openness mean he wasn't a Christian? Seay, for one, opined just the opposite. "I don't want to speak for (Stapp)," he told *New Man*, "but I've witnessed Scott's faith. He loves the Lord. That doesn't mean musicians are obliged to say they are a 'Christian band' simply because they are believers or that they need to stamp God's name on every song."[10]

AS THE POTTERY WHEEL TURNS

In hindsight, it might be easy for Stapp to see the difficulty of starting a family at the exact same time one is becoming a world famous rock star. Nonetheless, it was a challenge he gladly accepted in early 1998 with his marriage to nineteen-year-old model Hillaree Burns. Stapp was twenty-four at the time and admitted later that both were too young for the pressures they would soon face.[11] The marriage would produce a son named Jagger, a son who would change Stapp's life exponentially. His eternal commitment to Jagger would not translate to his marriage. He and Burns would divorce sixteen months later.

Professionally, Stapp was on the verge of even greater success. There was just one sticking point that kept creeping up. Despite the band's best effort, Creed was still having some trouble shaking the "Christian" label as they prepared to release the sophomore album *Human Clay*. Every interview, review, and web chat had at least one reference to the bands supposed spiritual nature. The talk was so strong, it become a point of contention for the band, and statements regarding faith eventually landed on their official website. "We are not a Christian band," Stapp wrote. "A Christian band has an agenda to lead others to believe in their specific religious beliefs. We have no agenda!"[12] It was obvious that Creed did, in fact, have no such agenda. But was Stapp inadvertently profiting from his life-long wrestling match with the demons of his past? Was the band reaping financial benefit from its dual appeal to both those disenfranchised with organized religion and those Christians hoping to latch onto the next big crossover act? If Stapp was perpetuating the myth, he claimed to do so innocently. "We never write with the intention of appealing to either audience," he told Launch.com. "We don't think we're walking a fine line and have to placate either side."[13]

On the surface, the issue was becoming a moot point. But behind the scenes, the implications were taking a toll on the other three members of Creed. Not only were they forced to answer questions on behalf of their tormented frontman, but lifestyle choices were sometimes limited. Stapp was well aware of the fact that many young listeners were allowed to enjoy his music based on the misconception that Creed was a Christian band. Again taking the less-traveled high road, Stapp was making unusual requests of his bandmates. "If they want to drink beers or whatever I'm like, 'will you please pour that in a cup before we go to the autograph session?' he told Seay and Bisgano. "'I just don't want you to influence some little kid and he thinks we are a Christian band. I don't want to be a stumbling block for him.' Now all of a sudden, they have a responsibility and they didn't ask for it. They wanted to be a rock star."[14]

Guitar player Mark Tremonti claimed it wasn't that big of an issue and usually only came up during interviews. "When we're writing music or playing live, it really doesn't come into play at all," he told the *Washington Post*. "We're just a rock band. Scott's the real spiritual one in the band."[15]

When addressing claims of the band's religious leanings, Tremonti acknowledged that the band's relatively clean-cut image was not an act. "The Christian rock thing is a big misconception," he told CNN.com "It's not entirely wrong. We all have morals, but that's it."[16]

In one instance that took place during the summer of 2000, Stapp's spiritual leadership took precedence over a band member's unwise comments. He openly reprimanded bass player Brian Marshall's off-the-cuff and disrespectful criticism of Pearl Jam. "There is no excuse for the arrogance and stupidity," Stapp wrote on the band's website. "I'm sorry if Brian offended anyone, and he has already apologized for his comments."[17] Just six weeks later, Marshall left the band to pursue other interests, but certainly his previous actions helped speed up the process. Stapp's handling of the situation invoked parable-like images of the separation of the wheat from the chaff. It was a show of integrity that continued to defy conventional rock 'n' roll wisdom.

If the band was so worried about misconceptions of their belief systems (as indicated by the constant need to address the issue), they didn't show intentions of watering down their spiritually charged diatribes. *Human Clay* was not an exact replica of *My Own Prison*, but there were still plenty of dancing embers to keep the fire brightly lit. The album's blazing opening track "Are You Ready?" could have been interpreted as a biographical admonishment. *Hey, Mr. Seeker, hold on to this advice*, Stapp wrote. *If you keep seeking you will find.* The self-proclaimed "seeker" alluded to some of the places he had already sought the truth. In "What If," Stapp declared that he had *been beaten down/ By the words of men who have no grounds*, perhaps referring to religious leaders, and another song lyric alleged that "somebody told me the wrong way."

"Faceless Man," the album's sixth track, allowed a ray of hope to shine through the cracks left in Stapp's trust-depleted soul. Using his typical ethereal style of writing, Creed's frontman described a scene in which he saw a face looking back at him from a pool of water. The identity of this mystery man was revealed when Stapp said, "His yoke is easy and His burden is light," referring to the words of Christ in Matthew 11:30. In the portrayed conversation, the "faceless man" reminded Stapp to "always do what's right." He even went as far as asking this unnamed person to "come inside and never go away." The Christian tenets of repentance, salvation, and righteousness are unmistakable, and Stapp's true feelings were unveiled when he told VH1.com that Jesus was the person he would most like to meet. "His message is one of love, peace, unity and grace," Stapp said. "Those are all messages our world could use to help solve our problems. Also, He died for his beliefs. I admire that."[18]

On the other hand, Stapp has never concurred with the Christian explications of his lyrics. Instead, he has often told fans to take whatever meaning from their songs that they want. Call it mystique or just plain stubbornness. Either way, Stapp's unwillingness to be frank when it comes to specifics has brought on more questions than answers. But for that one brief moment in time, during his interview with Bisagno and Seay, the singer did expose more of his true heart than ever before. Besides the highly publicized bout with his father over what he deemed religious oppression, Stapp talked candidly about whether or not he was a Christian, among other personal topics. And while the interview managed to fly beneath mainstream radar screen, it continues to give a great deal of insight into Stapp's conflict. "Someone asked me if I was a Christian," Stapp said. "I don't know. I still have a lot of questions that I wish I had answers for ... I know that I believe in God and I speak with Him every day and I have a relationship with Him and I feel like He speaks with me and I feel like He's instrumental in everything that I do."[19]

Stapp also suggested that God has used him despite himself. As a boy, he believed he had been called into the ministry. Stapp gave an account of how he used to ask God for wisdom and spiritual strength, then suddenly decided he did not want those things anymore. But had God blessed him with those gifts anyway? Stapp seemed to think that was the case. "You can't run from the truth, as much as you want to run," Stapp said. "You can't run when God has a calling on your life ... I think that I was running and I think that partly I'm still running to some degree. The ironic thing is that I'm running, and I ran right into Him ... I've affected so many people on accident, just like I was a minister."[20]

Human Clay's defining "ministry" moment came in the form of the smash hit number one song "Higher." The crunchy power ballad evoked images of a utopian dreamland, a place that the chorus would seemingly define as heaven or "the place where blind men see" and "the place with golden streets." But true to Stapp's nebulous approach, the method to reaching this place was left unspoken. Was it a relationship with Christ or a more humanistic approach as suggested on "Inside Us All," the album's closing song. *There's a peace inside us all*, Stapp wrote, *Let it be your friend/ It will help you carry on*. Creed's fans didn't mind the ambiguity one bit, but instead embraced it and pushed sales of the project to over 10 million copies. Riding the fence in politics may be a bad idea, but when it comes to entertainment, it's apparently a profitable policy.

ANGER MANAGEMENT

After recording two albums and touring nonstop for nearly three years, the members of Creed needed a break. Stapp in particular was dealing with high doses of stress. He was now balancing the demands of a full-fledged rock star with the newfound role of single parent. On occasion, it appeared that the pressures were taking their toll. Allegations of a drinking problem began to surface and Stapp's inability to control his temper turned into headline news. The first of two publicized incidents took place on February 8,

2001. Stapp verbally threatened a tattoo parlor owner after the man revealed Stapp's identity to other customers. Two months later at a nightclub in Florida, the singer started a fight that ended in a brawl after a drunken patron harassed him about Creed's music. The combination of Stapp's alcohol intake and references to Pearl Jam apparently pushed him over the edge.[21] A few months after, Stapp admitted that his temper was the one thing about himself that he most wanted to change. "These situations, I'm not proud of how I handle them," he told *Rolling Stone*. "Whatever anyone says, they're just words. I have to learn that."[22]

A more controlled Stapp had already been involved in a verbal feud with Limp Bizkit lead vocalist Fred Durst. The war of words started almost a year earlier (June 23, 2000) at New York station K-Rock's Dysfunctional Family Picnic in Holmdel, New Jersey. From the stage, Durst made several disparaging remarks about Stapp while Creed sat backstage waiting to perform. Afterward, the bands released a series of nasty barbs back and forth through the media. Creed went as far as sending Durst a copy of an anger management book and Stapp would later challenge him to a boxing match for charity. Durst declined the offer. Stapp would later state that Durst, "has worn out his welcome as an artist spokesperson for our industry."[23]

In contrast to the occasional turbulence, Stapp was transforming into a rock 'n' roll philanthropist. One of *Human Clay*'s biggest radio hits was the power ballad "With Arms Wide Open." The song was dedicated to Stapp's son Jagger even before he was born, inspired by first hearing the news that he would be a father. The video was full of spiritual imagery, including one scene that depicted Stapp dipping into a pool of water in an act of self-baptism. The lyrical celebration of a child would later lead to the creation of the Arms Wide Open Foundation, an organization dedicated to making disadvantaged children's dreams come true. At least one element of Stapp's search for purpose had seemingly been fulfilled.

OLDER, WISER, WEATHERED

By early 2001, Creed was winding down a hectic tour schedule and gearing up to prepare for a third album. But first, a few months off would help rest the band for the work ahead. For Stapp, there was a more personal benefit. "We needed a break from all this to absorb it and digest it and reconnect with our friends and our family and our loved ones," Stapp said.[24]

In particular, it was a chance to build a stronger bridge between him and his stepfather Steven. Fatherhood alone had given Stapp a greater appreciation for his strict upbringing. "It has changed my outlook towards my father completely," he told VH1.com. "It has helped me understand why he did what he did. Whether I feel like it is right or wrong, he did it to protect, teach and guard my heart."[25] The coming months would find Stapp spending more time with his family and on at least one occasion, he found himself attending Easter Sunday services with them. In Chris Heath's in-depth *Rolling Stone* interview with Stapp, he observed the Stapp family holding hands and saying grace over a meal. When Stapp's father asked him if the excruciating punishment of writing scripture verses had influenced his songwriting, he openly showed a renewed sense of appreciation. "They definitely influenced how I wrote," Stapp said. They are poetic and are written in a type of rhythm and a pattern ... and probably even got me thinking about a lot of things."[26] He would also tell *People* magazine that he saw his stepfather as "a strong man for coming into a situation where a woman had three kids."[27]

While on tour, Stapp had imposed a band rule that prohibited any song writing until just before hitting the studio. He also insisted that no one listen to music during this time. Stapp wanted the new offering to come from a pure, unadulterated place.[28] So in March of 2001, the process began. The result was *Weathered*, a decidedly heavier and darker affair (albeit with the obligatory ballad here and there) that would help reinvent the band. Gone was much of Stapp's overdone vocal intensity. Instead, restraint was in order, along with a more understated infusion of passion. Stapp sounded less like Eddie Vedder and Jim Morrison, and for the first time, this revitalized lead singer crooned confidently with his own voice.

Also missing was a great deal of the overt biblical references from the previous two albums. In a way, Creed found itself killing two birds with one heavy, slick stone. Except for one little problem—September 11. The day Creed was to begin mixing their fresh material, the process came to a standstill along with the rest of the country. Once things returned to relative normalcy, the band decided not to alter the lyrical content, all of which had been written and recorded before the fateful day.[29] In an eerie twist of fate, Creed's least spiritual sounding album suddenly took on prophetic meaning. Songs such as "Bullets," "Who's Got My Back," and "Signs" were drenched with imagery fit to provide the soundtrack for any national news broadcast. But it was one of the album's heaviest numbers, "Freedom Fighter," that stood above the rest. With great bravado Stapp proclaimed, *Our mission's set in stone, 'cause the writing's on the wall/ I'll scream it from the mountain tops, pride comes before a fall.* The chorus was particularly timely. *I'm just a freedom fighter, no remorse*, he belted out, *raging on in holy war.* Those chilling words took on new meaning during the war on terror and the conflict in Iraq.

There was still a remnant of Stapp's past found randomly strewn throughout *Weathered*. On the introspective "One Last Breath," he wrote, *I thought I found the road to somewhere, somewhere in His grace/ I cried out heaven save me.* Similar thoughts prevailed on the mid-tempo groove of "Hide," as Stapp admitted he had been *dancing with the devil way too long/ And it's making me grow old.* *Weathered*'s "With Arms Wide Open" moment came courtesy of the orchestrated power ballad "Don't Stop Dancing," a song that featured guest vocals from Stapp's younger sister Amie. The song opened with the frustrated realization that *at times life is wicked and I just can't see the light*. Stapp also used the song to convey the universal feeling of loneliness. *Hey God I know I'm just a dot in this world, have you forgot about me?* he rhetorically asked. Stapp's answer provided one of the few consistencies from previous albums: a reliance on self to move forward.

The most surprising aspect of *Weathered*'s release was an unexpected warming trend that critics were showing toward Creed. For the first time, positive reviews were cropping up in favor of a band that had previously been denied such a luxury. James Hunter of *Rolling Stone* described the band as "masters of hard-rock atmosphere" and declared *Weathered* as "rock of unusual focus and arrest, a beautifully distressed dance of sustained style and unapologetic emotion."[30]

But Creed was not lucky enough to escape without a partially bruised ego. *Entertainment Weekly* selected the album as the "#1 Worst of 2002." In a biblical parody, David Browne wrote, "On the seventh day, the Lord rested and decided to listen to the latest Creed album. Then He heard its preening ballads, apocalypse-now sermonizing, and tuneless attempts at headbanging, and He became really incensed."[31] Even the nastiest review could not keep fans from responding en masse. *Weathered* shot straight to the top of the charts and went on to sell more copies in the first week than any other rock album of 2001. That total has long since surpassed five million.

MAKING PEACE

The roller coaster that is Scott Stapp's spiritual journey continues in its state of perpetual motion. Living in the limelight doesn't give him the luxury of private inner conflict. It doesn't help that he writes his songs from within those deeply personal places. Stapp has often said he wants people to understand his music. That desire contradicts the fact that he rarely divulges the actual meanings of his songs. Instead, they are left with the task of reading into his lyrics and dissecting open-ended quotes from the press.

But since *Weathered*, Stapp seems to have toned down the anti-religious rhetoric. Perhaps watching his son Jagger growing up before his eyes has mellowed the harsh, unforgiving tone that came from his earliest offerings. "I'm at peace with it," Stapp said of personal belief system. "There's no guilt anymore. No condemnation anymore."[32] His newly discovered repose makes sense according to the words of the Apostle Paul. In Romans 8:1, he wrote, "There is therefore now no condemnation to them which are in Christ Jesus, who walk not after the flesh, but after the Spirit."[33] If Scott Stapp has truly applied this biblical principle to his life, then he is already miles ahead of the millions who have yet to uncover its power. And as long as Creed is still making music, the blueprint to his soul will be laid out for the rest of us to wonder.

1. Bob Briner, *Roaring Lambs* (Zondervan, 1993).
2. Rob O'Conner, "Review of Human Clay," Launch.com, September 28, 1999.
3. Steve Dougherty and Linda Trischitta, "Staying Alive," *People*, March 26, 2001.
4. Quoted from Creednet.com.
5. Tim Bisagno and Chris Seay, "MXTV Creed Interview," MissionX.org.
6. Quoted from Creednet.com.
7. Ibid.
8. Bill Carl, "Arms Wide Open," PraiseTV.com, February 5, 2001.
9. Tim Bisagno and Chris Seay, "MXTV Creed Interview," MissionX.org.
10. Bob Liparulo, "Solid Rock," *New Man*, November-December 2002.
11. Chris Heath, "Creed's Stairway to Heaven," *Rolling Stone*, February 28, 2002.
12. Quoted from Creednet.com.
13. Dave DiMartino, "How's the Weathered up There?" Launch.com, August 25, 2002.
14. Tim Bisagno and Chris Seay, "MXTV Creed Interview," MissionX.org.
15. Mark Jenkins, "Creed's True Calling," *The Washington Post*, September 28, 1999.
16. Donna Freydkin, "The Little Rock Band That Could," CNN.com, February 23, 1999.
17. Jaan Uhelszki, "Bassist Brian Marshall Leaves Creed," *Rolling Stone*, August 11, 2000.
18. Scott Stapp interview with VHI.com's "One-To-One," February 5, 2001.
19. Tim Bisagno and Chris Seay, "MXTV Creed Interview," MissionX.org.
20. Ibid.
21. Joe Hauler, "Stapp in Nightclub Brawl," *Rolling Stone*, April 20, 2001.
22. Chris Heath, "Creed's Stairway to Heaven," *Rolling Stone*, February 28, 2002.
23. Jennifer Vineyard, "Creed Takes Limp Bizkit to Task for TapRoot Threats," *Rolling Stone*, July 21, 2000.
24. Dave DiMartino, "How's the Weathered up There?" Launch.com, August 25, 2002.
25. Scott Stapp interview with VHI.com's "One-To-One," February 5, 2001.
26. Chris Heath, "Creed's Stairway to Heaven," *Rolling Stone*, February 28, 2002.
27. Steve Dougherty and Linda Trischitta, "Staying Alive," *People*, March 26, 2001.
28. Jenny Eliscu, "Creed Take You Higher," *Rolling Stone*, November 2, 2001.
29. Elysa Gardner, "Creed Stays The Course," *USA Today*, November 27, 2001.
30. James Hunter, "Review of Weathered," *Rolling Stone*, January 17, 2002.
31. David Browne, "5 Worst of 2002," *Entertainment Weekly*, December 13, 2002.
32. Chris Heath, "Creed's Stairway to Heaven," *Rolling Stone*, February 28, 2002.
33. Holy Bible: King James Version (B.B. Kirkbride Bible Company: 1982) New Testament, 166.

SEXINESS VS. SPIRITUALITY

By Denise Washington

Style. Strong vocals. Sex appeal. Independence. Words used to describe the Grammy award-winning group, Destiny's Child. With songs like "Independent Women, Part I" and "Say My Name," the trio has impacted the formulaic and often mediocre world of pop music by achieving a major coup—critical acclaim and commercial success. Openly Christian, these three women, Beyoncé Knowles, Kelly Rowland, and Michelle Williams, blend an interesting mix of faith, Christian beliefs, and sexy pop persona. As young fans support this unique and complex image that make up the group, some criticize the dichotomy of sexiness and spirituality, believing the members of Destiny's Child compromise their Christianity.

Despite the criticism, fans have embraced Destiny's Child's songs that combine R&B and dance with catchy pro-women lyrics in powerful anthems like "Survivor," as well as their contemporary gospel renditions of "Now Behold the Lamb" and "Jesus Loves Me." They have experienced commercial success with platinum albums, hit singles, and multiple awards.

But problems that plagued the group since it started have tarnished the stardom and success. Dramatic breakups, lawsuits, and attacks from the media have given them the reputation of being divas and having a controlling and demanding manager, Mathew Knowles (Beyoncé's father). But the women of Destiny's Child have continued to advance their career, and they credit their success and inner strength to their relationship with God.

All three women grew up in church and sang in the church choir. Two of these girls grew up in Houston, Texas, with dreams of becoming stars. Beyoncé Knowles, the daughter of a successful corporate manager father and a beauty salon owner mother, Tina, began singing at the age of seven. Her talent became apparent after she won her elementary school talent show by singing John Lennon's "Imagine." Knowles soon auditioned for a group called Girl Tyme. There she met Kelly Rowland, and the two became good friends. Doors of opportunity opened for the all-girl group, including an appearance on *Star Search*. But the girls lost the competition. The loss fractured the group but made Knowles and Rowland more determined to succeed. During this time, Rowland's mother was a full-time nanny and traveled extensively with the families that employed her, so Mathew Knowles invited Rowland to come live with Beyoncé.

Knowles and Rowland continued to practice while the group evolved through name changes and different lineups. It finally settled with the lineup consisting of Knowles, Rowland, LaTavia Roberson, and LeToya Luckett. "Less than a year later, we started going by Destiny, because my mom came across that word while reading the Bible," Knowles said.[1] "My dad went to check to make sure that there weren't any other Destinys, but there were about a hundred of them—so he came up with the idea of child. People said, 'Why not Destiny's Children since there are four of y'all?' And we said, 'No, it's going to be child, because we are a group that represents one person.' And that person is God. Only He knows how many hours of rehearsal time we put in," Rowland said.[2]

Seeing that the girls were serious, Mathew Knowles quit his day job to manage the girls. He arranged for them to perform for various record industry representatives. Eventually, the group signed with a division of Elektra Records, but the deal only lasted eight months. Mathew Knowles quickly arranged to meet with key decision-makers from Columbia Records in New York. They were quickly signed, and their first self-titled album released with a hit single, "No, No, No" (produced by Wyclef Jean). Destiny's Child created their signature style and transformed themselves from cute teen sensations into stylish trend-setting stars with the help of Knowles's stylist mother, Tina.

When their second album, *The Writing's on the Wall*, released, Destiny's Child thrived despite being in a crowded pop and R&B market populated with Christina Aguilera, Britney Spears, TLC, Mary J. Blige, and N'Sync. Songs like "Say My Name" and "Bills, Bills, Bills" established them as outspoken women who were not afraid to flaunt their sexiness and independence.

The Writing's on the Wall (a biblical title taken from the fifth chapter in the book of Daniel when he interprets a prophetic message on the wall for the king who does not honor God) sold more than ten million copies and earned them a 2000 Grammy for Best R&B performance by a Group or Duo with Vocal and a Grammy for Best R&B song for "Say My Name." Accolades grew as the group won *Billboard*, Soul Train, and MTV awards.

Destiny's Child was riding high, enjoying the success created by hard work and sacrifice. But, despite this achievement, dissention spilt the group apart. Just before the video shoot for "Say My Name," Roberson and Luckett tried to have Mathew Knowles replaced with a new manager. They alleged that he was a demanding manager and favored Knowles. Knowles told a journalist, "They felt like we would have to give them whatever they asked for. And, the day they sent it (a letter terminating Mathew Knowles as manager), we were devastated. For two weeks, I literally stayed in my room and did not move. I felt like I could not breathe. It hurt so bad."[3]

Knowles and Rowland turned to prayer for answers. Knowles told *Ebony* magazine, "We went on a praying week. We just prayed, prayed, and prayed. We said, 'God we are not trying to put a time limit on you, but we are asking you what to do. If you send two new members to us, then that is what will do. If not, then we know that you want Kelly and me to just finish out [promoting] the album."[4]

According to a September 2000 *Ebony* magazine article, Knowles and Rowland sought out pastoral advise. Through prayer and counseling, Knowles and Rowland decided to let Roberson and Luckett go. They soon invited two singers to fill in: Farrah Franklin, who danced in one of their music videos, and Michelle Williams, a backup singer for the R&B artist Monica. Franklin and Williams quickly learned the Destiny's Child signature sound, image, and dance moves. "They were definitely angels sent from God," said Knowles.[5] "It took a lot of hard work. There were struggles and tears and sweat, but we got through it."

At the time, Rowland and Knowles did not know if the women would be permanent additions to the group. To disguise the changes until the lineup solidified, they added three other dancers in the video. However, the fans and the media picked up on it immediately. Soon a flurry of speculation and accusation from the media hit, each wanting the exclusive true story. During this time, Roberson and Luckett filed a lawsuit, which was settled out of court and allowed them to form a new group.

Knowles, Rowland, Williams, and Franklin first performed live at the NBA All-Star weekend. But preparation for the tour would once again be plagued with drama and dissention. Newest member Farrah Franklin had failed to bond with the group. She spent time offstage alone instead of with the group, and during interviews she appeared unhappy. Things came to a head as the group prepared to tour Australia. Franklin flew back to L.A. because she was feeling sick. While Rowland, Knowles, and Williams waited to depart from Seattle's airport, Knowles called Franklin to convince her to come back. Franklin declined, saying she would stay in L.A. Feeling that Franklin did not want to be in the group, the members decided to let her go. "I kind of always knew that Farrah would leave the group," Williams said.[6] "The way she left was just so unfortunate because I kept trying to talk her out of it. But, Farrah could not let her concerns go—like the amount of time on camera. She'd say things like, 'How come they show Beyoncé more?' And I'd say, 'She is the lead singer.' At first, she acted like she wanted to be friends with us, but then when she finally got in the group, she was not happy."

After making the decision, the women flew to Australia and performed as a trio. The tour pushed them to a new performance level as they tried to compensate for one less member. Returning to Houston, they broke the news about Franklin and the new lineup. "People always ask us about Destiny's Child's decision to remain a trio instead of a quartet," Knowles said.[7] "Well, it wasn't really our decision—it was God's. Some may disagree, but He has His way of doing things, and we all just needed to hear and accept it."

The next stage for the group was the video shoot for "Independent Women Part I," the single from the hit movie *Charlie's Angels*. The song soared up the chart, proving again that Destiny's Child could rise from the ashes of another breakup. They went on a tour with Christina Aguilera and then returned to the studio to record their third album, *Survivor*. With Knowles taking control of songwriting and production, the women lyrically released the pent-up emotion of the past years. Fans identified. The song "Survivor" became a radio anthem for the year. The release came out simultaneously with the group's receiving two Grammy nominations—Best R&B performance by a group or duo with vocal and Best R&B song. The night of the 2000 Grammy Awards, Destiny's Child gained respect from the music industry elite as they performed "Independent Woman Part I" and "Say My Name." The night ended with them winning two Grammy awards. Destiny's Child surpassed the expectation of pop novelty with minimal staying power. They were three talented young women with a chance for longevity.

Knowles told MTV, "I think it is important to look good and to dance, but I think it's more important to be a true artist than half talent because beauty fades. If you don't have any substance and talent behind it, then after one or two albums, there is another beautiful band there take your place."[8]

Survivor went on to sell more than ten million copies, and Destiny's Child continued to win awards. In other projects, Knowles made her acting debut as Foxy Cleopatra in the 2002 Austin Powers' flick, *Goldmember*. Rowland branched out into solo work the same year, recording the hit single, "Dilemma" with rapper Nelly.

With chart-topping success, awards, critical acclaim, and an international fan base, Destiny's Child had amassed major stardom in the pop music world. Since their humble beginnings, the women relied on God to help them in their difficult journey.

At most of their concerts, the women lead the group and crew through prayers before performances, speak to the audience about God, and sing about their Christianity in original songs and gospel medleys. Rowland and Knowles fly home to Houston often to attend the Saint John's United Methodist Church. Williams attends Saint Paul's Church of God in Christ in Rockford, Illinois. Pastor Rudy Rasmus of Saint John's provides spiritual counseling to the women and asks the church pray for them and their endeavors. Knowles and Rowland have donated $500,000 to Saint John's to help build a youth center.[9] And Williams has given $148,900 to Saint Paul's.[10] Their active involvement inside and outside of the church is quite apparent.

"Beyoncé, Kelly, and I go to church every Sunday that we can," Williams said.[11] "We read our Bibles lots of times instead of going to a party. We get on our tour bus and have church in the back of the bus. We surround ourselves with Christians and people who are spirit-filled."

The group maintains that their beliefs stem from a faith that took root at a young age and is not a ploy to sell records. Knowles spoke candidly in their autobiography, *Soul Survivors: The Official Autobiography of Destiny's Child,* about being a Christian. "It's not easy being a Christian and living your life right by God all the time—especially in the music industry," she said. "There is a lot of temptation. Some people are only Christian when it's convenient, not all the time (mainly holidays). I know that I'm not perfect—everybody makes mistakes—but I try to be consistent even when it's not easy."[12]

Knowles grew up in Saint John's and said she was "born again" when she was baptized in her teen years. Rowland recalled her baptismal experience, "The water pouring over me was the most spiritual sensation of my life," she said. "One by one, my sins were washed away. I knew God wanted to give me another chance. I knew that was His will. I felt purified as a Christian. There is nothing like that feeling of being able to start over again; even performing onstage cannot come close to that."[13]

Williams spent most of her life in church, singing in the choir. She sang her first solo at the age of nine. Despite her background, or perhaps because of it, she hears much criticism about her choice of dress. Her perspective is, "It's important to keep an open mind. If you have been cooped up in a church all of your life, you're going to think smaller than if you have gone out into the world, you can get to know God yourself. Somebody might think I am going to hell simple because of the way I dress. But, I can't worry about what other people think or say about me, because in the end, it's going to be just Him and me. And, me and God, we're tight."[14]

On the road, the young women search for strength and direction from their faith. "No matter where in the world we are, if it is a Sunday, Beyoncé, Michelle, and I will join hands and pray together just as if were in church," said Rowland.[15] At home, church becomes a sanctuary where the women can shed the pop persona and be vulnerable in front of God and their congregation. They use the time to get spiritually recharged and find refuge and healing as they deal with painful experiences, insecurities, and professional pressures. It is also a time to give back to the community. The women help local at risk teens through their church's outreach programs.

Yet, many see contradiction and compromise in the group's image portrayed on magazine covers, television interviews, and award shows—from revealing clothes to suggestive dances and lyrics. Some believe that their appearance contradicts the group's Christian beliefs. (Yet, ironically, in the song "Nasty Girl," the women tell scantily clad girls to put some clothes on.) Knowles told the Associated Press, "A classy girl can wear something classy and still be sexy. It doesn't mean you're nasty because you dress sexy. It's how your carry yourself."[16]

Reporter Sharon Tubbs contested this in her article, "And God Made The World ... Bootylicious?": "Bootylicious Christians. Christians who happen to be bootylicious. Nope, no matter how you work it, these two words don't sound right together."[17] Tubbs interviewed G. Craige Lewis, a Texas minister and gospel artist about Destiny's' Child. "Members of Destiny's Child gyrate and make sexual moves. It's not anything of God. Christianity a lot of times is used as a tool for justification."[18] Tubbs and Lewis contended that Destiny's Child's actions do not coincide with the "traditional beliefs of right and wrong."[19]

Bob Waliszewski of *Plugged In* magazine, a publication from Focus on the Family, agreed. "The chart topping R&B stars speak openly about their Christian faith (and even sing about it now and then), causing much confusion among young people. It's a pop culture paradox. How can singers stump for Jesus, yet specialize in songs like 'Bootylicious'?"[20] Yet, Williams defended the song in the May 14, 2001, issue of *Jet* magazine. "It's G rated. It's about self-confidence and being confident about your body whether you're thick or tiny or petite. Whatever your size is, you're bootylicious. Be proud of who you are. Be bootylicious."[21]

Two issues arise when artists who are Christian work in the mainstream music industry. On one hand, the Bible says that God looks at the heart while man judges appearance (1 Samuel 16:7). Yet, on the other hand, the Bible also addresses the subject of modesty and not making your brother stumble (1 Corinthians 10-32-33, 1 Timothy 2:9-10). So, with Christians in a secular industry, how should they act and appear when both issues have equal weight? Author Patrick M. Morley addressed the issue of Christians being in the world and not of the world. "'In but not' is our *relationship* with the world. Biblical Christians are to be 'in' the world but not 'of' the world. It pertains to our *character*—the kind of life we lead."[22]

Destiny's Child's pastors and churches support the life they lead. Williams told *Gospel Today* magazine, "I talked to my pastor. He is supportive and keeps me in prayer. I know we sing R&B, but we don't promote premarital sex, drugs, and alcohol or do those things. I'm here to help change the world—not have the world change me."[23]

But Morley called that perspective cultural Christianity. "Cultural Christianity means to pursue the God we want instead of the God who is," he said. "It is sensing a need for God, but only our own terms. It is wanting the God we have underlined in our Bibles without wanting the rest of Him, too."[24]

Williams also defended the group's appearance in an interview for *Christian Reader* magazine. "I look at that as my job. That's not who we really are. When we are offstage, we've got on jeans and sweat suits. No one has a religious job all the time. It's no different than with any secular job. So, (Destiny's Child) is my job, and that is my uniform."[25]

Based on Williams' response, Destiny's Child's main focus is not on the clothes they wear, the songs they sing, or being pop icons. But, being witnesses to a world who does not know God. Williams explained further to *Christian Reader*, "You have to let your light shine wherever it is you go. That may be the reason why God has placed me in this. I think the fact that I am able to do this and still be myself is shining my light."[26]

So, despite the issue of appearance and lyrical content versus Christian beliefs, many young girls see that light and support Destiny's Child. In an article for the *London Institute for Contemporary Christianity*, the author searched for a deeper spiritual meaning in the some of their song lyrics instead of criticizing their attire. "I don't know whether their Christianity includes for example, a radical concern for the poor, but the Christian teenagers who looked at the song ['Survivor'] with me found much to affirm 'love your enemies,' 'forgiveness,' and 'no revenge.'"[27]

In a similar vein, Simon Weaver, a music and books critic, saw their paradoxical image as an asset rather than a detriment. "Throw in too, the Christianity quotient—the God-loving, God-fearing ingredient—and you have a vehicle ready to steamroll even an ardent and weakening Southern fundamentalist. In the U.K., such religious posturing is now so dangerously unfashionable that it would generally, in itself, guarantee instant failure on these shores, but so eye catchingly do Destiny's Child flaunt their physical beings that the ever cynical British audience has, it seems, proved capable of forgetting the group's claimed spiritual allegiances."[28] With Warner focusing more on the outer package than the spiritual message Destiny's Child tries to convey to a secular audience, he said, "Black and beautiful, these three glamazons, these simmering sirens of Jesus, may prove to have more than just staying power."[29] Blinded by their physical beauty, the spiritual message becomes diluted to critics like Warner.

The women continue to defend their faith, despite the negative comments. "I do know that I probably will get some negative feedback from people, but I can't let them discourage me and try to tell me that I'm not a Christian and I'm not saved because they are not God," Williams said.[30] "I know what God has done in my life and I know that God is still with me and He loves me."

Artists like Destiny's Child can defend their faith because they do not have a problem with integrating the sacred and the secular, singing gospel songs as well as suggestive pop songs. It is a reflection of the current postmodern society. In the past, things that were sacred remained in the church or in a Judeo-Christian setting. Non-churched people recognized the sacredness and respected its place in culture regardless if they agreed with it or not.

But, as time progressed, Judeo-Christian beliefs no longer shaped the larger culture. The sacred and the secular were integrating, especially in pop culture. An example is the movie *The Godfather* where Michael Corleone is at his niece's christening while, in juxtaposing shots, his henchman are assassinating major Mafia bosses. Or music videos such as "Like a Prayer," with Madonna making out with a black Christ figure one moment, then dancing and praising in the church with a gospel choir in the next shot.

Some of the older generation is used to the separateness, and most of the criticism about Destiny's Child arises from them. But, to some of the younger generation who were exposed to adult issues at an early age (media violence, school shootings, increased crime rates, broken homes), the women's appearance is not a major issue. They accept that aspect of the group since the issue may seem miniscule compared to what they have experienced or seen. The focus is more on what Destiny's Child represents—independence, survival, moral stances on premarital sex and drinking, and their spirituality.

Also, with their fans being mostly young girls, these girls have accepted the current image of the female pop singer—a dichotomy of sex and innocence. Some emulate their favorite star by wearing similar clothing styles—midriffs and hip hugger jeans. With a lot of young people facing major issues like despair, hopelessness, and a lack of purpose, many of them are turning to their pop music idols for answers instead of the church. Williams told *Gospel Today* magazine, "Right now there are so many things going on, and young people don't have a lot of people to look up to. I want to be an encouragement to people and let them know that their dreams can come true. I've always been prayerful. Every move that I've made, God has been there. I guess it's to encourage people because God is soon to come. It's my purpose to tell people that don't know Him to get know Him and He can change people's life."[31]

Writer Sarah Magill Mueller agreed. "Stay too long inside a 'Christian music white castle,' and you won't be able to support Christian artists who choose to exist outside its walls. Bands such as P.O.D., Over the Rhine, Pedro the Lion, and others serve as lights in the mainstream market. Pull up the drawbridge and you won't hear Destiny's Child divas tell an arena full of 14 year olds that they need to be on their knees thanking God every night."[32] Going beyond the walls of the religious community, Destiny's Child breaks the stereotypes of artists who are Christian by bringing a spiritual message that is palatable to the masses.

As Destiny's Child continues to evolve, the women have explored solo projects. Knowles pursued acting gigs in the movie *Carmen: the Hip Hopera* and *Austin Powers 3: Goldmember* and started in various television commercials. Rowland, diverging from the Destiny's Child sound, released an album infused R&B, rock and funk. And she also appeared in the television show *The Hughleys*. And Williams returned to her spiritual music roots and released a gospel album. Yet, with these solo pursuits, the women remain faithful to the group. "The group is solid," Williams said in *Jet* magazine.[33] "We're not breaking up. Nobody is going to leave and not come back. It's none of that going on. We are definitely here to stay. We're in God's will."

The debate will continue in Christian circles about how Christians in the spotlight should package and present spiritual messages to a secular market. As there are varying beliefs within Christianity, there will also be varying answers on how that presentation should be resolved especially when the integration of the sacred and the secular in a postmodern society will occur more often.

Pressure exists from both sides to be role models, absent of any imperfections. The secular music industry wants them to be perfect women with no physical flaws. Two-dimensional icons created to entertain the masses. The Christian world wants them to be perfect Christians, free from any struggles and have rock solid convictions in all areas of life. Despite the pressures, the women of Destiny's Child openly walk out their faith everyday with struggle and grace. Their imperfect faith gives the non-churched audience a facet of Christianity they have yet to see—the human dimension.

1. Beyoncé Knowles, Kelly Rowland, and Michelle Williams with James Patrick Herman, *Soul Survivors: The Official Autobiography of Destiny's Child* (New York: HarperCollins, 2002), 58.
2. Ibid.
3. Kelly Kenyatta, *Destiny's Child: The Complete Story* (Phoenix: Amber Books, 2001), 7-8.
4. Lynn Norment, "Destiny's Child: The Growing Pains of Fame," *Ebony*, September 2000.
5. Ibid.
6. Beyoncé Knowles, Kelly Rowland, and Michelle Williams with James Patrick Herman, *Soul Survivors: The Official Autobiography of Destiny's Child* (New York: HarperCollins, 2002), 117.
7. Ibid., 1
8. Ibid., 129.
9. "Destiny's Child Gives Back to Houston," *Business Wire*, May 25, 2001.
10. "Michelle Williams of Destiny's Child Makes Sizeable Contribution to Church," *Business Wire*, June 25, 2001.
11. "Destiny's Child's Michelle Williams," *Gospel Today*, April 2002.
12. Beyoncé Knowles, Kelly Rowland, and Michelle Williams with James Patrick Herman, *Soul Survivors: The Official Autobiography of Destiny's Child* (New York: HarperCollins, 2002), 268.
13. Ibid.,170.
14. Ibid.,172.
15. Ibid.,181.
16. "Destiny's Child Defends New Song," Associated Press, April 17, 2002.
17. Sharon Tubbs, "And God Made the World ... Bootylicious?" *St. Petersburg Times*, July 17, 2001.
18. Ibid.
19. Ibid.
20. Bob Waliszewski, "Sincere Faith or Mere Navel Grazing," *Plugged In*, May 2002, 3.
21. Margena A. Christian, "Destiny's Child: Hot, Sexy Singing Group Soars to the Top," *Jet*, 14 May 2001.
22. Patrick M. Morley, *The Rest of Your Life* (Grand Rapids: Zondervan Publishing House, 1998), 26.
23. "Destiny's Child's Michelle Williams," *Gospel Today*, April 2002.
24. Patrick M. Morley, *The Rest of Your Life* (Grand Rapids: Zondervan Publishing House, 1998), 65.
25. Edward Gilbreath, "Michelle Williams: Child of Destiny," *Christian Reader*, May 2002.
26. Ibid.
27. "Connecting with Culture 1: Godly Girls?" The London Institute on Contemporary Christianity, 2001.
28. Simon Warner, "Destiny's Child: Survivor," Pop Matters.com, May 2001.
29. Ibid.
30. "Destiny's Child's Michelle Williams," *Gospel Today*, April 2002.
31. Ibid.
32. Sarah Magill Mueller, "35 Reasons to Start Cheating on Your Christian Bookstore," *The Lutheran*, August 2001.
33. Margena A. Christian, "Destiny's Child: Hot, Sexy Singing Group Soars to the Top," *Jet*, 14 May 2001.

GOTTA SERVE SOMEBODY

By Scott Marshall

While touring Australia in 2001, the legendary Bob Dylan took a break to be hooked up to a worldwide satellite feed. The occasion was the seventy-third annual Academy Awards, and his recent composition, "Things Have Changed" (written for the film *Wonder Boys*), was one of five nominees for Best Original Song. Once it was announced that he won the coveted Oscar—beating out Randy Newman and Sting, among others—the focus of Tinseltown was upon Dylan, whose image was beamed from Sydney onto a large screen at the awards show.

"I want to thank the Academy who were bold enough to give me this award for this song," a surprised Dylan said, "which obviously ... is a song which doesn't pussyfoot around or turn a blind eye to human nature. And God bless you all with peace, tranquility, and goodwill. Thanks."

In an industry that often does seem to pussyfoot around and turn a blind eye to human nature, the songs Dylan has created over four decades have been a good antidote to wishful thinking. Dylan's hope for his audience—"peace, tranquility, and goodwill"—was oddly quaint, and a far cry from self-glorying in the moment.

163

There is little debate that the Jewish-born Dylan is an incredibly influential artist, one who has maintained his musical integrity and reluctantly dealt with the not-so-noble aspects of the entertainment business. He likened it to the "cotton candy business," telling Edna Gundersen of *USA Today* that the concerts he and his band played at "sell more junk out there than you can dream of. It has nothing to do with music."

1941–1960

On a spring evening in 1941—May 24 at 9:05 P.M., to be precise—Beatty Zimmerman gave birth to her first child in Duluth, Minnesota. Abraham Zimmerman, the son of Jewish immigrants from Odessa, Russia, was the proud new father.

In Hebrew, the Zimmerman's firstborn would be known as Shabtai Zisel ben Avraham (combining the names of his maternal great-grandfather Shabtai Solemovitz and his paternal grandfather Zigman 'Zisel' Zimmerman, with the standard "ben Avraham," or "son of Abraham"). In English his name would be Robert Allen Zimmerman, and before long, Bobby Zimmerman for short.

"The birth certificate is filed May 28, 1941, coinciding with the circumcision ceremony," wrote Dave Engel, author of *Just Like Bob Zimmerman's Blues: Dylan in Minnesota*. "Brit milah, or bris, signifies God's covenant with Abraham. The operation is performed by a religiously-schooled mohel in the presence of relatives and congregation members; a big party follows."

Dylan's father grew up in Duluth, in a family that spoke Yiddish (the common language of eastern European Jews) and eventually became a member of the local B'nai Brith lodge. His mother, a native of Hibbing, Minnesota, attended events sponsored by the Jewish Covenant Club and later became the president of the synagogue's sisterhood in Hibbing as well as the local chapter of Hadassah, a Zionist organization for women.

The nature of Dylan's parents' faith isn't clear (they never publicly addressed the issue and rarely spoke on the record), but their Jewish identity and religious tradition were important even if they weren't "practicing" or "observant." They didn't isolate themselves because of their ethnic identity or religion, and family was important.

"When I was young, my life was built around the family. We got together all the time," Dylan said. "There weren't many Jews around, and we never thought much about it one way or the other. Our family was close, but not narrow: one uncle married a Catholic, another married an Egyptian."[1]

Although Dylan's hometown of Hibbing was 92 percent Catholic (the remaining minority mostly Protestant), certain traditions were celebrated. On May 22, 1954, Bobby Zimmerman was bar mitzvahed; the witnesses at Agudath Achim—the only synagogue in Hibbing—heard the young boy coming of age read, in Hebrew, from the haftorah (selected readings from the Prophets), and listened to him speak on the moral duty of the Jew.

When biographer Robert Shelton asked Dylan's father if his son knew the whole Hebrew ritual and if he studied the biblical language, Abraham Zimmerman recalled, "Bobby could speak. He knew four hundred Hebrew words. Literally ... He could speak Hebrew like they do in Israel today. Rabbi Reuben Maier took great pride in him [during his bar mitzvah preparation in 1954] and took him to show him off one Friday night. The rabbi would say the sentence in English and Bobby would say it in Hebrew."[2]

As for Dylan's own memory of his bar mitzvah, he shared this touching account with Scott Cohen of *Spin* magazine in 1985:

"There weren't too many Jews in Hibbing, Minnesota. Most of them I was related to. The town didn't have a rabbi, and it was time for me to be bar mitzvahed. Suddenly, a rabbi showed up under strange circumstances for only a year. He and his wife got off the bus in the middle of winter. He showed up just in time for me to learn this stuff. He was an old man from Brooklyn who had a white beard and wore a black hat and black clothes. They put him upstairs above the café, which was the local hangout. It was a rock 'n' roll café where I used to hang out, too. I used to go up there every day to learn this stuff, either after school or after dinner. After studying with him an hour or so, I'd come down and boogie."

In the years that followed, Dylan attended Camp Herzl, a religious summer camp for Jewish kids in Webster, Wisconsin, from 1954 to 1958. One of its sponsors was his mother's local Hadassah chapter. Although Hebrew was taught and spoken at Camp Herzl, friend Steve Friedman recalled a rock 'n' roll moment when Dylan did a great Jerry Lee Lewis imitation, standing up at the camp piano and singing his heart out.

During a brief fling in college (three semesters at the University of Minnesota in Minneapolis), Dylan initially lived at the Jewish fraternity, Sigma Alpha Mu, but soon, living in others' apartments and listening to singers in coffeehouses became more appealing than the student/frat brother life. While growing up in Hibbing, Dylan's musical tastes had been influenced by a radio station out of Shreveport, Louisiana, that played blues and gospel. As for the gospel music, he shared with Dave Hoekstra of the *Chicago Sun-Times,* how he remembered hearing the unique sound of the Staple Singers for the first time in 1953. The gospel music was aired at midnight, and Dylan became acquainted with groups like the Swan Silvertones, the Dixie Hummingbirds, and the Highway QCs.

1961–1963

When Dylan moved to New York City, he became a student, and
eventually, a leader of the neo-folk scene. Part of the folk scene
in both Minneapolis and New York included the songs known
as spirituals, and he likely became more familiar with the gospel
themes woven into songs like "Jesus Met the Woman at the Well,"
"Streets of Glory," "Gospel Plow," "Wayfaring Stranger," and "Wade
in the Water."

Songs like "Jesus Christ" (Woody Guthrie), "Death Don't Have No
Mercy" (the Reverend Gary Davis), "Fixin' to Die" (Bukka White),
"In My Time of Dyin'" (Blind Willie Johnson), and "See That My
Grave is Kept Clean" (Blind Lemon Jefferson) also became pieces
of Dylan's history.

Dylan's first professional recording session included his harmonica
contribution to the gospel song "I'll Fly Away," which appeared on
Carolyn Hester's debut album for Columbia Records.

As for his own compositions of the early 1960s, many revealed a
fascination with spiritual matters: "Quit Your Low Down Ways"
noted the futility of the pretty mama who read her Bible and
prayed to the Lord, but just wouldn't quit her "lowdown ways."
The image of death creeping under one's door was on display in
"Whatcha Gonna Do?": *Tell me what you're gonna do/ When the
devil calls your cards/ O Lord, O Lord/ What shall you do.*

"Long Time Gone" with its line, *But I know I ain't no prophet/ An'
I ain't no prophet's son,* was lifted from an Old Testament passage
(Amos 7:14), and "Let Me Die in My Footsteps" reflected a familiarity with the words of Jesus: "There's been rumors of wars and wars
that have been" (Matthew 24:6).

167

While plumbing the depths of folk music in 1963, Dylan shared this with journalist Michael Iachetta of New York's *Daily News*: "There's mystery, magic, truth, and the Bible in great folk music. I can't hope to touch that. But I'm goin' to try."

As Dylan's pace of songwriting increased, the biblical allusions were evident. Even though he's generally been silent between songs, Dylan offered this up to his Carnegie Hall audience in New York City in 1963, prior to singing the apocalyptic "When the Ship Comes In": "Now days there are crueler Goliaths who do crueler and crueler things, but one day they're going to be slain, too, and people two thousand years from now can look back and say, 'Remember when the second Goliath was slayed.'"

1964–1966

Dylan was also writing epics like "Masters of War" and "With God On Our Side"—songs that showed a preoccupation with morality and the big questions. Yet, in 1964, we also see a search for an elusive God. "Know where God is?" asked Dylan. "The river, that's God. The river's right where you're standing, and it's up in the mountains, and it's down the bend, and into the sea. All the same instant. If there's a God, the river's Him."[3]

By the next year, in the documentary *Dont Look Back* [sic], Dylan responded to a reporter's question of whether he "believed" in something. "No, I don't believe in anything. No, why should I believe in anything? I don't see anything to believe in."

Was he just being cynical?

"No, I'm not cynical. I just can't see anything that anybody's offered me to believe in that I'm gonna believe in and put my trust and faith and everything in." Sensing other things when it came to Dylan's lyrical essence, Maureen Cleave of the *London Evening Standard* asked if he read the Bible. Dylan shrugged off the question, mumbling that he had glanced through it.

Dylan didn't claim a personal faith at this point, but clearly his lyrics showed a familiarity with the Bible. Some of this was indirectly from gospel and folk songs, but many direct allusions owed to more specific knowledge.

While one journalist later described Dylan's epic album of 1965, *Highway 61 Revisited*, as a "translation of the Bible in street terms." At the time of its release, critic Ralph Gleason of the *San Francisco Chronicle* wrote this: "I played portions of the new Dylan album for a young man studying for the priesthood. 'He's a preacher,' he said, 'he ought to be speaking in the cathedrals.'"

Although an interview with *Playboy* magazine in 1966 was filled with put-on responses, perhaps a serious moment was captured when Nat Hentoff asked Dylan what he had to look forward to: "Salvation, just plain salvation," came the simple reply.

If Dylan had, as he said in 1965, merely "glanced through" the Bible, then the season that followed his 1966 motorcycle accident provided an opportunity to read the Scriptures more carefully.

1967–1973

Dylan's mother revealed that there was one book in his Woodstock, New York, home that stood apart: "There's a huge Bible open on a stand in the middle of his study," Beatty Zimmerman told Toby Thompson for his book *Positively Main Street*. "Of all the books that crowd his house, [that] overflow from his house, that Bible gets the most attention. He's continuously getting up and going over to refer to something."

The album *John Wesley Harding*, composed in 1967, wasn't just juxtaposed against the times of psychedelic studio excess. With its acoustic guitar and bare bones sound, it reeked of morality, even by Dylan standards. "All Along the Watchtower" borrowed its image from the book of Isaiah, and "The Ballad of Frankie Lee and Judas Priest" was parable-like and biblically derived as well. "Sign on the Cross," an obvious example of a spiritually inclined Dylan from *The Basement Tapes* sessions of 1967, had Dylan suggesting (and worrying) that the sign mockingly placed above Jesus' head during His crucifixion, which read "King of the Jews," might be "the thing you need the most." Another reflective outtake was "Waltzing with Sin," which spoke of roaming about at parties with a cold heart and no true love, and "each time you're dancing, you're waltzing with sin."

After Dylan's father died in 1967, associate Harold Leventhal suggested he visit the Holy Land and gave him some books on Israel. "After his father died, Bob became quite conscious of his Jewishness," Leventhal said. "He was very excited about Israel when he got back."[4]

As Dylan's public was grappling with the new family man image presented in albums like *Nashville Skyline* (1969) and *New Morning* (1970), Dylan visited Israel in the summers of 1969 and 1970. By his third visit in 1971, where he privately celebrated his thirtieth birthday with his family, the Israel connection and Dylan's silence about it led to the following: While visiting Mount Zion Yeshiva, a theological training center in Jerusalem, Dylan was introduced by a resident rabbi to some American students. Why did he seem to avoid focusing on his Jewish roots? one student wondered. "I'm a Jew. It touches my poetry, my life, in ways I can't describe," Dylan replied. "Why should I declare something that should be so obvious?"[5]

Robert Campbell, writing for *Christian Century* in 1971, saw Dylan gradually being accepted as a poet by the cultural establishment but looked to a day when acceptance would come from other circles. "Perhaps the day will come when the clergy, too, open themselves up to Dylan's work," Campbell wrote. "For his music, even apart from its many references to Christ, God, and the Bible, has a general spirituality about it. This spirituality has endured in Dylan's music because of his determination to maintain his integrity, to continue to make an honest personal statement about his life."

During the Yom Kippur War of 1973, Harry Leventhal attempted to organize a benefit for Israel at Madison Square Garden. For whatever reason, Dylan declined. While recording *Planet Waves*, an album that included the classic "Forever Young," a United Jewish Appeal member sent a number of letters and telegrams to Dylan requesting his assistance. "He had seen Dylan at the Wailing Wall," wrote Stephen Pickering (photos were inadvertently taken by a UPI photographer during his Jerusalem visit in 1971), "and sensed Dylan's profound concern with his own soul." Reports said Dylan privately contributed to Israel's cause.

1974–1978

When Dylan hit the road in 1974, his first tour since the motorcycle accident of 1966, Pickering spoke to Rabbi Richard Rocklin (who grew up with Dylan and knew his family well) on the day of the Charlotte, North Carolina, concert, and discovered the rabbi had received a gift. "When Bob came by he left six tickets so I could give them to my confirmation class. It excited the kids, and instead of wanting to talk Jewish philosophy, they wanted me to tell them everything about Bobby," Rocklin said. "He'd make one helluva rabbi because he and I both grew up in homes with intense Jewish feelings ... You don't necessarily have to be a praying Jew to be a Jew. Bobby never lost his Jewish roots. Israel moved him very much. He was bar-mitzvahed like all of us."[6] During a tour stop in Miami, Dylan attended what has been labeled a "religious rally" at Peacock Park, but it was, more accurately, a rally to win souls for Jesus. Dylan chatted afterward with one of the speakers, Arthur Blessit, a man once known as "The Mod Minister of the Sunset Strip," who had a club in Hollywood called His Place, which catered the Gospel message to the counter-cultural crowd. A journalist from the *Miami Herald* filed this report: "Bob went up and talked to Blessit for about ten minutes. My feeling was that he just was inquiring. Art didn't want to say anything about it. He said, 'If anybody is going to talk about it, it'll have to be Bob Dylan.'"

After an Atlanta concert, Dylan was invited to a party at the governor's mansion. Governor Jimmy Carter's son, Chip, presented Dylan with a coin that was found at an Israeli archaeological dig and learned that Dylan was impressed by his father's visit to Israel in 1972.

Although Dylan informed Neil Hickey of *TV Guide* in 1976 that there was no special significance to his 1971 visit to Israel, he did acknowledge that he was interested in "what and who a Jew is" and knew that, unlike other Semitic people, the Jews were hated by a lot of people. "There's something going on here that's hard to explain," he concluded.

When asked how he imagined God, Dylan seemed to express a pantheistic view, saying he could see God in a daisy, at night, and in the wind and rain, but a fuller context revealed the monotheism that has seemingly been etched into his soul. "I see creation just about everywhere. The highest form of song is prayer: King David's, Solomon's, the wailing of a coyote, the rumble of the earth," he observed. "It must be wonderful to be God. There's so much going on out there that you can't get to it all. It would take you longer than forever."

Here we see Dylan's sense of his Jewish roots, where God is clearly proclaimed as the one and only Creator—an omniscient God, a God entirely aware of the goings on in His creation. But just over a year after this interview, Dylan told Ron Rosenbaum of *Playboy* that he wasn't a "patriot to any creed," stating that a devout Christian or Muslim could be just as effective as a devout Jew. He sensed a "heartfelt God" but didn't think God wanted him thinking about Him all the time. "He's got enough people asking Him for favors. He's got enough people asking Him to pull strings," Dylan said with characteristic wit.

One fascinating thing about this interview was how a decade-old memory from a national magazine revealed Dylan's agitation with the atheistic viewpoint: "I remember seeing a *Time* magazine on an airplane a few years back and it had a big cover headline, 'Is God Dead?' [incidentally, an issue dated April 8, 1966, cleverly scheduled to coincide with Easter] I mean, that was—would you think it was a responsible thing to do?" asked a perturbed Dylan. "What does God think of that? I mean, if you were God, how would you like to see that written about yourself?"

Then Dylan delivered the hammer blow: "You know, I think the country's gone downhill since that day." An amazed Ron Rosenbaum asked for clarification: "Really? Since that particular question was asked?"

"Yeah, I think at that point, some very irresponsible people got hold of too much power to put such an irrelevant thing like that on a magazine when they could be talking about real issues. Since that day, you've had to kind of make your own way."

When asked how we were doing in "making our own way," Dylan said we're born and then we die, and we're concerned with our journey from point A to Z. "But it's pretty self-deluding if you think that's all there is," he concluded.[7]

On the one hand, Bob Dylan certainly didn't follow the increasingly popular secular-humanist view, which denied the supernatural, neatly doing away with God. On the other hand, even though his monotheistic tendencies were evident, he didn't seem committed. There was some neutral ground; it wasn't a matter of either faith in Christ or unbelief, as he would later write. But the foundation for the teachings of Jesus was there.

And there were those people Dylan met along the road of life who claimed that Jesus was now dwelling inside of them: Noel Paul Stookey, after visiting Dylan in Woodstock in 1967, followed Dylan's advice to "read the Bible" and soon became a believer in Jesus; New York deejay Scott Ross, at the time of *New Morning*, in 1970, shared with Dylan that he had come to the realization that Jesus was the truth; Jimmy Carter, the governor of Georgia and then U.S. president, wouldn't shy away from sharing the fact of his faith; and a number of bandmates and close friends—Roger McGuinn, T-Bone Burnett, Steven Soles, and Jerry Scheff—either became believers in Jesus or reaffirmed their childhood commitments by returning to church not long after the *Rolling Thunder* tours of 1975-1976.

In 1977, journalist Ron Rosenbaum—by asking, "Do you think Christ is an answer?"—drew out Dylan's most revealing commentary about Jesus before his salvation experience of 1979.[8]

"What is it that attracts people to Christ?" Dylan asked. "The fact that it was such a tragedy, is what. Who does Christ become when he lives inside a person? Many people say that Christ lives inside of them. Well, what does this mean? I've talked to many people whom Christ lives inside; I haven't met one who would want to trade places with Christ. Not one of his people put himself on the line when it came down to the final hour."[9]

The following year, during a world tour, singer Helena Springs recalled Dylan experiencing some problems and asking her questions "that no one could possibly help with." Springs asked if he ever prayed, which apparently caught him off guard. "When I have trouble I pray," Springs confided. "He asked me more questions about it, he started inquiring. He's a very inquisitive person which is one good thing about him—he's always searching for truth, truth in anything he can find."[10]

Dylan's 1978 album, *Street-Legal*, is a document of the truth-seeking man that Helena Springs and others had witnessed. It is an album of journey, mystery, and painful soul-searching. "Changing of the Guard" referenced the good shepherd grieving, renegade priests, angels' voices, and Eden burning. "No Time to Think" cited the warlords of sorrow and queens of tomorrow who'll offer their heads for a prayer, but in the end, salvation is conspicuously absent. A discussion of destination is offered up in "Senor"—is it Lincoln County Road or Armageddon? On the closing number "Where Are You Tonight?" there's a long-distance train, the obscurity of truth, the fighting with his twin (the enemy within), a woman who divined his private thoughts, and a biting into forbidden fruit. Upon the album's release, Philippe Adler of the French magazine *L'Expresse*, asked Dylan if he believed in God. "Let's say, as He shows Himself," the singer responded.

Before long, it would be the twilight of 1978; Dylan would soon be having his life-changing encounter with Jesus. The Bible asserts that the angels in Heaven rejoice when a single sinner repents. The rock 'n' world wouldn't quite know what to do.

1979–1981

In early 1979, Larry Myers and Paul Emond, two pastors from the Vineyard church, visited Dylan's home in Brentwood, California (per Dylan's request), and shared the Gospel. Not long afterward,

Dylan came to faith in Jesus, was baptized, and enrolled in a discipleship class through the Vineyard.

Author Martin Grossman has noted how many of Dylan's Jewish fans were stunned to learn that the singer had been baptized and was studying and praying with an evangelical Christian group. "Some regard it as the most shocking act of apostasy since Shabtai Zvi, a messianic pretender of medieval times who converted to Islam and left millions of followers in despair."[11]

The praying and studying would soon be translated into Dylan exercising his God-given gift: The songs of *Slow Train Coming* were released in the fall of 1979 and served as confirmation that Dylan, indeed, had turned to Jesus. Millions of Dylan followers, it seemed, were in despair.

Larry Yudelson, of "Tangled Up in Jews," a website devoted to exploring Dylan's Jewish roots, recalled one Washington, D.C.-area rabbi who had "painfully excommunicated Dylan from his record collection when the singer converted."

For her part, Dylan's mother seemed at peace when interviewed by Fred Bernstein for his book, *The Official Jewish Mothers' Hall of Fame*. "What religion a person is shouldn't make any difference to anybody else. I'm not bigoted in any way," Beatty Zimmerman said. "Rabbis would call me up. I'd say, 'If you're upset, you try to change him.'"

Dylan's gospel tours of November 1979 through May 1980, a total of seventy-nine concerts where he only played his newly-penned songs of faith (and managed to preach a bit between songs), were a shock to many. The overwhelming majority of critics lambasted the "new Dylan" and seemed to relish it.

In May 1980, Dylan was introspective when he spoke to journalist Karen Hughes about the call of God on his life. "I guess He's always been calling me. Of course, how would I have ever known that? ... That it was Jesus calling me. I always thought it was some voice that would be more identifiable," Dylan observed. "But Christ is calling everybody, we just turn Him off. We just don't want to hear. We think He's gonna make our lives miserable, you know what I mean? We think He's gonna make us do things we don't want to do. Or keep us from doing things we want to do. But God's got His own purpose and time for everything. He knew when I would respond to His call."[12]

By November 1980, much to the delight of fans, Dylan began incorporating his older songs into the set lists. He told Robert Hilburn of the *Los Angeles Times* that he had made his statement with *Slow Train Coming* and *Saved* and didn't think he could've made it any better than he did in some of the songs from those albums. "I didn't mean to deliver a hammer blow. It might come out that way, but I'm not trying to kill anybody," he explained. "You can't put down people who don't believe. Anybody can have the answer I have. I mean, it's free."

Ultimately, Dylan paid a price, both commercially and critically, for the personal convictions that led to the so-called religious trilogy of *Slow Train Coming* (1979), *Saved* (1980), and *Shot of Love* (1981) and the accompanying tours: Many longtime fans scoffed while jumping ship. "My sense of estrangement was amplified at the end of that decade when Dylan chose the moment of new wave skepticism and ennui to embrace Christianity," wrote Vit Wagner of *Rolling Stone*, echoing the sentiment of countless others. "After that," he said, "I didn't think much about Dylan, one way or the other."

Some were thinking though; among them were Dylan's musician friends. Harvey Brooks was an old friend who shared Dylan's Jewish heritage and played bass during the electric concerts of 1965 and on two of Dylan albums, *Highway 61 Revisited* (1965) and *New*

Morning (1970). Clearly taken aback by Dylan's turn to Jesus, he recalled for John Bauldie of *The Telegraph* an opportunity he had to attend a 1981 concert. "I was a studio manager and producer in Atlanta, and he came to tour," Brooks remembered. "He had just converted to Christianity and I called up and got passes for the show, but to be honest, I had problems with his confusion and I just couldn't bring myself to go. It led to my own confusion."

When drummer Bruce Gary joined Dylan for the last six concerts of 1981 tour, he remembered Dylan was mixing in his religious songs with his hits, but noted, "he was still very much into the Jesus thing," and that anyone was free to join Dylan and others in the singer's dressing room before the show for a recitation of the Lord's Prayer.[13]

1982–1989

After these shows, Dylan wouldn't tour the U.S. again for nearly five years and would only briefly tour Europe in 1984, a tour that featured only a few of the religious numbers. His two album releases during this spell—*Infidels* (1983) and *Empire Burlesque* (1985)—contained a number of biblical allusions, but their overall thrust was entirely different from the overt statements of 1979 to 1981.

Since 1982 there have been persistent rumors that Dylan renounced his faith in Jesus, that he returned to Judaism, or that he somehow got over his "religious" hangover. Some private actions which were leaked to the public through press accounts—from attending his sons' bar mitzvahs to studying with some Orthodox Hasidic Jews, the Lubavitchers—led many to conclude that Dylan was no longer the property of Jesus. Additionally, when Dylan returned to touring on a regular basis in 1986, even though the so-called religious songs appeared, they were simply a part, not a dominant feature. What did this mean? If one works from the assumption that Dylan no longer believes in Jesus—and he no longer believes in the Bible, literally, like he obviously did during 1979 to 1981—then a huge problem remains: the numerous facts that fly in the face of this assumption.

In 1981, when Neil Spencer of *New Musical Express* asked if his interest in Judaism and his visits to Israel and the Western Wall [1969-1971] were "compatible" with his present beliefs [i.e., his belief in Jesus], Dylan responded: "There's really no difference between any of it in my mind."

Dylan's decision, in 1983, to study with the Lubavitchers, a group of Hasidic Jews, was just that—his decision. It revealed an increasing interest in his Jewish roots and Scripture, but there is no evidence that Dylan left behind his belief in Jesus (although clearly the Lubavitchers do not subscribe to this belief).

James Earl, writing for the University of Hartford Studies in Literature, didn't buy into the supposed contradiction of Dylan believing in Jesus and embracing his Jewish heritage. "Those who follow Dylan primarily through rumor or the press often ask if he hasn't gone back to being a Jew, but the question is wrong," Earl concluded. "After the first flush of his rebirth he rediscovered and reabsorbed his Jewishness in new and personal ways."

Earl's analysis was all but confirmed when Dylan shared the following with Martin Keller of the *Minneapolis City Pages*, a widely syndicated interview that made the rounds in 1983. Here we see a man firmly rooted in a literal interpretation of the Bible and someone who still saw the significance of Jesus appearing:

"My so-called Jewish roots are in Egypt. They went down there with Joseph, and they came back out with Moses—you know, the guy that killed the Egyptian, married an Ethiopian girl and brought the Law down from the mountain. The same Moses whose staff turned into a serpent. The same person who killed three thousand Hebrews for getting down, stripping off their clothes and dancing around a golden calf. These are my roots. Jacob had four wives and thirteen children, who fathered thirteen children, who fathered an entire people. Those are my roots too. Gideon, with a small army, defeating an army of thousands. Deborah, the prophetess; Esther the queen and many Canaanite women. Reuben slipping into his father's bed when his father wasn't there. These are my roots.

"Delilah tempting Samson, killing him softly with her song. The mighty King David was an outlaw before he was king, you know. He had to hide in caves and get his meals at back doors. The wonderful King Saul had a warrant out on him—a 'no-knock' search warrant. They wanted to cut his head off. John the Baptist could tell you more about it. Roots, man—we're talking about Jewish roots, you want to know more? Check up on Elijah the prophet. He could make [it] rain. Isaiah the prophet, even Jeremiah, see if their brethren didn't want to bust their brains for telling it right like it is. Yeah, these are my roots I suppose."[14]

For Dylan to mention the John the Baptist amid the long line of biblical prophets is not insignificant. Chronologically, he is the last prophet, and a question worth asking is, What was his prophetic role? According to the New Testament, when he saw Jesus walking toward him, John the Baptist proclaimed, "Look, the Lamb of God who takes away the sin of the world." Amid heckling, Dylan had told one of his audiences of the gospel tours this very thing. Besides his interview with Martin Keller in 1983, Dylan gave his only other interview to Robert Hilburn of the *Los Angeles Times*. Hilburn wondered if any *Slow Train Coming* songs would appear on future tours. "Yeah, I'll probably do a few of those," Dylan said. "I get letters from people who say they were touched by those shows. I don't disavow any of that."

Although the musical energy of the gospel tours was undeniable, clearly the lyrics and Dylan's stage raps were a significant issue. "I don't particularly regret telling people how to get their souls saved," an unrepentant Dylan remarked, "whoever was supposed to pick it up, picked it up."

Jim Keltner, Dylan's drummer from 1979 to 1981, has spoken about the burdens his friend faced during those heady days. "What I found to be really amazing was the amount of people who mistrusted Bob. There were so many Christian people that mistrusted him, saying, 'This is not for real.' 'He's a phony.' [And] people in the Jewish community mistrusted him," Keltner recalled. "They were offended, or mistrusted whether he was for real with it. Bob [was] offending everyone. And at the same time I know, from being out there with him, and talking with certain people, that a lot of people's lives were changed forever. In the Christian world, they say 'saved.' I know, for a fact, that happened to a lot of people."[15]

For all that has been made of Dylan's studying with the Lubavitchers in 1983, it is revealing that in 1984 Dylan expressed a biblical worldview that had not turned its back on Jesus and the New Testament. When Kurt Loder of *Rolling Stone* asked if he was a "literal believer" of the Bible, Dylan replied, "Yeah. Sure, yeah. I am," and when Loder asked if he thought the Old and New Testaments were equally valid, Dylan responded, "To me."

When Dylan was interviewed by Scott Cohen of *Spin* magazine in 1985, there was plenty of biblical talk, including how Dylan found out, subsequent to his bar mitzvah of 1954, that the rabbi was of the "orthodox" persuasion. Perhaps this served as a convenient launching pad because he immediately proceeded to debunk the self-imposed labels within both Judaism and Christianity. "Jews separate themselves like that: Orthodox, Conservative, Reform, as if God calls them that," Dylan dryly observed. "Christians, too: Baptists, Assembly of God, Methodists, Calvinists. God has no respect for a person's title. He don't care what you call yourself."

A staple of Dylan's tour of 1986 was "In the Garden," his biblical composition from *Saved* that pointed to Jesus as Creator and Messiah. Dylan also managed to participate in the Chabad telethon, an annual fund-raising event hosted by the Lubavitchers. Besides contributing a taped public service announcement that lent support for Chabad's drug rehab and educational programs, Dylan contributed, interestingly enough, a version of "Thank God," a gospel song Hank Williams was known to sing.

During his first concerts in Israel in 1987, Dylan had no problem singing songs like "In the Garden" and "Gotta Serve Somebody," leading some to believe he was sending a "mixed message," but the evidence has shown that Dylan has no problems with the co-existence of his Jewish roots and a belief in Jesus. However, a photo of Dylan onstage in Tel Aviv, circulated by the Associated Press, ran a caption that included this matter-of-fact statement: "Dylan converted to Christianity in 1979 but has since returned to Judaism." Presumably, "returning to Judaism"—the tired rumor that has followed Dylan since 1982—wouldn't allow for the belief that Jesus is God and the Messiah, yet the inclusion of "In the Garden" in Tel Aviv was expressing just that: a song, in essence, aimed at some of the religious leaders of Jesus' day who didn't recognize Him.

When asked by Robert Hilburn of the *Los Angeles Times* if people should interpret Dylan's visit to Israel in big statement terms, Dylan simply expressed warmth for Israel and said he'd play anywhere he was welcome. After having visited Egypt before the Tel Aviv concert, Dylan pondered his biblical roots and expressed frustration at the age-old conflict in the Middle East. Arabs and Jews, Dylan insisted, were really brothers who shared the same father. "If someone is anti-Semitic, they're anti-Arab as much as anti-Jew. The problem is politics. I'd like to play Egypt. I felt right at home in Egypt. I wasn't surprised because Egypt land is in all our [Jewish] blood. I didn't go to see the Pyramids: I wanted to see the prison where Joseph was in, and the place Abraham took Sarah.'"

What we now know as Dylan's "Never-Ending Tour" began in 1988, and by tour's end, during a four-night stint at New York's Radio City Music Hall, Dylan was prefacing "In the Garden" with a plea for Amnesty International to conclude their world tour with this song; the human rights' organization had, in previous years, chosen other songs of his to close out their campaigns ("I Shall Be Released" and "Chimes of Freedom"). One wonders why Dylan wanted to turn on the Amnesty world—a world that was ultimately protesting how we treat one another—onto his evangelical narrative about Jesus? If nothing else, it seemed a rather unorthodox stance for a legendary rock 'n' roller.

In the fall of 1989, Dylan made another appearance on the Chabad telethon, inevitably fueling further speculation of a Dylan returned to Judaism. As author Marty Grossman has noted, "Chabad denies the divinity of Jesus and works very actively to return straying Jews to Judaism." Yet Dylan was singing "In the Garden"—his song that affirmed the divinity of Jesus—in concerts just before his Chabad appearance, as well as afterward.

Mitch Glaser, a Jewish man who believes in Jesus (and president of Chosen People ministries), didn't see any problem. "Dylan's support for Chabad is not at all disturbing, because a lot of us support Jewish causes. It's not like we became Christians and all of a sudden we're no longer Jews," Glaser said. "We're very much Jews ... But it wouldn't matter to Chabad [if Dylan still believed in Jesus]; that would not keep them from inviting him. They're not like that."[16]

Just days after his Chabad appearance, Edna Gundersen of *USA Today* reminded Dylan how the media had dubbed him a "born again." "If that's what was laid on me, there must have been a reason for it," Dylan replied. "Whatever label is put on you, the purpose of it is to limit your accessibility to people."

In 1983, Dylan told Robert Hilburn of the *Los Angeles Times* that the born again label was a "media hype term" that "threw people in a corner and left them there."

Gundersen also heard how Dylan didn't view *Slow Train Coming* and *Saved* as albums of "religious content" at all; he didn't feel the word "religious" did justice to them. "People who work for big companies, that's their 'religion,'" he said. "That's not a word that has any holiness to it." How then, did he characterize the albums? "It's just based on my experience in daily matters, what you run up against and how you respond to things."

1990–1998

In 1990, Dylan was interviewed by Gundersen again and spoke about the moral state of contemporary music. "People say music is intended to elevate the spirit. But you've got a lot of groups and lyrics projecting emptiness and giving you nothing, less than nothing, because they're taking up your time," Dylan lamented. "It's not difficult to get people throbbing in their guts. That can lead you down an evil path if that's all they're getting. You gotta put something on top of that."

When interviewed by Joe Queenan of *Spy* magazine in 1991, Dylan reflected on the backlash he had received a decade earlier during the gospel tours. "People didn't like those tunes," he said. "They rejected all that stuff when my show would be all off the new album [*Slow Train Coming*]. People would shout, 'We want to hear the old songs.'"

Dylan's album releases of the early nineties, *Good As I Been to You*

(1992) and *World Gone Wrong* (1993), were a return to the roots music he so enjoyed and absorbed as a young singer coming up in the coffeehouses of Minneapolis and Greenwich Village. Blues and folk strands were woven throughout, as the powerful yet acquired taste of Dylan's voice, his acoustic guitar, and harmonica were in full force.

Within the liner notes to *World Gone Wrong*, there would be no shortage of apocalyptic Dylan writing. "What attracts me to the song is how the lunacy of trying to fool the self is set aside at some given point," Dylan wrote about the Doc Watson recording, "Lone Pilgrim." "Salvation and the needs of mankind are prominent and hegemony takes a breathing spell. 'My soul flew to mansions on high.' Technology to wipe out truth is now available. Not everybody can afford it but it's available. When the price comes down, look out! There won't be songs like these anymore."

In 1992, Dylan recorded Dallas Holm's "Rise Again," a song that appeared during the gospel tours. The song's first-person perspective revealed Jesus: *Go ahead and mock my name—my love for you is still the same ...'Cause I'll come again—there's no power on earth can keep me back/ Yes I'll come again—come to take My people back/ Go ahead and say I'm dead and gone/ But you will see that you were wrong.*[17]

In June of 1993, Dylan returned to the Holy Land, playing concerts in Tel Aviv, Beersheba, and Haifa, and including biblically inspired numbers like "I and I," "Little Moses," and "Cat's in the Well," the latter of which was a recent composition, with its farewell line of "May the Lord have mercy on us all."

By 1995, a journalist questioned Dylan specifically on a lyric written in the same year he received Jesus. "I remember the lines, *You talk about Buddha/ You talk about Muhammad/ But you never said a word about the One who came to die for us instead.* Those were fearless words," said John Dolen of Fort Lauderdale's *Sun-Sentinel*. "How do you feel about those words and the songs you wrote during that period now?"

"Just writing a song like that probably emancipated me from other kinds of illusions. I can't say I would disagree with that line," Dylan remarked. "On its own level, it was some kind of turning point for me, writing that."

Dylan continued supporting Jewish charity causes, such as the benefit at the Simon Wiesenthal Center in Los Angeles in 1997, and continued to prompt people to scratch their heads with a performance before the Pope in the same year at a concert for the Catholic Eucharistic Congress.

In December of 1997, Dylan would be welcome as one of five honorees at the Kennedy Center Honors as Shirley Caesar, at Dylan's request, belted out "Gotta Serve Somebody" in what seemed to be a preview of things to come. "In fact, he told me that he wasn't even gonna show up unless they had me [there] to sing in his honor," Caesar said. "I praise God for that."[18]

By the following summer, Dylan had re-introduced this same song to his stage repertoire and was—like the gospel tours of 1979 to 1981—opening his concerts with it. In the meantime, Dylan's 1997 album, *Time Out of Mind*, had received critical and commercial success (his first top ten album since *Slow Train Coming*), winning the Grammy for Album of the Year. The album sounded like a man full of blues-drenched world-weariness, yet who stayed above water with the underpinning of hope. Author Ronnie Keohane saw the album as a "believer's blues" type affair, where Dylan was writing an open letter to his Lord, lamenting his status in the flesh but not willing to give up the hope from on high—his Lord who was his "shield" and would not lead him astray.

Although Dylan toured constantly between 1988 and 1998, singing mostly his time-honored classics from the 1960s, he always included the spiritually inclined songs from all periods of his career and his testimonials from the gospel albums of 1979-1981. But by 1999, songs about Jesus began to appear more often.

1999–PRESENT

In fact, since 1999 Dylan has trotted out hymns like "Rock of Ages" and "Pass Me Not, O Gentle Savior" and traditional gospel songs like "Hallelujah, I'm Ready to Go," "Somebody Touched Me," and "A Voice from On High," as well as apocalyptic fare like "This World Can't Stand Long." Additionally, "I Am the Man, Thomas" was, lyrically, as overt as anything from *Slow Train Coming* or *Saved*, and Dylan chose to open numerous concerts with the song. For those who had been certain that Dylan was merely tipping his troubadour hat to American roots music but not reflecting his experience of 1979, explanations were in short supply, as Dylan also re-introduced songs like "Solid Rock" and "Saving Grace," which were his own songs about this Creator and Redeemer who had "saved his soul from sin."

In March 2002, following *"Love and Theft"*—another landmark album filled with distinctly American music—Dylan entered a Los Angeles studio with a rewritten version of "Gonna Change My Way of Thinking" for the tribute album *Gotta Serve Somebody: The Gospel Songs of Bob Dylan*. The song was transformed lyrically and musically, but its overt sentiments were still evident: *Every day you got to pray for guidance, every day you got to give yourself a chance … / Oh, Lord, you know I have no friend without you.*

Dylan told Mikal Gilmore of *Rolling Stone* in 1986 he hated to keep "beating people over the head with the Bible," but it was the only thing that he knew "that stayed true."

1. Laurence A. Schlesinger, "Trouble in Mind: A Rabbinic Perspective on Bob Dylan's 'Religious Period,'" *On the Tracks* #4 (Fall 1994), p. 32.
2. "Boston Herald's 1978 Interview with Bob Dylan by Barbara Kerr," *On the Tracks* #18 (Spring 2000), p. 8.
3. Ian Woodward, "The Robert Shelton Minnesota Transcripts: Interview with Abe and Beatty Zimmerman," from *Isis: A Bob Dylan Anthology*, Derek Barker [Editor], (London: Helter Skelter Publishing, 2001), p. 21.
4. Stephen Pickering, *Bob Dylan Approximately: A Portrait of the Jewish Poet in Search of God: A Midrash*, (New York: David McKay Company, Inc., 1975), p. 60.
5. Ibid., p. 82.
6. Robert Shelton, *No Direction Home: The Life and Music of Bob Dylan*, (New York: Da Capo Press, 1997), p. 413 (originally published in 1986, Beech Tree Books, New York).
7. Pickering, *Bob Dylan Approximately*, p. 80, 82.
8. Ron Rosenbaum, "Bob Dylan: A Candid Conversation with the Visionary Whose Songs Changed the Times," *Playboy*, March 1978, p. 90.
9. Ibid.
10. Chris Cooper, "Helena Springs: A Conversation with Chris Cooper," *The Telegraph* #34 (Winter 1989), pp. 72-73.
11. Martin Grossman (with Ronnie Schreiber and Larry Yudelson), "Tangled Up in Jews," *On the Tracks* #22 (Fall 2001), p. 46.
12. Karen Hughes, "Dylan Follows Christ with a Passion," *The Dominion*, August 2, 1980, p. 8.
13. Clinton Heylin, *Bob Dylan: Behind the Shades Revisited*, (New York: William Morrow, 2001), p. 543.
14. Martin Keller, "Times Are A-Changin': In Search of the Latest Bob Dylan," *Dallas Times-Herald*, November 6, 1983, H-1.
15. Howard Sounes, *Down the Highway: The Life of Bob Dylan*, (New York: Grove Press, 2001, p. 331).
16. Author interview with Mitch Glaser, 2001.
17. Dallas Holm, lyric excerpt from "Rise Again," Copyright 1977 by Dimension Music/SESAC (all rights controlled by The Benson Company, Inc., Nashville, Tennessee).
18. Author interview with Shirley Caesar, 1999.

LENNY KRAVITZ

MULTICULTURAL SEEKER

By Chad Bonham

Lenny Kravitz has been called a lot of things in his life. He's been labeled a fraud, a chameleon, and an impostor. He's been described as derivative, gratuitous, overindulgent, and pretentious. Those are some of the harsher words that have been levied against him despite spending more than ten years as one of rock 'n' roll's most enduring artists. However, it hasn't all been bad press for the four-time Grammy Award winner. Some people have actually said nice things about Kravitz, praising him for his diversity, his positive lyrics, and his uncanny ability to break stereotypes. Others have gone as far as calling him a brilliant musician.

But strangely enough, one of the things Kravitz has worn most boldly on his sleeve is one of the adjectives that fans and critics alike seldom use—Christian. Beyond the media hype and the glitz and glamour of the rock star lifestyle, Kravitz has always subscribed to a deeply rooted faith. As if the consistent Gospel messages placed indubitably within his song lyrics aren't enough, Kravitz bears a tattoo across his back proclaiming "My Heart Belongs to Jesus Christ." Yet somehow something else always ends up the focus: relationships, musical influences, fashion sense, politics, anything but the part of his life that Kravitz himself deems the most important.[1] Looking at his life and his career leads to some interesting questions about just how focused he himself has stayed on his faith. On the song "In My Life Today" from *Circus*, Kravitz alluded that he had always known about the need for God in his life. This inherent need would crop up in his music and in many of his interviews, giving credence to what may have been perceived as empty claims.

POSTER CHILD FOR MULTICULTURALISM

It was the marriage of a Russian Jewish man named Sy Kravitz to Roxie Roker, a black Christian woman who was raised in a strict West Indian family, that laid the groundwork for Kravitz's unordinary life. Even by East Coast standards, this kind of interracial, bi-religious marriage was well before its time. Sy was a television news producer for NBC and Roxie a young actress still ten years away from her big break playing Helen Willis on *The Jeffersons*. In an appropriate twist of fate, her character would also be married to a white man.

When asked about the Star of David and the cross that Kravitz wears around his neck, he explained that the objects represented both sides of his family heritage. "But I follow the teachings of Christ," Kravitz said, "who obviously was a Jew."[2] His politically correct answer might sound like religious appeasement, but understanding the equality by which he was raised helps make sense of the abnormal circumstance. "It was really cool because I'd go to church and temple," Kravitz explained to *Interview* magazine. "I'd have Easter, I'd have Passover, I'd have Christmas, I'd have Hanukkah ... I went to Hebrew school and all the kids stared at me because it was like, no black kid ever walked into Hebrew school."[3] Not only was Kravitz the product of a pioneering multicultural family, he showed early signs of being a true musical multi-linguist. He understood and appreciated great music no matter what the genre. Kravitz took in all of the big shows, from jazz greats such as Duke Ellington and Ella Fitzgerald to the pop icons of his youth, such as Stevie Wonder and the Jackson 5. Later on, he would begin to diversify even more by diving into the music of the Beatles. One of the last influences on Kravitz's music would come during the early eighties in the form of enigmatic artist Prince. This open-ended embrace of multiple genres would be a blessing and a curse as Kravitz began to make his own music as a teenager.

Lenny Kravitz was born on May 26, 1964, in Brooklyn, New York. It's no coincidence he was born right in the middle of the twentieth century's most influential decade. Although his formidable teen-age years were in the seventies, the music and the message of the sixties has made a lasting impression. The difference with Kravitz has been a noticeable absence of lyrics promoting illicit drug use and "free love." Instead, he has preached a consistent message of "peace on Earth" with a teetering blend of humanism and Christianity. In some cases, Kravitz has managed to espouse both ideals in the same song. On his album simply titled *Lenny* (2001), he cried out to a higher power in "God Save Us All," but simultaneously maintained, *If we really try, maybe we can make it.* The balance between faith in God and faith in mankind is a duality that would find its way into much of Kravitz's music, perhaps as a sort of balancing act between his need to proclaim his faith yet remain unobtrusive and never preachy.

Musically, his ties to the music of both the sixties and the seventies have gained him worldwide appeal but only sparse critical acclaim. Kravitz was highly influenced by the Beatles, Led Zeppelin, Jimi Hendrix, and Sly and the Family Stone, among other retro icons. While some recent media darlings have found this approach to be conducive to early success (i.e., Norah Jones and John Mayer), it would take Kravitz years before shaking the label of rip-off artist. Publicly, this seemingly hypocritical treatment has never appeared to bother him. When speaking to *Interview* magazine, he recognized the disparity by comparing his plight to that of English pop/rock band Oasis. "I have influences like anybody else," Kravitz said. "(Oasis is) not just influenced by the Beatles, they actually take stuff. Then they get praised for the same thing I got dumped on for."[4] Mostly though, Kravitz has left the issue alone and forged ahead to make the music he wanted to make, not the music that others might have expected.

ROCK STAR 101

By 1979, a fifteen-year-old Kravitz left home against the wishes of his parents. He split time sleeping in his Pinto or staying with different friends in the neighborhood. Somehow this two-year routine did not affect his ability to graduate from Beverly Hills High School. But education was the least of Kravitz's concerns. He was aiming for a different life—the life of a rock star.

Kravitz may have been influenced by a number of artists whose time had long since past, but it was the style and image of a brand new musician that turned a young dreamer's creative wheels. Just as the psychedelic seventies were morphing into the new wave eighties, Prince and his "revolutionary" band were set to change the musical landscape with a brand new sound that blended pop, rock, R&B, and funk. Kravitz had found himself a new hero. Prince made such an impact on him, he gave his own image a complete overhaul and donned the stage name "Romeo Blue." Kravitz straightened his hair, wore blue contact lenses and dressed like a flashy bohemian with long coats and flare cuff shirts fit for the most stylish of Buccaneers. During an Internet chat that took place in November of 2002, one fan asked if he and Prince were related. "We are not related other than spiritual brothers, as we all are," Kravitz responded. "But we're very good friends. Yes, he inspired me very much being a multi-instrumentalist, writer, and producer."[5] His new age approach in answering the question suggested that he and Prince were more than just linked musically, but philosophically as well.

Kravitz may have met his soul brother in Prince, but his soul mate came in the form of actress Lisa Bonet, who played Denise on the top-rated comedy *The Cosby Show*. The two met backstage at a New Edition concert and quickly became close friends. Not long after, they began living together before ultimately eloping to Las Vegas in 1987. His parents had divorced a few years earlier, so Kravitz was determined not to repeat their mistakes. Sadly, he would not be so fortunate. But in the early days of their marriage, Kravitz and Bonet experienced great bliss, and the two had a daughter named Zoe.

Living inconspicuously in Bonet's shadow, Kravitz began working on his first solo record. Record labels didn't know what to make of this black musician with rock 'n' roll sensibilities. "I decided that I was tired of people telling me that I wasn't black enough, I wasn't white enough, I wasn't Chinese enough," Kravitz said.[6] He decided to shun the skeptics and make his own record without their support. Still in need of financial help, his father bankrolled the first record. With the help of noted producer Henry Hirsch, Kravitz recorded the songs that would become *Let Love Rule*. After eight years of striving for that all-elusive record deal, the finished project caught the attention of Virgin Records in a fifteen-minute meeting. It was a humble beginning that set the stage for the rest of the young musician's long career to come.

MUSICAL HISTORY LESSONS

Kravitz was in love, and hence the mood of his first album reflected as much. *Let Love Rule* was all about the idealistic views of the sixties, and it had the psychedelic music (and clothes) to match. *Love is gentle as a rose*, Kravitz gently preached. *And love can conquer any war.* He was calling for a new era of worldwide brotherhood a la John Lennon. Critics were skeptical. Anthony DeCurtis of *Rolling Stone* wrote: "As if compelled to self-destruct, Kravitz courts artistic disaster by continually evoking his betters."[7] It was a charge that he would constantly fight for years to come. There would always be a musical legend that had already done it better.

Perhaps the difference came in his words. With the exception of Bob Dylan, most of Kravitz's predecessors rarely mentioned Judeo-Christian beliefs unless speaking negatively of organized religion. For an artist who claims to "stay connected with God on a daily basis," the early show of spiritualism was simply part of his regular routine. It made sense to come out in his music. "I Build This Garden For Us" painted a picture of Kravitz and his love walking in harmony amid the natural setting of a garden on a farm. *Glory glory for the day He came*, Kravitz proclaimed, and later even paraphrased the Lord's Prayer.

Another strong statement of Kravitz's Christian faith came in the song "Empty Hands," a retelling of Christ's momentous ride into Jerusalem just days before his crucifixion. It paid tribute to the peaceful ways by which Kravitz has patterned his own personal philosophy. *He came to fight in a battle/ With no guns or money*, he wrote. *Just with his empty hands*.

The album was not without its contradictions. On one hand Kravitz purveyed salvation as the way to peace. The song "Rosemary" implored the subject in question to *keep the faith in your soul*, and added, *Your heart can turn to gold/ All you need is Christ to receive it*. But on "Flower Child," Kravitz claimed, *meditation is the key*, and because of that new age tradition, *her soul and mind are free*. The song "Fear" veers down the same path in the promotion of religious tolerance. Presumably referring to the much-maligned Muslims of the Middle East, Kravitz opined, *their search for God is just the same*, and warned that we not forget, *they're human too*. A positive message, yes, but its ideology that there are many ways to God is off key from traditional Christian thought.

Kravitz was by no means a major player from day one, but his early success generated enough interest to land him a spot opening for Tom Petty and the Heartbreakers. Once Kravitz hit the road, problems began to arise in his union with Bonet. Rumors of marital infidelity ran amuck. Fellow artist and friend Nenah Cherry showed her frustration by writing the song "Buddy X." It was a hit radio single for Cherry that was based on her alleged knowledge of Kravitz's illicit behavior. Adding fuel to the fire was his working relationship with Madonna. Kravitz had written the provocative and chart-topping song "Justify My Love" that would produce an even more controversial video (it was actually banned by MTV). Those implied accusations were, in a humorous twist of fate, unjustified.

The turmoil surrounding Kravitz's life had a major impact on the lyrical content of his sophomore release *Mama Said*. The fact that the project took a swing at the seventies as opposed the sixties-flavored *Let Love Rule* was due to his musical restlessness and admitted love affair with multiple genres. A good portion of *Mama Said* dealt with his guilty complex and an overriding desire to win back his separated wife's heart. "More Than Anything in This World," "The Difference Is Why" and "All I Ever Wanted" were just a few of the songs that made reference to his damaged relationship with Bonet. "Stand By My Woman" and the Top 40 radio hit "It Ain't Over 'Til It's Over" were particularly heart-wrenching numbers. Kravitz and Bonet separated in 1990, and by the time *Mama Said* was released, the marriage had already ended in divorce.

Throughout the recording process, Kravitz managed to exhale just long enough to retain his light-hearted side with songs like "Flowers for Zoe," a tribute to his infant daughter. *God is for Zoe*, he told her. *And Heaven's for Zoe*. The hope-infused "When the Morning Turns To Light" encouraged a struggling drug addict to *follow the*

Son, He'll take you where/ The night and the seas are all full of light.

Yet again, the critics swung for the fences in an effort to knock Kravitz out of the rock 'n' roll ballpark. They continued to compare him to the influences he wore unabashedly on his sleeve. Elysa Gardner of *Rolling Stone* described Kravitz as "maddeningly derivative." She went on to describe *Mama Said* as a "rather disjointed album that lacks freshness and distinction."[8] Undaunted, Kravitz continued to grow as an artist. He was persistent in his mission to make the records he wanted to make. In the process, Kravitz also began to learn from his personal mistakes.

EVERYTHING'S GOING MY WAY

By 1993, the sting of Kravitz's breakup with Bonet was finally wearing off. The divorce was now final, but her influence in his music would continue to make its presence known throughout the next ten years. Yet with reckless abandon, Kravitz proved that at least musically speaking, he was ready for the next phase of his career. His third album, *Are You Gonna Go My Way*, made the resonating statement that would finally push him over the proverbial hump.

For the first time in three attempts, Kravitz was finally shaking the critics. He was also amassing unprecedented radio play and record sales, largely due to the success of the riveting title track and its accompanying video. Even DeCurtis, one of Kravitz's most vocal critics, was inclined to give the much-maligned artist some credit this time around. "Lenny Kravitz began to find his own voice," DeCurtis told VH1's *Behind The Music*. "I think even in the title, he had a sense that things were beginning to come his way."[9]
If listeners assumed "Are You Gonna Go My Way" was a blatant, predestined invitation to Kravitz's coming out party, they were

sadly mistaken. As he would later reveal, the song was actually a last-minute addition to the project, birthed out of a jam session between he and guitarist Craig Ross. The lyrics were originally written on a paper bag.[10] Amazingly, the impromptu song would translate into one of Kravitz's biggest hits ever, a song that to this day is usually saved for last at his live shows.

Beyond its infectious guitar riff and MTV award-winning video, the song spoke volumes of Kravitz's personal philosophy. *I was born long ago/ I am the chosen I'm the one*, Kravitz boldly declared. *I have come to save the day/ And I won't leave until I'm done.* Was he posing as some sort of rock 'n' roll messiah, or was the song intended as a metaphor for his spiritual belief in Christ? One thing is for certain, "Are Your Gonna Go My Way" preached Kravitz's ubiquitous message of peace on Earth, a message that was not with contradiction. From song to song, and sometimes within a single set of lyrics, Kravitz displayed a confused state of mind regarding how exactly this supposed peace might come about. Would it be through divine intervention, human cooperation, or a combination of both? Kravitz's balancing act between spiritualism and human-ism was a part of his music from the beginning, and this record was no different.

In fact, listeners would only have to look as far the album's sec-ond track to hear their first dose of Christian thought. Musically, "Believe" espoused a distinct John Lennon flair, but lyrically, its directive called for a relationship with God as the answer to both individual and global freedom, a theme that was far removed from the late (and openly anti-religious) Beatles legend. Again wearing his convictions on his sleeve, Kravitz wrote: *The Son of God is in our face/ Offering us eternal grace. It was a song that Kravitz said was inspired by the words of his grandfather.* "'Believe' deals with believing in God and believing in yourself as well," Kravitz told in-terviewer Dan Neer. "I was taught by my grandfather that anything that your mind can conceive, you can have it. It's a reality. It begins in your mind. That's the beginning of the reality."[11]

But most of the remaining songs from *Are You Gonna Go My Way* evoked a number of issues surrounding the human condition and in particular, personal relationships. The dirty funk of "Come on and Love Me" accompanied an equally seductive lyric complete with falsetto, breathy vocals a la Prince. *I need you and I need love*, Kravitz crooned. *I need truth and I need God.* While most artists might seem uncomfortable blending their spirituality with their love life, Kravitz shamelessly invited God (and the rest of the world) into his bedroom. He took a more conventional approach on "Just Be a Woman" and "Sugar" but invoked one of the most overused Christian clichés when opening his heart on "Heaven Help." The song reminded any future loves that Kravitz was still hurting from his recent divorce. He was, in a sense, praying for the well being of any woman who might take a chance on his fragile emotional state.

Not only was the album a huge leap from an artistic standpoint, it was also the first sign that Kravitz was turning into a commercial success. *Are You Gonna Go My Way* received two Grammy nominations for Best Rock Song and Best Rock Vocal Performance. His struggles as a black man making "white man's music" made the success that much sweeter. Unfortunately for Kravitz, an unexpected personal crisis would cut the celebration all too short.

LIFE UNDER THE BIG TOP

After nearly two years of maniacal touring amid the illness of his beloved mother (she would later succumb to cancer), Kravitz was both emotionally and physically spent. When he went into the studio to record his fourth album, Kravitz was unfocused, and his life was a haze. Instead of riding the wave of his last project, he wrote, produced, and recorded what he described as "this weird record."[12]

When the critics got their first listen, the fallout was immediate and hardly positive. Although the album was a huge hit overseas, Japan in particular, Kravitz took hits from the American press for both the album's musical and lyrical content. Just one album after shaking the originality issue, many reviewers again cried foul, comparing the project to a rehash of seventies acid rock legends Led Zeppelin. *Rolling Stone*'s Mark Kemp described the effort as a dive "headfirst into the shallowest regions of the classic-rock watering hole."[13]

Kravitz would later theorize that *Circus* performed poorly in the United States and received little critical praise due to the album's overt spiritual content.[14] He had infused faith into his music before, but never to this extreme. In the end, *Circus* became a bizarre blend of pure worship, raw sexuality, and social commentary. Kravitz described it as "a dark record, not dark meaning evil, just dark ... I was basically just crying out to God."[15] The album's lead track, "Rock and Roll Is Dead," set the tone with its heavy-handed Jimmy Page influenced guitar riffs and equally harsh lyrics. Kravitz lashed out against a music business machine that he perceived as perpetuating big egos and unruly lifestyles. *All the money in the world/ Can't buy you from the place you're going to*, he warned those who might fall prey to rock 'n' roll's countless temptations.

Any vagueness was tossed aside on several other songs that could have easily passed for "contemporary Christian music," a segment of the recording industry that was coming into its own at the same time. "God Is Love," for instance, was blatant modern worship long before bands like the U.K.'s Delirious practically invented the catch phrase. The stripped-down, yet slightly psychedelic ballad boldly proclaimed, *God is love/ Through all your trials and tribulations/ God is love/ He'll get you through all situations*. Kravitz didn't stop there. The very next track, "In My Life Today," again extolled the virtue of his relationship with God. *I was bare and I was lost*, Kravitz wrote. *But You were there and now I'm born/ You are the force and strength/ In my life today.*

Circus' most impassioned moment came at its very end. "The Resurrection," the album's eleventh and final track, employed a dramatic build of "Stairway To Heaven" proportions. *If you could feel what I could feel*, Kravitz rhetorically asked. *Well then you'd know His love is real/ If you could hear what I could hear/ Well then you'd know the King is near.* He left even less doubt as to his Christian leanings (as opposed to his father's Jewish upbringing) with a powerful chorus that lauded the reality of Christ's resurrection and the impending second coming.

But the most intriguing aspect of *Circus* wasn't its overt spirituality. By now, most of Kravitz's fans had grown accustomed to his Bible-based views. Rather, it was the confusing marriage of those ideals with an unbridled measure of sexuality. The conflict didn't appear in the lyrics as much as something more superficial, the album's artwork and photography. Of the eleven gratuitous photos, five depicted a naked Kravitz, in some cases posing as a Minotaur, a half-man, half-bull character from Greek mythology.

The concept did bleed into the music on one blaring occasion. "Beyond The 7TH Sky" describes a mystical place where Kravitz and his lover are in perfect harmony with God and the universe. *As the spirit covers our electrified rage*, he crooned over a thick layer of deliberate, dirty funk rock. *Hold me mama/ And we'll fly across the sea/ Way beyond the moon and stars and sky/ I'm talkin' bout you and God and I.* Even the average secular journalist noted the conflicting messages. Kemp called it an "embarrassing sexual-spiritual manipulation."[16] While the act of sex is never actually described, the vivid word imagery leaves little for the imagination. He followed that track with "Tunnel Vision," an upbeat funk song that threw ambiguity to the wind. No spiritual references here, just a hot and heavy proposal: *Tunnel vision goin' through my head/ Lay me down inside your flying bed.*

Unlike many pop and R&B artists who have used sexuality as a marketing tool, Kravitz's infatuation with such passionate indulgence appears to have originated from a purer place. For the most part, his lifestyle has conveyed an unspoken appreciation for monogamous relationships. While still married to Bonet, however, he allegedly had multiple affairs while touring the world. To this day, Kravitz has yet to admit to infidelity, which, if it in fact happened, likely cost him his marriage. By most rock star standards, he has kept his libido in check ever since. His occasional celebration of sexuality instead exudes a certain biblical charm akin to the steamy prose of the Song of Solomon (also referred to as the Song of Songs). While Kravitz has never cited the Old Testament book as an inspiration for his sensual offerings, comparisons could easily be made. Solomon's writings have been said to be both literal and metaphorical. So when Kravitz compares sex to an encounter with God and the angels, it might not be such a stretch, but uncomfortable nonetheless.

THE PERFECT NUMBER

It took Kravitz three years before releasing a follow-up to *Circus*. Rampant touring that was supposed to be therapeutic after the death of his mother only masked the pain temporarily. Kravitz desperately needed time off, so he spent a few months in Jamaica with his daughter and grandfather. During his vacation, he made an important reconnection with a long lost love. Bonet, now going by the name Liloquois Moon, helped the healing process as a reconciled friend. She convinced Kravitz it was time to lose the dreadlocks that had symbolically collected a decade's worth of painful memories. He would later describe the event as "beautiful."[17]

The music that emerged from troubled times proved to be much more upbeat than critics expected. Kravitz's fifth album, aptly titled *5*, was a triumphant celebration of life. The album was filled with joyous funk-infused tunes, such as "Live" and "Fly Away." The latter was a last-minute addition to the project that would shoot Kravitz's superstar status through the roof. There was also Kravitz's obligatory mixed bag that included songs about social issues ("Black Velveteen," "Take Time," and "Can't We Find A Reason") and love ("I Belong To You," "It's Your Life," and "You're My Flavor"). *5* also pulled at heartstrings with two touching tributes. Kravitz found inspiration in the death of his mother ("Thinking of You") and the young life of his daughter Zoe ("Little Girl's Eyes").

Direct spiritual themes were not so prevalent this time around, but as Kravitz himself once said, "God is always in my life and that's the most important thing to me."[18] One of *5*'s rare glimpses into Kravitz's faith came on the disco-funky "Supersoulfighter." The song tells of a *Soul brother space man/ Flying through the sky/ Fighting wars and battles/ Defending you and I.* It goes on to proclaim, *The lord of the wasteland/ He don't want us to be free/ But he can't stop our hero/ On his supersonic V.* While some may have seen this song as an egotistical biography in which Kravitz is posing as a musical Superman, others may have noticed the spiritual analogy or in simpler terms, a classic battle of good versus evil. Applying a Christian worldview, the "Supersoulfighter" in question might represent Jesus Christ, while "the lord of the wasteland" could describe Satan. The simple chorus of "super soul fighter's coming" (a reference to the second coming of Jesus) seems to back up this theory.

The spiritual slant of "Thinking of You" is much less ambiguous and even more personal. Dedicated posthumously to his mother Roxie, Kravitz asked, *Tell me mama, how is freedom?* He makes other heavenly implications as he continued: *Tell me mama, no more sleeping/ Tell me mama, no more weeping.* Instead of crooning a sad tune, Kravitz kept in step with the album's overall theme by portraying his mother as looking down and observing her son from heaven.

After the bump in the road that *Circus* created, *5* clearly put Kravitz's career back on track. For the most part, the critics gave the project a collective thumbs up. But even amid the positive remarks, comparisons continued to be made to other artists. Ken Micallef of Launch.com called him an "easy mark"[19] and proceeded to name some of the usual suspects (i.e., Sly and the Family Stone) and a few new ones (i.e., Marvin Gaye, Earth Wind and Fire, the O'Jays, and the Ohio Players). But even Micallef couldn't deny Kravitz's "way with a melodic hook, and the diversity with which he swings his nostalgic wooly-bully."[20] *Rolling Stone*'s Greg Kot was another critic caught up in a love-hate relationship, describing parts of *5* as "a doozy of a flashback" and having lyrics that "exude a dippy romantic's charm."[21] Not exactly glowing reviews, but for Kravitz, it was a long way from much earlier in his career when he endured nasty attacks on his creative ability.

Despite the minor setbacks, like *Are You Gonna Go My Way*, record sales and peer recognition were forthcoming. Kravitz racked up yet another multi-platinum album and received Grammy Awards for "Fly Away" (1999) and "American Woman" (2000). The latter, a remake of the Guess Who's classic seventies hit, was recorded for the *Austin Powers: The Spy Who Shagged Me* movie soundtrack and also added to a special re-release of *5*. Amid his United States tour, with opening acts Smashmouth and Buckcherry, Kravitz received another honor that solidified him as much more than just an artist, but also as a cultural icon. On December 20, 1999, he was named "Most Fashionable Male" at the VH1/Vogue Fashion Awards. Something to especially proud of when you pick out your own clothes as Kravitz once said he indeed does.

WHAT'S IN A NAME?

By the year 2000, conventional wisdom would have lent itself to a brand new Kravitz recording. Instead, Virgin cleverly decided to capitalize on the success of *5*. It was the label's opinion that millions of new fans had met Kravitz for the first time. As he entered his tenth year as a recording artist, what would be more appropriate (and profitable) than a *Greatest Hits* project? Initially, Kravitz was unexcited about the album, feeling like a "best of" collection should come toward the end of a career. "I never would have thought of putting out a greatest-hits album," Kravitz told MTV.com. "The record company did, and I thought it was strange. I didn't realize I had that many [hits] to make an album ... I do things and I move on. I don't think about the past."[22] He did warm up to the idea long enough to add a brand new song, "Again," which garnered a third consecutive Grammy Award. A multitude of newcomers to the Kravitz legacy were also introduced to early gems such as "Can't Get You Off My Mind," "Mr. Cab Driver," and "Always On The Run." The label's marketing plan worked masterfully, and Kravitz's creative integrity remained in tact.

When the time finally arrived for Kravitz to write and produce his sixth studio project, he married the concept of using vintage and retro instruments with the digital production elements he incorporated throughout the recording of *5*. This new approach resulted in *Lenny*, a self-portrait of an artist coming to terms with his own stardom. For the first time in six studio albums, Kravitz did not include horn arrangements. Consequently, the elements of funk that his fans had grown accustomed to were not as prevalent. What the album did do, however, was rock. Returning to his roots, he performed, wrote, and arranged the majority of the songs. The bravado was back from the first downbeat of "Battlefield of Love," in which Kravitz referred to himself as "a soldier, a casualty of love." The song took on spiritual meaning when describing his earthly plight. *I've been from heaven all the way to hell*, Kravitz wrote, as if to suggest a messianic calling. The biblical mantras continued on the Grammy-winning "Dig In." The guitar-driven anthem gave simplistic instructions: *When the mountain is high/ Just look up to the sky/ Ask God to teach you/ Then persevere with a smile.*

Par for the course, Kravitz provided listeners with an intimate look into his soul. The driving rock ballad "Stillness of Heart" showed the artist to be in constant search of inner peace. The more tender ballad "Yesterday is Gone (My Dear Kay)" was based on a friend of Kravitz who was struggling with her past. But the album's second track, "If I Could Fall in Love Again," proved that Kravitz himself still has issues that need to be confronted. He sang of falling in love with a "goddess" at a young age. But when the relationship ended, he said, "She took my power and the love I had inside." Kravitz displayed an inability to truly fall in love based on the pain he still felt from his broken marriage.

The most personal confession came on the techno-flavored "You Are in My Heart." Kravitz portrayed himself as a man looking to do the right thing, aspiring to follow "the master's plan." He spoke of demons surrounding him in his sleep and temptations abounding at every turn. Kravitz went on to dispel the myth of happiness through money and fame. The blood of Jesus was "running through my veins," he wrote, allowing him to rise above it all. Yet Kravitz remained conflicted and openly admitted to struggling with the age-old battle between righteousness and sin. *Even though you took my place*, Kravitz wrote, *I'm somehow bound to fall.*

The song's chorus brought home a message that could easily have been inspired by the writings of the Apostle Paul found in Romans 7:18-19: "I know that my selfish desires won't let me do anything that is good. Even when I want to do right, I cannot. Instead of doing what I know is right, I do wrong." Paul conveys hope to this dilemma in verses 24-25: "What a miserable person I am. Who will rescue me from this body that is doomed to die? Thank God! Jesus Christ will rescue me."[23]

For Kravitz, it was a vivid description of his personal "valley of the shadow of death." In one interview, he explained that the song was dealing with "this sin nature" and telling God, "Even while I'm sinning, you're in my heart. You're with me, I'm with you, but the flesh fails, at certain times. That's the way it is. But when I'm in that mode of some kind of sin, I haven't forgotten, what it is I really should be doing, or forgotten Your presence."[24]

More importantly, the song represented the most heartfelt search for truth in his twelve-year career. Not since *Circus* had Kravitz poured out such brutal honesty. The only difference was that *Lenny* was recorded in a much happier time. *Circus* was admittedly a dark record that was born out of the frustration of watching his mother succumb to cancer. There was no such crisis this time around. It was simply Kravitz being more transparent than normal.

HUMAN ERROR

Kravitz' mixing of spiritual and secular thought has fascinated journalists and fans alike. In an online chat, he was asked if people confuse spiritualism with religion. Kravitz responded by saying, "being religious doesn't necessarily mean anything in particular. You can be a religious anything. It's about connecting with God."[25] For Kravitz, that connection can be achieved through something as specific as the teachings of Jesus Christ and an open appreciation of basic Bible principles such as Creation. "If you look around at the world and all the beautiful things that God provided us with, you know, that's what it's all about," Kravitz said. [26]

But most of the time the translation is much looser. Kravitz often relies on heavy doses of humanism with special attention paid to universal love and world peace. "People want to be loved and want to love," he said. "That is what we were put here for. That is what we were created to do."[27] His faith in such new age staples as a horoscope sign (Kravitz is a Gemini) only adds to the pseudo-spiritual mystique.

Lenny Kravitz might be the quintessential seeker. Not only does he ponder life's big picture, he writes countless songs on the topic. Kravitz' version of thinking out loud ends up on platinum-selling records that music lovers have increasingly embraced over his career of nearly fifteen years. The critics may scratch their heads and wonder why this artist they labeled derivative, gratuitous, overindulgent, and pretentious is still around. Perhaps they need not look any further than the mass appeal lyrical themes that resonate with the millions of seekers who join Kravitz on his daily quest. "It's hard being a spiritual person in any world," he told Guitar.com.[28]

Early on in his career, that simple truth (accompanied by his relentless addressing of the issue) was sometimes too hard for the average fan to stomach. As he and his audience have grown older and wiser, it's a reality that both seem eager to face together. Or perhaps the public has simply accepted Kravitz for who he is.

But make no mistake, Kravitz is his own man and his own musician. His spiritual contentment never has and never will be defined by fame. It's more personal than that. And just maybe, that's the way it should be.

1. Tracey Pepper, "Deep Joy," *Interview*, July 1998.
2. Lenny Kravitz live chat with America Online, October 2, 2000.
3. Tracey Pepper, "Deep Joy," *Interview*, July 1998.
4. Ibid.
5. Lenny Kravitz live chat with MSN.com, November 27, 2002.
6. "Behind The Music: Lenny Kravitz," VH1, 1999.
7. Anthony DeCurtis, "Review of Let Love Rule," *Rolling Stone*, September 7, 1989.
8. Elysa Gardner, "Review of Mama Said," *Rolling Stone*, April 18, 1991.
9. "Behind The Music: Lenny Kravitz," VH1, 1999.
10. Don Zulaica, "Interview With Lenny Kravitz," LiveDaily.com, October 2, 2000.
11. Dan Neer, "Interview With Lenny Kravitz," LennyKravitz.com, 2000.
12. "Behind The Music: Lenny Kravitz," VH1, 1999.
13. Mark Kemp, "Review of Circus," *Rolling Stone*, September 21, 1995.
14. Tracey Pepper, "Deep Joy," *Interview*, July 1998.
15. "Behind The Music: Lenny Kravitz," VH1, 1999.
16. Mark Kemp, "Review of Circus," *Rolling Stone*, September 21, 1995.
17. "Behind The Music: Lenny Kravitz," VH1, 1999.
18. Tracey Pepper, "Deep Joy," *Interview*, July 1998.
19. Ken Micallef, "Review of 5," Launch.com, May 12, 1998.
20. Ibid.
21. Greg Kot, "Review of 5," *Rolling Stone*, June 11, 1998.
22. Lenny Kravitz interview with MTV.com, October 25, 2001.
23. Holy Bible: Contemporary English Bible (New York: American Bible Society, 1995) 733- 734.
24. Davin Seay, "Interview With Lenny Kravitz," LennyKravitz.com, 2002.
25. Lenny Kravitz live chat with MSN.com, November 27, 2002.
26. Lenny Kravitz live interview with MuchMusic.com, September 16, 2002.
27. Davin Seay, "Interview With Lenny Kravitz," LennyKravitz.com, 2002.
28. Sandy Masuo, "Lenny Kravitz Let's Rock Rule," Guitar.com, 1999.

T-BONE BURNETT

SPARK IN THE DARK
By Scott Marshall

When actor Matthew McConaughey and pop divas Gloria Estefan and Janet Jackson took center stage at the 2002 Grammys, their assignment was simple enough: Present arguably the most prestigious Grammy—Album of the Year—to one of the five nominees. On this February evening in Los Angeles, the audience at the Staples Center, along with millions watching worldwide, were reminded of the nominations: India.Arie's *Acoustic Soul*, Bob Dylan's *"Love and Theft,"* Outkast's *Stankonia*, U2's *All That You Can't Leave Behind*, and the "various artists" soundtrack to the Coen Brothers' movie, *O Brother, Where Art Thou?*

Pre-show murmurings had U2 bringing home the award with relative ease. After all, they had made a formidable record, were enjoying another peak in popularity, and had recently performed at the Super Bowl. Some were betting on Bob Dylan as a darkhorse contender, since many thought *"Love and Theft"* to be superior to his previous release, *Time Out of Mind*—which did win the Grammy for Album of the Year in 1998. Talk on the street had India.Arie and Outkast being up against too much veteran competition, and everyone knew that various artists albums (like the T-Bone Burnett-produced *O Brother* soundtrack) do not win Album of the Year.

So when Jackson opened the sealed envelope with Estefan and McConaughey eagerly looking on, and uttered these words—"And the Grammy goes to ... *O Brother, Where Art Thou?*"—shockwaves rippled across the musical world. Estefan's startled look reflected the moment well.

The cameras panned to the audience and captured a member of the *O Brother* entourage raising his hands in joy, but then quickly placing them on his head in a show of disbelief. An equally stunned T-Bone Burnett embraced his friend, bluegrass legend Ralph Stanley, who was sitting next to him (and who contributed two tracks to the album). Dressed in a dark, double-breasted blazer and sporting some darkened sunglasses that featured a tuft of hair teetering over one of his lenses, the six-foot, six-inch Burnett led an entourage of no less than twenty people up to the stage as "Man of Constant Sorrow" filled the airwaves at the Staples Center.

After being given his Grammy by Janet Jackson, the fifty-four-year-old Burnett made a couple of nervous gestures and pulled out a piece of paper, presumably written in the off chance that the producer would be in front of the world. He spoke these words: "The Coen brothers [Joel and Ethan] have performed an extraordinary alchemy. They've made a movie that has replicated itself in actual life over and over again," Burnett explained. "James Joyce said that if you took any town in the world, as a whole, that the entire odyssey of Ulysses would be repeated in that town every day. These epics are not to be taken lightly. This version of this epic had a happy ending of sorts, and then one happy ending after another, but not even minds as elliptical as the Coen brothers could've written this ending," Burnett added with a wry laugh. "We are filled with gratitude not only that you have chosen to honor this work in this way, but also that we were afforded the chance to make it in the first place; and for the great joy that making it was. Thank you so very much."

Ironically enough, a quarter of a century earlier, Steven Soles—Burnett's bandmate in the Alpha Band—had quoted James Joyce's idea of an epiphany in an interview while discussing their album, *Spark in the Dark*: "seeing past the material aspects of what's going on, to a more spiritual realization." Perhaps this was the very reason why the soundtrack to *O Brother, Where Art Thou?* was so successful (though it caught everyone off guard)—it reeked of spirituality, of honesty and truth, things that don't exactly jibe with, say, selling millions of records.

Later on in the Grammy program, Stevie Wonder and Celine Dion joined Bonnie Raitt, who announced that the Grammy for Producer of the Year had, earlier in the day, been presented to T-Bone Burnett. "We'd like to ask him to stand now and be acknowledged for such fine work," Raitt said. "And congratulations." T-Bone stood, then sat down, amid thundering applause from the Los Angeles crowd.

His love for music had, in a way, come full circle at the Grammys in 2002. "You Are My Sunshine," one of the tracks found on the award-winning album (written by Jimmie Davis and Charles Mitchell and performed by Norman Blake), had been a part of Burnett's repertoire when he was performing solo sets in intimate venues in 1984. Go back nearly two more decades, and you'd find a teenaged Burnett at the helm of a recording studio in Forth Worth, Texas, producing blues albums.

One thing seems certain about the man who was born January 14, 1948, in St. Louis, Missouri, and grew up in Forth Worth, Texas (and who was named after his grandfather, J. Henry Burnett Sr., a secretary of the Southern Baptist Convention for twenty-five years): He will be remembered for his talent as a producer. A partial listing of artists and groups he's worked with over the years is downright staggering: Tony Bennett, Ralph Stanley, Roy Orbison, Maria Muldaur, Elvis Costello, Bruce Cockburn, Los Lobos, Marshall Crenshaw, Peter Case, The BoDeans, Counting Crows, The Call, Natalie Merchant, the Wallflowers, k.d. lang, Gillian Welch, and Leslie/Sam Phillips (his wife since 1989).

And whether he lends out his able guitar work or co-writes a tune (or even an occasional engineering or liner note gig), Burnett has also appeared on the recordings of well-known artists, such as Bob Dylan, Kris Kristofferson, Kinky Friedman, Emmylou Harris, Bob Neuwirth, Jimmie Dale Gilmore, and John Hammond, Jr.

When it comes to producing or working on soundtracks to films—even if you omit the watershed event of *O Brother, Where Art Thou?*—Burnett's résumé isn't too shabby. Here's a working list: *Sylvester* (1985), *Great Balls of Fire* (1989), *Until the End of the World* (1991), *Break Like the Wind* (1992), *Pret-A-Porter (Ready to Wear)* (1995), *Stealing Beauty* (1996), *Clay Pigeons* (1998), *Hope Floats* (1998), *Horse Whisperers* (1998), *The Big Lebowski* (1998), *Down to You* (2000), *Keeping the Faith* (2000), *Jay and Silent Bob Strike Back* (2001), and *The Divine Secrets of the Ya-Ya Sisterhood* (2002).

Still, this is only part of this artist's odyssey—one that has been filled with good doses of adventure and hardship, the kind of stuff life consists of. Burnett seems to embrace it all.

ROOTS

Burnett, who said his early theological influences came from his parents, admitted to not getting a very clear picture of religion and spirituality from his church leaders, with the exception of a Sunday school teacher who told him something "magnificent" that he had no problem recalling more than three decades after the fact. "We were talking about Providence, and she started drawing lines on a piece of paper and crossing them in every direction until the piece of paper was just completely black—'that's Providence.' That was a pretty abstract thing to tell a ten-year-old," remembered Burnett.[1]

This same Sunday school teacher planted another seed that Burnett clearly remembered. "'The will of God is like a rubber band that you're attached to. It goes from one spot to another. As you walk along this road, the band will let you go as long as you want to, but God will bring you back at some point.' I don't know if I decided to see how far I could go, or if that rubber band's the way it really is, but that's how my life has been."

When the teen years hit, Burnett's interest became increasingly focused on music—all kinds of music—and church didn't fit into the new equation. All he had to do while growing up, as he put it, was drive down the streets of Texas to hear blues, country-western, honky tonk, and rock 'n' roll. He traveled to the other side of his hometown of Forth Worth to Rosedale Street, where he first heard the particular sounds of Jimmy Reed, Muddy Waters, Slim Harpo, and Howlin' Wolf, as well as Tex-Mex musicians, R&B singers, rockabilly guitarists, and other regulars of the South's "chitlin circuit."[2]

1975–1976: THE DAYS OF ROLLING THUNDER

Twenty-seven-year-old Burnett got his first professional touring gig when he was hired by Bob Dylan in 1975. His first taste of life on the road had him contributing his skills as a guitarist, singing a song or two (covers and originals), and engaging in stage antics that were part and parcel of the free spirited affair that was the *Rolling Thunder Revue* tour of 1975-1976.

Seen from the eyes of Larry "Ratso" Sloman, who traveled with the entourage and wrote *On the Road with Bob Dylan*, a book chronicling the tour, Burnett was never out of range of the journalist's watchful gaze.[2] At Gerdes Folk City in Greenwich Village, Sloman described him as the "lanky stringbean of a Texan, ambling onstage to join [Bob] Neuwirth" to do a quick song; he was also referred to as the "lanky Texan discovery of Neuwirth's," and two crew members viewed Burnett as a "once obscure Texas songwriter" (Dylan quickly changed anyone's obscurity level).

Although Burnett was recruited for the tour because of his association with longtime Dylan friend Bob Neuwirth (Burnett was playing in Neuwirth's band in 1975), he still recalled the insanity of the instant acclaim. "It was seventy-five crazy maniacs, mostly people dragged right off the street to be rock 'n' roll stars. It does crazy things to one's psyche," Burnett remembered. "I watched what was going on from the shadows. I watched the fact that Bob Dylan could make somebody famous just by sitting across the table from him. And I saw onstage, the right spot to be was singing on the same mike as Bob. That repulsed me so much that I got as far away from his mike as possible—not as a virtuous thing, but just as reverse snobbery."[3]

Someone who also watched from the shadows was writer/ playwright Sam Shepard (also a member of the *Rolling Thunder* entourage), who described his friend Burnett as someone who could easily fulfill the role of rock 'n' roll maniac. "He was ... a man of instant hunger. If he wasn't served when the hunger hit him, he would systematically set about demolishing the entire restaurant, beginning with the menu and working his way up to the chandeliers," Shepard wrote in his 1977 book, *Rolling Thunder Logbook*. "He has a peculiar quality of craziness about him. He's the only one on the tour I'm not sure has relative control over his dark side."

Burnett's response?

"There's not much I can say about that," the singer said six years later, in 1983. "Talk to my shrink about it. I was real mean and sarcastic—I thought I was laughing in the face of death."

For all the loony anecdotes about the excesses of life on the road, there were a number of songs that seemed to temper the scene, addressing some heavy spiritual issues: non-Dylan compositions like "People Get Ready," "What Will You Do When Jesus Comes?," and "Little Moses," which were aired during rehearsals for the tour with Dylan on piano—as well as Dylan's own songs that aired during the tour like "A Hard Rain's A-Gonna Fall," "I Shall Be Released," "Oh, Sister," and countless others that expressed yearnings beyond the material plane. Clearly something was going on in the spiritual realm. "I have no idea what happened on that tour, but it is interesting that so many people either became Christians or went back to church by the time it ended," Burnett reflected.[4]

Steven Soles, a friend of Burnett's and one of those musicians who became a Christian, commented on the downside of the adulation brought on by touring with Dylan. "We received a lot of resentment from that association, everybody thought we were just trying to capitalize on it. People didn't realize we'd been around a long time [as musicians]."[5]

1976–1978: THE ALPHA BAND

The alleged "capitalization" from the Dylan association stemmed, in part, from the fact that within two months of the dust settling from the *Rolling Thunder Revue*, T-Bone Burnett, Steven Soles, and David Mansfield had formed the Alpha Band. Before 1976 had concluded, the band had a big-time contract with Arista Records and soon completed their self-titled debut record. But it wouldn't be until well into the next year when Soles and Burnett had their respective spiritual awakenings. In the meantime, it wasn't easy in the days that followed the *Rolling Thunder Revue*. "The pressure was ridiculous," Burnett remembered. "We had a $6 million deal with Arista as an unknown band that had been together for three weeks, and [label head] Clive Davis was saying we were the most important band since the Stones, the Beatles and Dylan. It's so typical of the disease of the Seventies."[6] The "disease" Burnett appeared to be addressing was the monster of marketing, which has often been accused of putting a stranglehold on creativity and freedom.

In retrospect, though, band member David Mansfield noted how good they actually had it under Clive Davis at the time. "If we'd had any premonition of where the music industry would wind up, we would have kissed the ground he walked on for letting us be creative. A few years later there would be no chance of it," Mansfield concluded.[7]

If freedom is important in the creative realm, then it seems obvious that freedom in the spiritual realm would be likewise. For Burnett, an evolution had taken place between his days as an acolyte in the Episcopal church in Forth Worth, Texas, as a young boy, and his days in the limelight as a young man.

"Well, personally I'd been what you might call a Christian mystic. I'd been raised in the church, but somewhere down the line I'd gotten hold of books like *The Aquarian Gospel of Jesus Christ*," Burnett recalled. "Mystical weird books. I never could finish them, or get serious about them, but I was looking. So I'd been touched by God as a kid, and I'd started looking for Christ, but in my wanderings I had become very mystical. The more I went in that direction, the further I got from personal contact. Then at some point I started returning to a biblical basis for the spiritual search. Right at that stage was when we did that second record [the Alpha Band's 1977 release, *Spark in the Dark*]."[8]

Who knows what Clive Davis was thinking when he took in the
Alpha Band's sophomore effort, *Spark in the Dark*, and the fact
that Burnett and Soles had both been reading their Bibles. Burnett
viewed the album as "a revelation" and said that before the album,
things had looked pretty dark, "but I turned around to where I
could see the spark—The Light." Bandmate Steven Soles described
Spark in the Dark in terms of what James Joyce called epiphany—"seeing past the material aspects of what's going on to a more
spiritual realization."

The Statue Makers of Hollywood (1978)—the Alpha Band's final
album—seemed liked a farewell to the entertainment industry and
a scathing indictment of the materialism of the age. There was no
doubt about this one: The songs were reflecting a biblical worldview. Although reluctant to buy into any single "moment of truth"
(instead, it was a personal God who met him at different junctures
in his life), Burnett would nonetheless claim that he was redeemed
by Jesus during this time period.

David Mansfield remembered the context of their last record for
Clive Davis as "a very good recording experience," but also noted
how the Alpha Band's leader wasn't exactly bashful about ap-
proaching his boss. "T-Bone basically went to Clive and said, 'I got
the idea for this record but it's completely non-commercial. It's
going to be really weird. If you want to let us out of the contract,
please do, but if you don't, I'm not going to make any compromis-
es.' I don't know if T-Bone said it quite that diplomatically either.
I'm not sure how he put it, but the message he gave Clive was:
'We're going to do this—take it or leave it. If you want to let us go,
and cut your losses now, do so.'

"We went in and in many ways that record was pretty fierce. It
was incredibly radio unfriendly. But T-Bone (and Steven Soles in
a lesser sense) had this mission having been recently converted
to Christianity. Besides being sort of wacky musically on many of

the songs, he did this Old Testament jeremiad kind of take on the whole thing. It was his chance to take the moral high ground, to do all the social and political criticism, unexpurgated and un-moderated, to get that all out in the open, out of his system. So it was very intense on both those levels. The lyrics were very confrontational and the music was eclectic to the 'nth' degree. Some of it was anyway, and after that Arista dropped us."[9]

One reviewer who teetered on assessing it as good but just couldn't swallow the morality-laced lyrics was none other than rock critic legend Dave Marsh. In his review for *Rolling Stone*, he informed readers that the opening track, "Tick Tock," was a retelling of the biblical Genesis and that the album obviously was concerned with man's fall from grace, although "unfortunately the subject is treated with too much cold-bloodedness, lacking almost completely in humor." If it wasn't for the inclusion of the closing track—Hank Williams' "Thank God"—the album wouldn't have acquired "an appropriate blend of rock and religion."

The last few sentences of Marsh's review pointed to the fact that a rock album based on biblical principles would indeed be a hard sell: "Man's expulsion from paradise is a fact, perhaps unchangeable, perhaps not. Judging from the inner-sleeve motto ('Where there is division, confusion and perversion, may there be unity, clarity and purity'), the Alpha Band does hold out some hope for all us sinners. While one can hardly help thanking them for that, one wonders if next time they might stop looking down their noses at the rest of the planet long enough to explore a few of their own flaws. Good as they are, they've got 'em."[10]

The irony here is that Burnett and friends weren't unaware of their own flaws—far from it. They were, in fact, becoming acutely aware of them—and Burnett's career, in particular, would become well-known for the exploration of his own flaws. Because of this tendency, many have observed how he's been able to "get away" with such hard pronouncements on the human condition known as sin, a condition the Bible presupposes.

Little did Dave Marsh and others in the rock critic community know, but less than a year after the release of *The Statue Makers of Hollywood*, the story of Jesus invading Bob Dylan's life (and music) would become the unavoidable subject. The Alpha Band would be disbanded by 1979 when Dylan's album *Slow Train Coming* was released and his gospel tours commenced; many thought it was now Dylan who was looking down his nose at the rest of the planet (however, if one listened to Dylan's lyrics and interviews closely, this proved to be a shallow assertion).

Not long after Dylan's gospel-only tours had ended, Burnett came forth with *Truth Decay*, his first solo effort since his debut album of 1972; it was (and is) one of Burnett's most critically acclaimed albums, although it certainly set no *Billboard* charts afire. *The Boston Phoenix* claimed *Truth Decay* was what "the Old Testament would sound like if set to a rock 'n' roll beat." Considering a number of songs in the Burnett catalog would ultimately fight against the vanity of the moment or the age, it wouldn't be unreasonable to assume Burnett cherished commentary like this.

Although Ken Tucker, in his review of the album for *Rolling Stone*, concluded that Burnett resembled "a hardheaded, perverse Christian like William Blake, fashioning his own mythology with commonplace materials and then creating urgent, ineluctable works from them." The album was, for Tucker, almost "a rockabilly version of Blake's *Marriage of Heaven and Hell*."

For these words to have even been written—much less in the pages of *Rolling Stone*—showed that T-Bone Burnett was making some waves in a community not usually known for being receptive to songs that took the moral high ground.

Burnett's state of mind was on display when he was interviewed by Bill Bentley of *L.A. Weekly* in the summer of 1980.[11] "[In] all lyrics, all literature—nobody's speaking in a vacuum and everybody's presenting some view of the world," he insisted. "And I don't think there's any view that knows a man better than Christianity. So what I think happens is, I get strength from it. If you don't go for the easy thing, which is, 'Oh, now I'm a religious person so I've got to quit all this because I don't want to offend anybody,' even though Jesus offended just about everybody. But if you don't go for that and take a hard look at things, I believe you can relate a lot more about life in your work."

Bentley asked if it was difficult to be both a Christian and a rock 'n' roller. "I forget who said this, but I don't think *I* made it up. If Jesus is the light of the world, there's two kinds of songs you can write," Burnett said. "You can write songs *about* the light, or you can write songs about what you *see* from the light. That's what I try to do. I'm still looking."

Clearly this journalist, who had also listened to *Truth Decay*, wasn't offended by the approach. "T-Bone Burnett has found a stripped-down model of modern rock to give some weight to the theory," Bentley wrote, "that musicians with religious beliefs can stay out of preacher's robes and still connect their convictions to their music."

Journalist Mark Humphrey, writing for *L.A. Weekly*, called Burnett "a rock 'n' roll ironist whose Christianity is tempered with more wit than piety," and added, "it's a danceable sort of wit."[12]

"The medium of pop music lends itself to certain points of view—sex, drugs, power, money. It seems to be more on the surface than Disneyland, where he [Disney] shows you this realm, but you can't touch it—there's nothing there," Burnett explained. "The Disneyland stuff is deceptive, illusory. Rock is more blatantly preaching."

Burnett felt that the genre of rock 'n' roll could touch people in a positive way, and definitely could give them something worthy to think about. He told Mikal Gilmore of *Rolling Stone* that he felt rock 'n' roll was the most potent medium going. But the problem—and it was no small one—was that "it's been inundated by too many one-dimensional, self-serving messages, all those pronouncements of repackaged nihilism and Epicureanism that say, 'Eat, drink, and kill yourself—there's no hope,'" Burnett observed. "Or, on the other side, those people who say, 'Well, yeah, the world's an awful place, but *I'm* saved, so everything's great.' Those people are all blowing a big chance. Rock 'n' roll touches people deeply, and therefore the question it raises is, 'What are you going to do with that responsibility, that opportunity to touch people deeply?'"

This would be a trait of T-Bone Burnett's in the years to come: not letting the non-believer or believer off the hook too easily.

While on a tour with Elvis Costello in 1984, Burnett gave an interview to Bill Flanagan who was at work on a book of interviews on "rock's greatest songwriters." Flanagan noted how Burnett, in his songwriting, never fell into "Born Again polemics." Burnett explained how there is a real temptation among new converts to want to bring everyone else along for the ride. "If you find a good book you want to show it to your friends," he explained. "There's a very fine line you walk, 'cause people say, 'I was so screwed up and now I'm straight and I feel great! You're still screwed up! You ought to get straight like me!' It's real easy to talk down to people that way. I don't think it's quite that simple. I don't think there's a bolt of lightning that straightens your life out. Maybe in an eternal sense, but not day to day. Life's still a complicated and difficult affair."

Burnett may have been chatting with *Rolling Stone* and *L.A. Weekly*, but he still maintained a penchant for doing interviews in obscure Christian-based publications, and in 1984, he spoke with the *The Wittenburg Door*, a magazine known for their vicious satire and wit. "A lot of 'Christian' artists make it seem as though all they do is sit around and read the Bible all day long and go to church," Burnett lamented. "They give the impression that they never go to a baseball game or play with the dog. That's demeaning." As he had recently noted in interviews, we discover again that Burnett's life as a Christian wasn't the bowl of cherries some might portray it as. "I've found that being a Christian makes life one hundred thousand times more difficult than just being a sort of standard, run-of-the-mill hedonist," he said.

When asked if he viewed himself as an artist and a musician, he avoided the easy one-word answer and issued this pronouncement: "I see myself as a man standing up trying to give my point of view as clearly as I can. I want people to understand that life is worth living, that this world is an incredible place to live, and that it's wilder than anyone's fantasy. I don't think I have to be perfect to say those things. I am a mass of contradictions myself."

In addition to producing the 1986 releases of Elvis Costello, *King of America* and *Blood & Chocolate*, Burnett produced and played guitar on The BoDeans' *Love and Hope and Sex and Dreams* and Peter Case's self-titled debut. His guitar work could be heard on Bob Dylan's *Knocked Out Loaded* album.

The year 1987 saw the release of a second Burnett-produced Los Lobos album (*By the Light of the Moon*) and another Costello effort (*Out of Our Idiot*), and also provided an opportunity to work with one of his heroes—fellow Texan Roy Orbison—on *In Dreams: The Greatest Hits*, which included newly recorded versions of the crooner's classic offerings. Additionally, Burnett produced the taping of a show from an L.A. nightclub, *A Black and White Night*, which featured Orbison and musicians who played behind him in an evening of tribute, artists ranging from Bruce Springsteen, Jackson Browne, and Elvis Costello, to Tom Waits, k.d. lang, and Bonnie Raitt.

For all the busy activities of 1987, there would be nothing more significant in Burnett's personal life than his meeting up with Leslie Phillips, a twenty-seven-year-old singer who had been releasing albums in the contemporary Christian music market. He produced and played guitar on her 1987 album, *The Turning*, which received great praise and wound up being a farewell of sorts to the folks who, she said, wanted "political and religious propaganda."

If there were ever two kindred spirits, it seemed Burnett and Phillips fit the bill. Consider the following: their mutual love for music, their shared talent at songwriting, and a sometimes vicious predisposition towards certain segments of Christianity, i.e., those lumped into the "Religious Right" category—those who have a penchant for mixing politics (or bad music for that matter) with the Gospel.

"She came out of gospel music, and not many people realize that she threw away a good career because she felt what she was doing was becoming so compromised, so she went from making a lot of money to making no money," Burnett said. "She sacrificed a lot for the truth. And since she went through that, having something she loved compromised, she's been the most uncompromising person I've ever worked with."[13] Burnett would often be a presence in the future releases of Sam Phillips (the artist formerly known as Leslie Phillips).

Burnett's next solo project, *The Talking Animals* (1988), saw him compose an album of songs that featured the overarching theme of mercy, as he told John Platt of WNEW-FM, New York City. It wasn't a country-tinged effort like his previous album. It was, well, hard to categorize, just as Burnett probably liked it.

"Life is mostly tedious," remarked Burnett to Sharon Liveten of *Creem* magazine, "so you have to have a certain amount of humor—and mercy." As for the record business, Burnett informed

Liveten that the current joke in the industry was that the easiest way to squelch a "hit song" was to perform it with just acoustic guitars—then it would instantly become a "non-hit" (a great irony considering what happened in the future with *O Brother, Where Art Thou?*).

Even with a solo effort to promote, other releases were coming out in 1988 that seemingly testified against Burnett's own indictment of his work ethic: He produced Elvis Costello's album, *Spike*; he produced and played on Sam Phillips' *Indescribable Wow*; he contributed vocals and played mandocello on his old buddy Bob Neuwirth's latest album, *Back to the Front*; he produced and played on Tonio K.'s *Notes from the Lost Civilization*; and produced and played on the Los Lobos release, *Pistola y El Corazon*.

After doing Costello's *Spike*, he pondered the thought of hanging up his hat as a recording artist and studio wizard. He packed his bags and headed back to Fort Worth. He visited his ex-wife and kids. He relaxed. He thought about things. "I wanted to just go back and become a part of ordinary life again, and feel all the things that ordinary people feel," he said. "I think poets have to be ordinary people, and are ordinary people, in fact. I got taken over by the business out here [in Los Angeles]."[18]

To think Burnett took off work for a couple of years, though, would be a mistake. After the sudden tragedy of Roy Orbison's death in late 1988, Burnett produced his posthumous *Mystery Girl* release. Ever the man involved with countless projects, Burnett also produced Elvis Costello's *Girls Girls Girls*, the original soundtrack to *Great Balls of Fire*, the film about rock icon Jerry Lee Lewis, and assisted on Peter Case's album that would be setting no records for the brevity of its title—*The Man with the Blue Post-Modern Fragmented Neo-Traditionalist Guitar*. Additionally, 1989 was the year Burnett and Sam Phillips tied the marriage knot.

In the early '90s, Burnett again played the field: He produced and contributed vocals for The Call (*Red Moon*), a Christian band; produced and played on his wife's album, *Cruel Inventions*, as well as Bruce Cockburn's *Nothing but a Burning Light*; lent his guitar skills to Kris Kristofferson's effort, *Third World Warrior*; and remixed and produced the 1967 song, "Rainy Day Sun" for Spinal Tap's *Break Like the Wind* album (really, that was the title).

All of this hard work for others ultimately led to a Burnett who, by 1992, was ready to come out with a new album of his own. After a shift in the administration of Columbia Records and a subsequent meeting that Burnett attended, a spark of life came from an admonition. "They told me, 'Don't try to make a hit, just make the truest record you can.'" Additionally, between the counsel of his mother and his old pal Bob Neuwirth, Burnett broke through with an important revelation about who he was, where he had come from, and where he needed to go.

His mom's advice? Forget about the record business and learn how to play the guitar better. And Neuwirth made him conscious of some wrong turns he'd made in the past. "He said, 'Let's make this album about the songs, about you.' I never wanted to make a record about me, myself, back in those days [those records in the 1980s]," Burnett remembered, "because I felt ashamed or embarrassed. Everything was a threat to me." The often ego-driven record business had him living in a constant state of fear that his music didn't measure up. "I don't want to compete anymore, because everybody else is: record companies, radio stations, newspapers, but for poets to compete creates a metaphysical doubt that poisons everybody," Burnett insisted. "I mean, getting a gold record—what does that mean? The songs are either gonna be around in hundreds of years or they're not."[14]

Although his 1992 effort, *The Criminal Under My Own Hat* (co-produced with Neuwirth) was nominated for a Grammy, it didn't sell truckloads of records. *Rolling Stone* reviewer John Milward even concluded that Burnett was fully aware that he'd never be a pop star: "On 'Kill Switch,' he sings of those who play for fame and adds, perhaps wistfully, *There are still those who only play for the love of the game*," Milward wrote. "The ornery artistry of *The Criminal Under My Own Hat* makes it easy to excuse Burnett's hubris."

"I Can Explain Everything," one of the more angry songs from *The Criminal Under My Own Hat*, encouraged the masses to rise up against crooked preacher/politicians and "throw all of these liars off television." Burnett—no fan of Religious Right posterboy Pat Robertson—had recently penned an article in *Spin* magazine where he referred to the tele-evangelist "as power-mad a religious figure as anyone since Rasputin." Burnett's lament was that anyone who disagreed with Robertson and company were, in certain Christian circles, unfairly dismissed as "radicals."

He explained to journalist John Mackie that he had, at times in his life, run away from God, ignored and denied God, and ignored his own feelings, but what seemed to irk Burnett most were those, like Pat Robertson, who weren't sticking to the nitty-gritty of true Christianity; he issued a strong charge indeed—that Robertson and his ilk were misrepresenting true Christianity:

"Pat Robertson and those people place the law of the U.S. above the Bible, they're only interested in the kingdom of the United States, that's the way I view it. They should be horse-whipped, they're smug, self-righteous, pretentious ... that's why I say they're like FBI infiltrators who've just come to give Jesus a bad name. Jesus was the exact opposite of that: He was powerless, He emptied Himself of all power. He was accepting, He was always saying 'suffer the little children, come to me.' He was hanging out with whores, He was hanging out with tax collectors, and the Pharisees and Sadducees were people like Pat Robertson, who were saying, 'Aw, but you can't do that because you know this, and these are unclean.' They had a thousand rules that they were trying to enforce on everyone, and Jesus said 'Sorry, but that's not it. That's not the way it is.' That's what I'm saying: Pat Robertson and those people, that's not the way it is. They're deceivers."[15]

Boston Globe reporter Jim Sullivan noted that Burnett was "a Christian who describes himself as 'not as angry as Bruce Cockburn, more bemused.'"

There were those communities of believers that Burnett didn't mind mingling with. Take, for example, the folks at *Radix*, an obscure magazine out of Berkeley, California, whose mission and focus was this: "In the questions we are called to raise and the issues we face, we realize that we are called to be a people radically set apart from the world system because of our rootedness in Christ. Jesus Christ is our base for analysis, our measure of truth, our hope for living."

Burnett had been interviewed by *Radix* back in 1978 with his Alpha Band friends and had been a contributing editor for the magazine from time to time. Following the release of *The Criminal Under My Own Hat*, he was interviewed again by Sharon Gallagher. "A segment of the fundamentalist church in this country—Sam calls it 'the political church'—is so bent on assigning blame that's it's not even functioning as the church anymore," Burnett concluded, "but rather as a propaganda wing for the right wing political movement in this country." Not willing to suffer fools gladly, Burnett fearlessly pursued sacred national cows. "This would be a good time to face reality and stop pretending that George Washington never told a lie and that he was a wonderful Christian man," he said. "He was the richest man in America and he lied as much as anyone else and he wasn't a Christian at all; he was a deist." Burnett's rants also included America's history with the Russians, Native Americans, and the atom bomb.

231

It was almost as if Burnett came out and made his statement, with his new album and the slew of interviews—and just when he was all over the radar screen (flirting with a Grammy and even hopping onstage again with Bob Dylan for a gig), he slipped off into the shadows and once again devoted his time to the work of others. Various album releases that Burnett produced (and played instruments on) included the following releases in 1993: Counting Crows' *August and Everything After*, Bruce Cockburn's *Christmas*, and the BoDeans' *Go Slow Down*; and in 1994, there was Sam Phillips' *Martinis and Bikinis* and Cockburn's *Dart to the Heart*.

Cockburn has credited Burnett with teaching him to find a song's essence, keeping instrumentation to a minimum, and having as a goal the sincere interpretation of a song (which often used first cuts as final takes).

In 1996, he produced another one of his wife's albums (*Omnipop*), Gillian Welch's *Revival*, and also the Wallflower's smash success, *Bringing Down the Horse*, which sold millions (Burnett had known a young Jakob Dylan—lead singer of the Wallflowers, and youngest son of Bob Dylan—during the days of Rolling Thunder). The following year Burnett produced the title track to Jackson Browne's *Next Time You Hear: The Best of...*

Gillian Welch again enlisted the production help of Burnett for her 1998 release, *Hell Among the Yearlings*, and this same year saw Burnett really diving into the role of movie soundtrack producer (*Hope Floats*, *Horse Whisperers*, *Clay Pigeons*, and the Coen brothers' *The Big Lebowski*).

In 1999, in keeping with his interactions with communities of Christian believers over the years (*Contemporary Christian Music* magazine, *Radix* magazine, and the record label What?) Burnett spoke before a crowd of students at Calvin College, an undergraduate school in Grand Rapids, Michigan. He gave an afternoon lecture on "The Christian Artist's Role in Society" and an evening concert at the college's fine arts center. In writing a preview of Burnett's appearance, the arts and entertainment editor for the *Chimes* (Calvin's student-run newspaper) knew their guest was no easy-going believer. "In fact, I'd call his attitude toward the clean, well-lit, self-assured, hide-behind-the-pulpit church proper downright acerbic," Tim Thompson wrote.

About a hundred people attended Burnett's "lecture," which actually consisted of some introductory comments and then a fielding of questions for nearly ninety minutes. During his opening remarks, Burnett talked of a letter the Reverend Jerry Falwell had written to the *Los Angeles Times* criticizing President Clinton for not being truly repentant for the recent scandal. This naturally led to a subject that has often been the target of some of his sharpest criticisms: the "E-church," or the Evangelical church/ Electronic church, that particular group of people with the propensity to package Jesus, with politics, for consumption by the masses.

At one point, Burnett asserted that "we are Christians because we are redeemed" and said how artists like himself, Bruce Cockburn, Bono, and Bob Dylan "have tried to bring love and perspective and Christ to people who can't hear Jerry Falwell." "For the last twenty years I have been endeavoring to truly be in the world but not of the world," said Burnett in a moment of humility, "but I'm horribly of the world and I screw up."[16]

As for his concert—his first in six years—when he walked onstage, he greeted his audience with a "Welcome to my first rehearsal." "And it showed," observed Joe Lapp for the *Chimes*, "yet through all the cracks and unpolished vocals and interrupted songs, an unpretentious honesty seeped through, giving the performance an authenticity that no polished musician will ever achieve. Burnett sang with the conviction of a performer who has been through all the hype and has forged his own ideas and identity."

1. Sharon Gallagher, "Faith and Hope and Rock and Roll: An Interview with T-Bone Burnett," *Radix*, (Volume 21 Number 3, Spring 1993), pp. 8-11, pp. 28-29.
2. Mikal Gilmore, "T-Bone Burnett's Moral Messages," *Rolling Stone*, November 11, 1982, p. 46.
3. Larry "Ratso" Sloman, *On the Road with Bob Dylan*, (New York: Three Rivers Press, 2002) [originally published by Bantam Books, New York, 1978].
4. Steve Pond, "T-Bone Burnett: Surviving the Wild Side," *Rolling Stone*, November 24, 1983, p. 62.
5. Steve Turner, *Hungry for Heaven: Rock 'n' Roll & the Search for Redemption*, (Downers Grove, IL: InterVarsity Press, 1995), p. 170.
6. Michael Barackman, "Alpha Band Soup: After the Thunder, A Band is Born," *Rolling Stone*, April 7, 1977.
7. Pond, *Rolling Stone*, November 24, 1983.
8. Larry Jaffee, "An Exclusive On the Tracks Interview: David Mansfield," *On the Tracks* #17 (Fall 1999), p. 35.
9. Sharon Gallagher, "Alpha Band Interview," *Radix* (November-December 1978), p. 5.
10. Jaffee, On the Tracks #17 (Fall 1999).
11. Dave Marsh [album review of *The Statue Makers of Hollywood*], *Rolling Stone*, July 27, 1978.
12. Bill Bentley, "T-Bone Burnett: Born Again But Still Looking," *L.A. Weekly*, August 8-14, 1980, p. 56.
13. Mark Humphrey, "T-Bone Burnett's Rock 'n' Roll Testament," *L.A. Weekly*, March 26-April 1, 1982, p. 16
14. Gilmore, *Rolling Stone*, November 11, 1982.
15. Bill Flanagan, *Written in My Soul: Rock's Greatest Songwriters*, (Chicago: Contemporary Books, 1986), p. 52.
16. "The Wittenburg Door Interview: T-Bone Burnett," *The Wittenburg Door* #80 (August-September 1984), pp. 20-21.
17. "The Record Producer's Life," *Orlando Sentinel*, December 4, 1992.
18. Steve Appleford, "Exile's Return: T-Bone Burnett's Feverish Mixed Emotions Permeate a New Album Tinged with Idealism and Outrage," *L.A. Times*, October 18, 1992.
19. Greg Kot, "Burnett Steps into Spotlight: Record Producer Finally Has Found His Own Groove," *Orlando Sentinel*, December 4, 1992.
20. John Mackie, "Amen and Farewell, America," *Vancouver Sun*, September 5, 1992.
21. Gallagher, *Radix* (Spring 1993).
22. Mark Feldbush, "Live at Calvin College with Ralston Bowles," *TrueTunes*, April 9, 1999.

BONO

THE GOSPEL OF HEAVEN AND HELL

By Steve Beard

His father called him Paul, the White House affectionately calls him The Pest, and the rest of the civilized world simply refers to him as Bono. He's as well known to presidents and prime ministers for his dogged political lobbying as he is to music fans as the lead singer of the Irish rock band U2. In 2000, the cover of *Newsweek* asked, "Can Bono Save the Third World?" Two years later, the cover of *Time* upped the ante by asking, "Can Bono Save the World?" How is that for heightened expectations for a man who once sang, *I don't believe that rock 'n' roll can really change the world*?

Within the last few years, U2 was named band of the year by both *Spin* and *Rolling Stone*, given MTV's Video Vanguard Award for lifetime achievement, and asked to perform the halftime Super Bowl show (800 million worldwide viewers) in the shadow of the September 11 terrorist tragedy. For Bono's part, he was named the most important man in the music industry by the influential British magazine *Q*, honored as MusicCare's Person of the Year, and nominated for the Nobel Peace Prize for his work on behalf of alleviating third-world debt and combating AIDS in Africa.

The band he leads has sold more than 100 million albums around the globe since the release of *Boy* in 1980. They collect Grammys (fourteen in all) as if they were baseball trading cards—the recognition spanning from Album of the Year with *The Joshua Tree* in 1987 to Record of the Year in 2001 for "Walk On."

During the recent *Elevation* tour, Bono audaciously announced that they were reapplying for the job of the best rock band in the world. For most groups made up of aging rock stars, that would have been considered fanciful hubris. But in the case of U2, how could it not be taken seriously? There are several bands whose longevity spans twenty years; U2 is the only one, however, that still matters in a culturally innovative sense.

Twenty years ago, one music journalist pointedly observed: "Bono is adored. He dangerously treads the fine line between adulated rock star and parodying that role."[1] One wonders if he would have laughed or cried hearing comedian Drew Carey at a humanitarian event say, "I'm so glad that God sent Bono down to save us from our sins. Do you want to see my wristband? It says, 'What would Bono do?' He's like Christ, I'm telling you. He's like Christ and Bob Dylan rolled into one."[2] Jarring in its apparent sacrilege, it is worth pointing out that while Carey may have been kidding, he was not mocking. What is it about the silver-tongued, do-gooding, poet-theologian that elicits this Bonotheistic adoration?

Bono is the kind of guy who, with his trophy in hand, can gently chide the previous recipients at the Grammy Awards ceremony by stating: "I would like to thank God and my mother also. But I just have this feeling, this picture in my head of God looking down on people like us on occasions like this and going, 'Uh-oh. Don't thank me for that song. There's no hook, the chorus is weak, and they'll never play it on the radio.'"[3]

He seems to have the ability to do and say exactly what you would not expect from him. Who else talks breezily about the theologi-

THE GOSPEL OF HEAVEN AND HELL

cal superiority of grace over karma to jaundiced rock journalists, writes the forward to a specially-packaged book of Psalms, convinces Jesse Helms to help African AIDS victims, and use his time on national television to pray the Scriptures?

One music writer found it frustrating to be able to nail down a sturdy critique on Bono, saying instead, "He simultaneously inflates himself into the most grandiose, arrogant, self-righteous rock star and deflates himself with self-mockery and modesty."[4] He is, after all, the one who sang, *All I have is a red guitar, three chords and the truth*—no small amount of presumptuous moral certainty.

During an anti-apartheid sermonette on the 1988 *Rattle and Hum*, Bono asked, "Am I bugging you? I don't mean to bug you." Somehow you knew that was not exactly sincere. For more than twenty years, Bono has used his global stage to pester and prod us—lyrically, politically, and spiritually. It is, of course, this last element of sin, redemption, grace, betrayal, angels, demons, guilt, and forgiveness that is most intriguing—especially coming from a rock star.

THE THIRD DIMENSION

"I sometimes think I have a kind of Tourette's syndrome where if you're not supposed to say something, it becomes very attractive to do so," he once confessed. "You're in a rock band—what can't you talk about? God? Ok, here we go. You're supposed to write songs about sex and drugs. Well, no I won't."[5]

Better than most, he understands the medium of journalism, the soundbite, and the verse. In turn, he drops the most memorable lines.

- I believe that Jesus is the Son of God. I do believe that, odd as it sounds" (*Mother Jones*).[6]

- "Sadomasochism is not taboo in rock 'n' roll. Spirituality is" (*Rolling Stone*).[7]
- "The belief that there is love and logic at the heart of the universe is a big influence on me. It's a big subject. If there is no God, it's serious. If there is a God, it's even more serious" (*Irish Independent*).[8]
- "I'm very interested in music that even attacks Christianity, because I think it's more real, because at least it acknowledges the Third Dimension. At least it's entering the realm of the spirit" (NME).[9]
- "I don't know anyone who's not interested in the idea of religion, either whether they're opposed to it or for it. Yet no one talks about it. It's taboo. People will talk about penis rings easier at a dinner table these days than the idea of grace. It's like, '*Eurghhhhh.* Don't go there'" (*Rolling Stone*).[10]
- "It says somewhere in the Scriptures that the Spirit moves like a wind—no one knows where it's come from or where it's going. The Spirit is described in the Holy Scriptures as much more anarchic than any established religion credits" (Beliefnet.com).[11]
- "Religious fundamentalism is where you get to shrink God; you remake God in your own image, as opposed to the other way around" (*Rolling Stone*).[12]
- "I'm a believer, but sometimes I think religion is the thing, you know, when God, like Elvis, has left the building, you get religion. But when God is in the house, you get something else" (*Oprah*).[13]

Bono is rock 'n' roll's most limber and enigmatic spiritual provocateur. He sees every stage as a pulpit and every coliseum as a cathedral—focusing on the fire of Pentecost, the grace of the Gospels, and de-emphasizing the Law of Moses. "Our music is church to me; where else are we going to talk about these things?" he has asked.[14]

British poet and music biographer Steve Turner observed, "More than any other act in the history of rock, they (U2) have forced God, Jesus, the Bible and a Christian worldview on to the agenda. Rock critics could ignore the Jesus rock of the 1970s (and they did!), but they couldn't ignore U2; they had to voice an opinion about the values [U2] stood for."[15]

While America was still reeling from the September 11 terrorist attacks, U2—an Irish band—was asked to perform at the 2002 Super Bowl halftime show in New Orleans. As the names of the victims were displayed over a huge backdrop, Bono began to pray Psalm 51:15: "O Lord, open my lips, so my mouth shows forth thy praise. O Lord, open my lips, so my mouth shows forth thy praise." U2 then launched into a stunning version of "Where the Streets Have No Name." In the firepower of the moment, Bono pulled open his jacket to display the Stars 'n' Stripes sewn into the lining. You could almost hear the collective national gasp before the cheers crescendoed into madness. He is 100 percent Irish, but he lives the life of a resident alien that knows no borders.

Bono's approach seems to be: *For those that have eyes to see, let them see. For everyone else, let's rock!* He pulled a similar Scripture recital at the 2001 NBA Championship halftime show. Bono was beamed across the airwaves saying, "What can I give back to God for the blessings he poured out on me. I lift high the cup of salvation as a toast to our Father. To follow through on the promise I made to you" (Psalm 116, *The Message*). Yesteryear, the networks had to worry about Elvis shaking his hips; today, it is Bono on his knees.

GOSPEL OF HEAVEN AND HELL

Whereas John Lennon invited us to imagine a world without a heaven, Bono inverted the plea to ask us to imagine heaven in a closer proximity. "I don't expect this pie in the sky when you die stuff," he once remarked. "My favorite line in the Lord's Prayer is 'Thy Kingdom come, Thy will be done on earth as it is in heaven' (Matthew 6:10). I want it all, and I want it now. Heaven on earth—now—let's have a bit of that."[16]

Bono attended Glide Memorial United Methodist Church in San Francisco during *The Joshua Tree* tour (and has been a frequent visitor since). He said, "their kinda church is what we in Ireland, would call a riot. People were jumpin' in the aisles and the preacher was rappin' …" He described the preacher as being "right out there with them [the congregation] and he went from the grimy, grainy bottom line of life to the ecstasy, right up and down into the depths of experience. It was all there—the gospel of heaven and hell. That's what I want from rock 'n'roll. That's where I want U2 to go."[17]

Bono is a flag-waving fan of the unseen kingdom of heaven, yet he finds the structures and attitudes of its institutional expressions to be claustrophobic. That becomes less difficult to understand considering his upbringing in Ireland—a country divided with sectarian barbwire and religio-political quagmires. "My mother was a Protestant, my father Catholic; anywhere other than Ireland that would be unremarkable," he said. "I had a foot in both camps, so my Goliath became religion itself; I began to see religion as the perversion of faith."[18]

Bono's disdain for religion would prove to be an overriding theme throughout his career. "I have no time for it, and I never felt a part of it. I am a Christian, but at times I feel very removed from Christianity. The Jesus Christ I believe in was the man who turned over the tables in the temple and threw the moneychangers out—substitute TV evangelists if you like," he told *Rolling Stone* in 1987. "There is a radical side to Christianity that I am attracted to. And I think without a commitment to social justice, it is empty." [19]

Bono attended the Mount Temple Comprehensive School in Dublin, the first progressively non-sectarian island in a sea of Roman Catholicism. It was also the birthplace of U2. The school underwent a fiery revival while he was there. "Charismatic things started happening," Bono recalled. "That was when we became involved in the Shalom group. We were studying the Scriptures and it was amazing. When everyone was learning how to get served and how to score, we were all completely wrapped up in this."[20]

"I didn't have Sunday school on my back," Bono said. "We had something far stronger—a bright white light. It was *too* hot. But it will never leave us. And it made the Sunday school notion of God seem *squeaky*. Squeaky clean."[21]

In 1981, Bono explained the vision of U2 in this way: "I'd like to think that U2 is aggressive, loud and emotional. I think that's good. I think that the people who I see parallels with are people like John the Baptist or Jeremiah. They were very loud, quite aggressive, yet joyful, and I believe they had an answer and a hope. In that sense, I think we have a love and an emotion without the flowers in our hair, and we have an aggression without the safety pins in our noses."[22]

Before his death, Bono's father Bob Hewson recalled the Shalom days. "I've always been a little bit cagey of those people who say they have all the answers. We never had rows but we used to debate the Bible for hours and hours on end. Because he [Bono] seemed to think he knew all about the Bible. We used to have great arguments, go on for hours. We still do sometimes," Hewson laughed. "I was a little skeptical. But then as he grew older it seemed to be working all right with him, so I didn't object."[23]

Those were heady and confusing times for the band. The charismatic Shalom house-church was a wonderful cocoonish type of fellowship that allowed for Bono, Larry, and the Edge to be nurtured and disciplined. Adam was never part of the U2 trinity of believers. "Three of us are Christians and Adam isn't," Bono said matter of factly in 1981. "That doesn't mean we're going to say to him at any time, you're not in the club."[24]

While that was true, the struggle between the three believers and the two other vital members of U2—Adam and manager Paul Mc-Guinness—should not be underplayed. The three Shalom members were battling the inner urges to abandon the rock 'n' roll life in order to pursue the vibrancy of their Christianity.

In a 1989 interview with the left-wing magazine *Mother Jones*, Bono confessed that the band was being pulled in two opposing directions. "A lot of it was based on the idea of the ego. We'd been reading a lot of Watchman Nee, a Chinese Christian mystic. His idea was: 'Unless the seed shall die and be crushed into the earth, it cannot bear fruit.'" Rock 'n' roll, on the other hand projected an arrogance, pride and self-centeredness, as if to say, "Out of my way, looking out for number one" and "I Can't Get No Satisfaction!" Bono pointed out that Nee's attitude to that would be: "So what? What's so important about you anyway?"[25]

"We felt almost subconscious pressure being applied to us by a lot of people we looked up to within that spiritual community that we were in and out of," he said. "In the end, I realized it was bulls---, that what these people were getting close to with this idea was denial, rather than willful surrender. It was denial, which is the next-door neighbor to self-flagellation, and that awful idea that 'through pain is gain.' Yes, there is pain. Yes, you may gain from it. But you don't get into your car looking for a traffic jam."[26]

The group decided that it was going to straddle the two kingdoms, typified by the lyrics, *I have spoke with the tongue of angels/ I have held the hand of the devil.* Those words, of course, are taken from "I Still Haven't Found What I Am Looking For"—which may prove to be a lasting legacy of the spiritual outlook of the band. When it was recorded for the *Rattle and Hum* album, the elegance of the struggle is placed within the tongues-of-fire context of gospel at its finest. There is a precision and succinctness to the Christian idea of redemption: *You broke the bonds/ You loosed the chains/ You carried the cross/ And my shame/ And my shame/ You know I believe it.* One wonders about what it means on a spiritual plane when 20,000 Japanese fans in Osaka sing along to such an overtly biblical affirmation.

Of course, we all say things (or sing things) that we really don't believe—but they often do have an unexpected effect on us. As Bono has said, "I love to think that music can be an instrument of grace, that there might be mercy in melody and that at the very least a great song can fill the silence of indifference we sometimes find in our hearts."[27] Twenty years ago, U2's music was called "transcendently eclectic, refreshingly realistic, naively passionate, and elusive pop music."[28] There is no reason to tamper with that description. If there has been one word that would characterize U2's musical journey, it would have to be *transcendent*, unfolding a world beyond the things that can be merely seen and rationally grasped.

KISSING THE CONTRADICTIONS

"Rock is really about the transcendent feeling," Bono told *Time* magazine. "There's life in the form. I still think that rock music is the only music that can still get you to that eternal place where you want to start a revolution, call your mother, change your job or change your mind. I think that's what rock music can do."[29]

A few years ago, my family visited the Rock and Roll Hall of Fame in Cleveland, Ohio. It was there, captured in one of their documentary films about the history of rock music, that Bono observed,

"The greatest rock and roll is produced by those either running toward God or running away from Him." It is in that spiritual wrestling—which often includes wandering away and returning home—that the creativity and freshness of art is often engaged.

"Around the time of *October* and *War* we weren't even sure if we wanted to be in a band," Bono recalled. "I thought rock 'n' roll was really just vanity and there didn't seem to be a place in it for some of the spiritual concerns in my writing. But I've since realized that a lot of the artists that have inspired me—Bob Dylan, Van Morrison, Patti Smith, Al Green, Marvin Gaye—were in a similar position. They all had three sides to their writing—sexual, spiritual and the political. In our own way, U2 have that same three-dimensional thing. That's why I'm more at ease."[30]

Some Christian fans were perplexed by Bono's confession of still not having found what he was looking for—despite the dramatic affirmation of faith. There was that, "Yes, but ..." factor to it all that did not sit well with a tidy and well-manicured theology. Whether we want to or not, most of us create within our minds a picture and concept of God that fits neatly within a three-volume systematic theology text that we can proudly display on our bookshelves. Bono was having none of it. He is a fan of the Psalms, Song of Solomon, Lamentations, and Job—filled with anxiety and doubt and loaded with questions.

"People expect you, as a believer, to have all the answers, when really all you have is a whole new set of questions," Bono said. "I think that if 'I Still Haven't Found What I'm Looking For' is successful, it's because it's not affirmative in the ordinary way of a gospel song. It's restless, yet there's a pure joy in it somewhere."[31]

He feared becoming a preacher in the "glass cathedral of rock 'n' roll" and was horrified by America's expression of fundamentalist Christianity, particularly the way that it was played out on television. When asked if he was ashamed or embarrassed about his faith because of the televangelists, he responded, "I'm not ashamed. I'm just not going to go around and flog it like a second-hand car salesman."[32]

Bono knew he was walking a tightrope and living a compromised life, as some would see it. At one point he decided, "Instead of running away from the contradictions, I should run into them and wrap my arms around them and give 'em a big kiss."[33] He found a new lease on life as an artist. "I've found that there is a great freedom when you have your feet in two so-called mutually exclusive worlds—the world of irony and the world of soul, the world of flesh and the world of the spirit, the world of surface and the world of depth," he said in 1992. "That's where most people live. That's where U2 lives."[34]

Bono explored the dark side of the "gospel of heaven and hell" by dressing up as Macphisto—a sleazy alter-ego character with white mime face, devil horns, and gaudy outfits—during the Zoo TV tour in the mid-1990s, but some observers simply did not get it. "The problem is, can anyone empathize with U2's stodgy idea of fun?" asked on music journalist. "Having lived their life in reverse, the Irish foursome began their career preaching Christian moderation like seen-it-all elder statesmen, before regressing into an adolescent playpen where wearing daft sunglasses and devil costumes apparently denotes Bacchanalian debauchery. Who else but virginal head prefect Bono could possibly consider making joke phone calls and watching television to be subversive acts?"[35]

Whereas some found the whole sarcastic rock schtick simply childish, others were worried for Bono's mortal soul. In the summer of 1994, U2 came through Cardiff, Wales. As is custom, Bono would bring one very excited female fan up onto the stage to waltz with him during a section of "Love Is Blindness." As the two dance gracefully around, Bono is instructing her to calm down and listen to the music. That night, however, Bono happened to pick out a woman who was intent on grilling him about his character.

"What are you doing?" she asked as she attempted to wipe the white make-up off his face. "Are you still a believer? If so why are you dressed up like the devil?"

"It's Ecclesiastes," Bono whispered while dancing as if they were on a prom date. She looked unconvinced and upset. "Have you read *The Screwtape Letters*?" he asked the young woman. Bono said that his whole philosophy of mock-the-devil-and-he-will-flee-from-you was inspired by the reading of C.S. Lewis's story of how a senior devil teaches a young demon how to torpedo the faith of the faithful. As they waltzed, he told her, "That's what this is."

"Oh." She thought about it, nodded, put her arm on his shoulder, and gave in to the dance. "I want to bless you," she said. Looking back on the experience, Bono said, "It took U2 fifteen years to get from Psalms to Ecclesiastes. And it's only one book!"[36]

It would be unfair to target the young woman as merely naïve and compulsively over-concerned. Admittedly, the band was stretching its wings and flaunting a spiritual libertarianism and do-it-yourself theology that rubbed many Christian observers the wrong way. The band had done several things that caused even their most tolerant and open-minded fans to scratch their heads—all within the wide-angle lens of a watching world. Had they opened up a Pandora's box? What did Jesus say about the man who gains the whole world and loses his soul? Even Bono refers to the nineties as a time when the band wandered far from joy. "We got darker and darker, but the lights were all the brighter at our concerts"—an age-old defense mechanism known as over-compensation.[37]

The case could be made that overtly faith-filled songs such as "I Still Haven't Found What I'm Looking For" or ghoulishly parabolic characters such as Macphisto are the exceptions, rather than the rule for the way in which U2 relates their faith to the art. Sometimes they reflect seasons that the band as individuals and corporately were experiencing. This should not come as a shock. When a band has a career as long as U2's, it is better to look at it as a film rather than a photograph. Sometimes the moment you see is a computer-enhanced glamshot, and sometimes it is merely a bad hair day.

DRAWING THEIR FISH IN THE SAND

Bono admitted that they have discovered different ways of expressing their faith and recognized the power of the media to manipulate such signs. "Maybe we just have to sort of draw our fish in the sand," he said. "It's there for people who are interested. It shouldn't be there for people who aren't."[38]

When Bono spoke of drawing a fish in the sand, he was referring to one of the oldest symbols of the Christian faith. During times of persecution, the symbol was used by the early Church as a secret insignia and the symbol of Christ. It is said that when two Christians needed to meet in a public place, one would use the end of his walking stick to draw a half crescent in the sand. The other believer would then draw the other half, thereby making the symbol of the fish. To the uninitiated, the fish was merely decorative and commonplace; to the persecuted Christian, it was a discreet sign of faith.

The principle of the fish is perhaps best illustrated by the cover of *All That You Can't Leave Behind*. Bono had the photo doctored so that the airport gate in the background reads J33-3→. It turns out that this is a reference to Jeremiah 33:3 ("Call to me and I will answer you and tell you great and unsearchable things you do not know"). Bono told *Rolling Stone*: "It was done like a piece of graffiti. It's known as 'God's telephone number.'"[39]

Aside from the practicalities of the symbol, the fish also became a synonymous symbol with the depth of life—representing the spiritual world that lies beneath the world of surface appearances. This could go a long way in explaining many of the multi-layered meanings of U2 lyrics. Since the beginning, fans have scoured the lyrics, scratching for the double entendres like code-breakers in World War II movies. Is he talking about the Second Coming of Christ or a nuclear holocaust? Is he referring to a lover or the Holy Spirit? Is Grace a girl or a theological concept?

Steve Turner compared Bono's lyrics to a hologram. "With ordinary perception we see the flat surface we call reality, but by turning the card we notice another dimension which was there all the time but not visible to us," he wrote. "Bono gazes at the commonplace but is soon transported into realms only the Christian can see, and then back again."[40]

To the biblically literate listener, Judas and his kiss of betrayal of Jesus makes appearances in U2 songs such as "Pride (In the Name of Love)" and "Until The End of the World." In the latter, the reference reads, *In the garden I was playing the tart/ I kissed your lips and broke your heart.* When asked about the perspective in the song, Bono said, "Yeah well I played Jesus for so long, I decided I needed a break! Judas, from whatever way you look at it, is a fascinating creature, because in one sense, by committing his crime, he introduced us to grace. It's kind of bizarre."[41]

The theological issue of grace would take on a major theological emphasis of Bono's thoughts and lyrics as evidenced with the song by the same name on *All That You Can't Leave Behind (Grace, she takes the blame/ She covers the shame/ Removes the stain/ It could be her name).*

Bono told Anthony DeCurtis, a long-time U2 observer for *Rolling Stone*, that grace is the "most powerful idea that's entered the world in the last few thousand years." In typical fashion, he said, "I sometimes feel more like a fan [of Christianity], rather than actually in the band. I can't live up to it. But the reason I would like to is the idea of grace. It's really powerful."[42]

On "Grace," Bono sings, *She travels outside karma/ When she goes to work/ You can hear her strings/ Grace finds beauty in everything.* Karma is a popular term within many cultures. In its simplified form, it is the idea of a universal cause-and-effect in the moral order. "We hear so much of karma and so little of grace," Bono observed. "Every religion teaches us about karma and, well, what you put out you will receive. And even Christianity, which is supposed to be about grace, has turned, you know, redemption into good manners, or the right accent, or, you know, good works or whatever it is. I just can't get over grace—(it's) so hard to find."[43]

In Christian theology, grace is the unmerited favor and love of God toward men and women that comes in the form of forgiveness and redemption. Bono expressed it poetically in this way: *What once was hurt/ What once was friction/ What left a mark/ No longer stings/ Because Grace makes beauty/ Out of ugly things.*

This thematic expression took on an interesting twist with Bono's relationship with Noel Gallagher of the mega-popular band Oasis. During the fall of 2000, Gallagher made news when he went off in a foul-mouthed tirade against religion in the pages of *Gear* magazine. "At school I wasn't interested in anything they had to say to me. Once I learned to read and write I thought, well f--- the rest of it, who needs to learn math. Then I got sent to religion classes. What do I want to learn about that s--- for, f------ Jesus and all that bollocks."[44]

A year later, *The London Sunday Times Magazine* ran a fascinating article about Gallagher. When the subject of his friendship with Bono came up, Gallagher confessed that he peppered the rock legend with questions about religion. "Look, you believe in it all," Gallagher said to Bono. "I'm Catholic same as you. Can you explain it to me?" Bono sat down for several hours and explained his faith. "We had a good three-hour conversation about his religious phi-losophy, which is basically, 'Go to God, tell Him what all your flaws are and say, 'Can you work with me?'" Gallagher even asked how a wealthy rock star prays. Gallagher remarked that "he made tons of sense."

Apparently, Bono sent a package a few days later to Noel and his girlfriend Sara that included Philip Yancey's book, *What's So Amazing About Grace?* Bono had attached a little note to the gift: "I don't know if you were serious the other night, but here's some-thing that might give you a bit more of an understanding."

"Bono's father had just died. How difficult must that be?" Gallager asked. "Takes time out because two people were interested. What a guy." He went on to say, "I'll tell you, I'm going to read 'em from cover to cover."[45]

INSPIRATION FOR THE GOTHS

Throughout his career, Bono made no secret to rock journalists that he read Francis Schaeffer, Watchman Nee, Walker Percy, and Flannery O'Connor during various seasons of his life. The one book that has been a constant for his inspiration, however, has been the Bible.

When *Rolling Stone* asked him in 2001 what he was reading, Bono responded: "There's a translation of Scriptures—the New Testa-ment and the Books of Wisdom—that this guy Eugene Peterson has undertaken. It has been a great strength to me. He's a poet and a scholar, and he's brought the text back to the tone in which the books were written. A lot of the Gospels were written in common kind of marketspeak. They were not at all highfalutin' like the King James Version of the Bible, from which all Goths get their inspiration."[46]

The singer has been anything but timid in promoting *The Message* (NavPress), a version of the Bible in contemporary language written by Peterson, a well-known theologian and professor emeritus at Regent College in Vancouver, B.C. Shortly after the death of his father last year, Bono told the Irish magazine *Hot Press* that he had read *The Message* aloud at his father's bedside. He went on to recommend Peterson's translation of the Bible: "It's just incredible stuff."

In an interview with Angela Pancella of AtU2.com, Peterson was asked what he knew about Bono and U2. "A year or so ago (maybe less) their chaplain/pastor who was traveling with them at the time, called and asked me to come to Chicago to meet them," Peterson responded. "I wasn't able to get away at the time but I had a lovely conversation with him. And many of my younger friends and ex-students keep me posted on the latest from U2. When the *Rolling Stone* interview with them came out a few months ago, I got clippings sent to me from all over the world!"

And what was his reaction to having *The Message* quoted in concert arenas around the world? Peterson said: "Pleased, very pleased. Bono is singing to the very people I did this work for. I feel that we are allies in this. He is helping get me and *The Message* into the company of the very people Jesus spent much of his time with."[47]

Bono has even gone so far in his admiration to provide a videotaped endorsement of *The Message* and special thanks to Peterson.

"I wanted to sort of video message you my thanks, and our thanks in the band, for this remarkable work you've done translating the Scriptures. Really, really a remarkable work." Bono went on to say, "You brought the musicality to God's Word that I'm sure was there, was always there in intention. There have been some great translations, some very literary translations, but no translations that I've read that speak to me in my own language. So I want to thank you for that."[48]

Endorsing *The Message* is not Bono's only foray into promoting Bible reading. A few years ago, a company in the United Kingdom published individual books of the Bible with the forewords written by prominent literary or cultural figures. Bono penned the foreword to the book of Psalms, making the case that it was the first collection of blues songs. "Abandonment and displacement are the stuff of my favorite psalms. The Psalter may be a font of gospel music, but for me it's despair that the psalmist really reveals the nature of his special relationship with God. Honesty, even to the point of anger. 'How long, Lord? Wilt thou hide thyself forever?' (Psalm 89), or 'Answer me when I call' (Psalm 5)."[49]

The Irish singer wrote, "Words and music did for me what solid, even rigorous, religious argument could never do, they introduced me to God, not belief in God, more an experiential sense of God. Over art, literature, reason, the way into my spirit was a combination of words and music. As a result, the book of Psalms always felt open to me and led me to the poetry of Ecclesiastes, the Song of Solomon, the book of John. My religion could not be fiction but it had to transcend facts. I could be mystical, but not mythical and definitely not ritual."[50]

Bono also noted his affection for the psalmist David, who he referred to as the "Elvis of the Bible." He wrote, "That the Scriptures are brim full of hustlers, murderers, cowards, adulterers and mercenaries used to shock me. Now it is a source of great comfort."[51]

BANGIN' THE DUSTBIN LIDS

On Sunday, December 1, 2002, Bono found himself sitting on the front row of a church through two infant baptisms and a traditional lighting of the Advent wreath before he took the stage. He was not there to sing; he was there to launch a weeklong AIDS awareness tour through the Midwest. He christened the event at Saint Paul United Methodist Church in Lincoln, Nebraska. Launched on World AIDS Day, the seven-city "Heart of America Tour: Africa's Future and Ours" was sponsored by DATA (Debt, AIDS, Trade in Africa), a political advocacy organization that Bono helped found.

The Sunday morning program included a dynamic youth choir from Ghana called the Gateway Ambassadors and the sobering testimony of Agnes Nyamayarwo, an HIV-positive Ugandan nurse who lost her husband and six-year-old son to AIDS.

Saint Paul pastor, the Reverend David Lux, offered Bono (donning his blue Romeo Gigli sunglasses) the pulpit, but the singer jokingly responded, "I don't know about a rock star in the pulpit." Later, however, when his lapel microphone failed, Bono jumped at the chance to use it. "I've always wanted to get into one of these," he said. During his presentation on why he was activated to fight against AIDS in Africa, one of the newly baptized babies began to cry. As the father was taking the child out of the sanctuary, Bono recalled the child's name and said, "Where are you going, Alexander?" The congregation howled.

Lux found Bono to be "personable, friendly, compassionate, and articulate," he said. "He challenges Christians to live out the teachings of Christ in specific ways, like responding to the horrific AIDS crisis in Africa which is ravaging families and children."[52]

African issues have been on Bono's front burner since he and his wife went there in 1985 with World Vision and saw the incredible starvation tragedy that unfolded before their very eyes. Other political concerns have been expressed in songs such as "Silver and Gold," "Mothers of the Disappeared," and "Bullet the Blue Sky." They have also promoted causes such as Amnesty International, Greenpeace, the Belfast Peace Agreement, the release of Burmese opposition leader Aung San Suu Kyi, and Jubilee 2000—an endeavor to reduce or eliminate debts for poor nations.

This trip to the American heartland, however, was to draw attention to AIDS in Africa, which is devouring the continent with cataclysmic speed. An estimated 42 million people worldwide live with HIV, with 75 percent of them living in sub-Saharan Africa. AIDS kills 6,500 Africans everyday, and a projected 2.5 million Africans will die next year because they lack the medicine to fight the virus.

Near the end of his weeklong tour, a handful of journalists were able to ask Bono a few questions before the presentation that evening at the Northeast Christian Church in Louisville, Kentucky. At my first opportunity, I asked him how his Christian faith inspired his activism.

"Well, you know, I am not a very good advertisement for God. So, I generally don't wear that badge on my lapel. But it is certainly written on the inside. I am a believer," he said. "There are 2,103 verses of Scripture pertaining to the poor. Jesus Christ only speaks of judgment once. It is not all about the things that the Church bangs on about. It is not about sexual immorality, and it is not about megalomania, or vanity," he said jokingly as he ran his fingers through his hair.

Bono is a tippy-toe talker, holding on to the side of the lectern, leaning in—engaged. You can see the Irish dander and passion brew even when he tries to be sedate. "It is about the poor. 'I was

naked and you clothed me. I was a stranger and you let me in.'"
he said. "This is at the heart of the Gospel. Why is it that we have
seemed to have forgotten this? Why isn't the Church leading this
movement? The Church ought to be ready to do that." [53]

Bono's work on behalf of the world's dispossessed, forgotten,
and hungry has placed him in seemingly incongruent company.
Nevertheless, he seems to get along well with them all. There is
the rather humorous meeting where Pope John Paul II gave Bono
rosary beads and in turn wanted to try on the singer's infamous
sunglasses. Photos of the exchange were never released. "The
Vatican didn't have the same sense of humor as the Pontiff," Bono
said. "But he was cool."[54]

His lobbying efforts have stretched him. "I really have had to swallow my own prejudice at times," he confessed. "Because I was suspicious of the traditional Christian church, I tended to tar them all
with the same brush. That was a mistake, because there are righteous people working in a whole rainbow of belief systems—from
Hasidic Jews to right-wing Bible Belters to charismatic Catholics."[55]

The most popular picture of President Richard Nixon is the one
he took with Elvis. Perhaps one of the strangest images to have
emerged within the past several years has been the pictures of
Bono and Senator Jesse Helms from North Carolina—an essential
ingredient to getting the U.S. Senate to move forward on third-
world debt reduction legislation. The two stand in contrast in so
many ways, but it was Bono who brought the famous conservative
to tears as he shared about the hungry children in Africa. "Well,
I never heard of him, but the guy is impressive," Helms recalled.
"The thing that impressed me is he is a deeply religious man ...
He is here to sincerely get something going to feed the starving
children in Africa."[56] Bono even invited Helms to the U2 concert in
Washington, D.C. during the *Elevation* tour. The senator accepted
and attended his very first rock show, where he was forced to cover

his ears. It was not out of ingratitude, but because it "was the noisiest thing I ever heard," he said.[57]

Bono is very persistent and persuasive when it comes to his lobbying efforts. "The most amazing thing was that he kept coming back," said Bobby Shriver, part of the Kennedy political family and Bono's political door opener. "He went to one meeting and they were like, 'Nice guy.' He came to a second meeting, and they were like, 'Smart guy.' Then he came to a third meeting and they were like, 'Who is this guy?' By the fourth meeting, they thought, 'We're never gonna get rid of him!' And that has a big influence in Washington. When you keep coming back—and you know your stuff—people pay attention."[58]

Throughout the Midwest tour, Bono hit college campuses, truck stops, churches, and newspaper editorial offices. "Christ's example is being demeaned by the church if they ignore the new leprosy, which is AIDS," he has said. "The church is the sleeping giant here. If it wakes up to what's really going on in the rest of the world, it has a real role to play. If it doesn't, it will be irrelevant."[59]

He also went after the notion that there is a hierarchy of sins—with sexual immorality rating higher than, say, institutional greed. "Somewhere in the back of the religious mind was this idea [that people with AIDS] reaped what they sowed—missing the entire New Testament, the New Covenant, and the concept of grace," Bono said. "Evangelicals in a poll, only 6 percent thought that they should be doing something about the AIDS emergency ... I'm sure that made you, as it made me, wince."[60] The polling data is actually worse than that. According to Barna's poll released November 22, 2002, only 3 percent of evangelicals said they would "definitely" help children orphaned because of AIDS. The survey showed that evangelical Christians were one of the least likely groups to qualify as supportive of the HIV/AIDS causes.

While in Chicago, the group met with Bill Hybels, pastor of Willow Creek Community Church—the largest church in the United States. For his part, Hybels told *Christianity Today*, "After a two-hour private meeting in my office, I came away convinced that Bono's faith is genuine, his vision to relieve the tragic suffering in Africa is God-honoring, and his prophetic challenge to the U.S. church must be taken seriously."[61]

Bonomania then hit Wheaton College, the highly-respected evangelical school outside of Chicago. He was greeted with a welcoming telegram from Billy Graham—the school's most influential alumnus—and the college's president announced, "We want to stand in solidarity with what this tour is about." Recognizing the volatility of the AIDS issue, Bono told the students: "Our discussion may divide some of us tonight. Why? Because I believe that if the Church doesn't respond then it will become a largely irrelevant body that preaches, 'Love Thy Neighbor,' and does nothing. It will be the salt left on the side of a plate." He went on to say, "'Love your neighbor' is not advice. It is a command."[62]

Bono was not taking offerings at any of the DATA events. He was asked if there was particular legislation that he was wanting support for. "I think we are keeping it broad. We are just saying, 'Call your congressman, call the president. Let's grow a movement'... I am absolutely sure that if we start banging the dustbin lids and telling the politicians that there is a vote here, they will switch on it."[63]

From the Church, he is expecting much more. "There should be civil disobedience on this," he told Cathleen Falsani of the *Chicago Sun Times*. "You read about the apostles being persecuted because they were out there taking on the powers that be. Jesus said, 'I came to bring a sword.' In fact, it's a load of sissies running around with their 'bless me' clubs. And there's a war going on between good and evil. And millions of children and millions of lives are being lost to greed, to bureaucracy, and to a church that's been asleep. And it sends me out of my mind with anger."[64]

He emphasized, "I'm not here as a do-gooder. This is not a cause; it's an emergency." The tour was not a fund-raising effort; instead, it was a consciousness-raising educational event—which very often doubled as a revival meeting with the Gateway Ambassadors youth choir singing, praying, and dancing with fervor and zeal.

After Agnes Nyamayarwo, the HIV-positive Ugandan woman, shared her testimony in Louisville, Bono said, "Let me say this in the house of God: If there is anybody here who wants to pass judgment on a woman like Agnes and her children—and indeed the man who gave her the virus, her husband—maybe they should leave now. God will be the judge—not anyone in this church." The congregation applauded. "Let he without sin throw the first stone," he remarked soberly.

"I guess that would clear the place. I'll be out of here," Bono said with a smile. Serving as a benediction, Bono said, "I am normally not too comfortable in churches. I find them often pious places and the Christ that I hear preached doesn't feel like the one I read about in the gospels. But tonight, God is in the house."[65]

WHEN GOD IS IN THE HOUSE

Bono often said that he does not feel comfortable in churches, but one gets the feeling that it may be more of a throwaway line than reality. When Bono makes comments like that, he is protecting himself from getting sucked into a bloated religious industry—making fast bucks off of Jesus—that he remains justifiably skittish about. The truth is, one gets the feeling that Bono may love the Church more than he leads on. After all, he is well aware that it is most likely the only institution on the planet that can actually get the ball rolling on the issues that he cares so deeply about.

"I find solace in places I never could have imagined ... the quiet sprinkling of my child's head in Baptism, a gospel choir drunk on the Holy Spirit in Memphis, or the back of a cathedral in Rome watching the first cinematographers play with light and color in stained glass stories of the Passion," Bono said. "I am still amazed at how big, how enormous a love and mystery God is—and how small are the minds that attempt to corral this life force into rules and taboos, cults and sects. Mercifully God transcends the Church ..."[66]

Although *All That You Can't Leave Behind* garnered praise from every quarter of the music scene, it was interesting to note how many people talked about spiritual epiphanies at their live shows. In writing her review of a U2 concert for the *Chicago Sun Times*, Cathleen Falsani observed: "I drove 200 miles this week to go to church in a gymnasium at the University of Notre Dame. With 11,000 strangers. And one Irish preacher with a familiar face." She confessed, "In light of recent events that have sent me—like so many millions of others out there—diving back toward a place we call faith, the lyrics [Bono] sang were imbued with new meaning. It was sacred, joyful, healing. Like how church is supposed to be."[67] Other observers have also testified to similar mystical experiences.

"I found myself singing the songs, very aware of God's gracious presence," testified Randy L. Rowland, a pastor from Seattle, about his time at a U2 concert. "At times during the concert, I found myself praying in the gaps between songs or during instrumentals."

"When the concert was over, I realized that I had been involved in worship even though I hadn't really expected to worship," related Rowland in the pages of *Worship Leader* magazine. "I hadn't been all that conscious of what I was being caught up in, but there I was, worshiping the risen Lord at a rock concert."[68]

Bono touched upon this phenomena when he discussed the Elevation tour with *Rolling Stone.* "God is in the room, more than Elvis," he said. "It feels like there's a blessing on the band right now. People are saying they're feeling shivers—well, the band is as well. And I don't know what that is, but it feels like God walking through the room, and it feels like a blessing, and in the end, music is a kind of sacrament; it's not just about airplay or chart positions."[69]

According to the Barna Research Group, a majority of people who attend Christian worship services leave without feeling that they've experienced God's presence. Less than one-third of the adults feel as though they truly interacted with God. Stunningly, one-third of the adults who regularly attend worship services say that they have never experienced God's presence at any time during their life. According to George Barna, "The research shows that while most people attend church services with a desire to connect with God, most of them leave the church disappointed, week after week. Eventually people cease to expect a real encounter with God and simply settle for a pleasant experience."[70]

So what happens when people settle for the pleasant experience at church and discover the real encounter at a rock concert? One need not be a theologian to realize that something transcendent, mystical, joyful, and perhaps even holy is going on here. Somehow, I think Bono understands it.

1. Paul Morley, "U2 can make it in the rock business," NME (New Music Express), March 22, 1980.
2. "He's like Christ, I'm telling you," (Dublin) *Hot Press*, February 18, 2002.
3. "Gag me with a Grammy," Salon.com, February 22, 2002.
4. David Plotz, "U2: Their Vague Majesties of Rock," Slate.com, January 25, 2002.
5. David Fricke, "The Wizards of Pop," *Rolling Stone*, May 29, 1997.
6. "Bono Bites Back," *Mother Jones*, May 1989
7. Christopher Connelly, "Keeping the faith," *Rolling Stone*, March 14, 1985.
8. Neil McCormick, "Bono: The Pain, the Pride, the Passion," *Irish Independent*, August 25, 2001.
9. Stuart Bailie, "Rock and Roll Should be this Big," NME, June 13, 1992.
10. Chris Heath, "U2: Band of the year," *Rolling Stone*, January 18, 2001.
11. Anthony DeCurtis, "The Beliefnet Interview with Bono," Beliefnet.com, February 2001.
12. Anthony Bozza, "Bono: Fighting the Good Fight in the Name of Love and Rock & Roll," *Rolling Stone*, December 6-13, 2001.
13. Bono interviewed on *The Oprah Winfrey Show*, September 20, 2002.
14. Edna Gunderson, "Bono honored as 2003 MusiCares Person of the Year," Grammy.com, February 20, 2003.
15. Steve Turner, *Imagine: A Vision for Christians in the Arts* (Downers Grove, Ill.: InterVarsity Press, 2001), 106.
16. Liam Mackey, "I Still Haven't Found What I'm Looking For," (Dublin) *Hot Press*, December 1988).
17. Sean O'Hagan, "The Gospel of Heaven and Hell," NME, December 19-26, 1987.
18. Bono, Introduction to Pocket Canons Psalms (Edinburgh, Scotland: Canongate Books, 1999), ix-x.
19. David Bresken, "Bono: The Rolling Stone Interview," *Rolling Stone*, October 8, 1987.
20. Niall Stokes, *Into the Heart* (London: Omnibus Press, 1996), 27.
21. Bill Flanagan, *U2 at the End of the World* (London: Bantam Press, 1995), 433-434.
22. Steve Turner, *Hungry for Heaven* (Downers Grove, Ill: InterVarsity, 1995 revised edition), 178.
23. Bill Flanagan, *U2 at the End of the World* (London: Bantam Press, 1995), 314.
24. Richard Cook, "A Dreamboat Named Desire," NME, February 27, 1981. In 1994, Bono was asked by Bill Flanagan if he and Larry and The Edge were still on the same spiritual wave length. Bono responded: "What about Adam? Adam's the same. I mean, nobody is exactly the same, but Adam's a believer. I think that the spirit will more and more become the important thing over the next ten years when it becomes clear that God isn't dead, Nietzsche is." (U2 at the *End of the World*, page 480.)
25. Adam Block, "Bono Bites Back," *Mother Jones*, May 1989.
26. Ibid.
27. A portion of the endorsement that Bono gave to Steve Turner's book *Amazing Grace* (New York: HarperCollins, 2002). Provided by the publisher.
28. Paul Morley, "U2 Can Make it in the Rock Business," NME, March 22, 1980.
29. Lisa McLaughlin, "Can Rock and Roll Save the World?" *Time*, September 23, 2001.
30. Adrian Thrills, "Cactus Worldviews," NME, March 14, 1987.
31. Steve Turner, *Imagine: A Vision for Christians in the Arts* (Downers Grove, Ill.:InterVarsity Press, 2001), 112-113.
32. Niall Stokes, *Into the Heart* (London: Omnibus Press, 1996), 34.
33. Bill Flanagan, *U2 at the End of the World* (London: Bantam Press, 1995), 56-57.
34. Steve Turner, *Hungry for Heaven* (Downers Grove, Ill: InterVarsity, 1995 revised edition), 184.
35. Stephen Dalton, "Animal Lightweight," NME, July 3, 1993.
36. Bill Flanagan, *U2 at the End of the World* (London: Bantam Press, 1995), 56-57. Also, Joe Jackson, "In Search of Elvis," *Irish Times*, November 1, 1994.
37. Chris Heath, "U2: Band of the Year," *Rolling Stone*, January 18, 2001.
38. Bill Flanagan, *U2 at the End of the World* (London: Bantam Press, 1995), 480.
39. Chris Heath, "U2: Band of the Year," *Rolling Stone*, January 18, 2001.

40. Steve Turner, *Imagine: A Vision for Christians in the Arts* (Downers Grove, Ill.: InterVarsity Press, 2001), 107.

41. Stuart Bailie, "Rock and Roll Should Be This Big," NME, June 13, 1992.

42. Anthony DeCurtis, "Beliefnet Interview with Bono," Beliefnet.com, February 2001.

43. Gary Graff, "U2 Plans To Bring Grace To The Concert For New York City," Launch.com, October 18, 2001.

44. "Oasis Create Another Row with 'Jesus' Jibe," Q4music.com, September 11, 2000.

45. Robert Crampton, "Oh Brother," *London Sunday Times*, September 29, 2001. Also *Q magazine*, March/April 2001.

46. Anthony Bozza, "Bono: Fighting the Good Fight in the Name of Love and Rock & Roll," *Rolling Stone*, December 6-13, 2001.

47. Angela Pancella, "U2 Connections: Eugene Peterson," atU2.com, *http://www.atu2.com/news/connections/peterson/*

48. "Easy-to-Read Bible Translation is Spreading God's 'Message,'" *Colorado Springs Gazette*, July 13, 2002.

49. Bono, Introduction to Pocket Canons Psalms (Edinburgh, Scotland: Canongate Books, 1999), viii.

50. Ibid., ix.

51. Ibid., xi.

52. Steve Beard, "Bono Launches AIDS Awareness Tour," *Good News*, January/February 2003.

53. Ibid.

54. Paul Robicheau, "You Can Do the Impossible, Bono Tells Harvard Grads," Yahoo.com, June 8, 2001.

55. Anthony DeCurtis, "Beliefnet Interview with Bono," Beliefnet.com, February 2001.

56. Albert Eisele and Betsy Rothstein, "Helms: I'd Quit the Senate to Help Starving Kids," *The Hill*, October 11, 2000.

57. "Sen. Helms Take in U2 Concert," Associated Press, June 16, 2001.

58. Andrew Essex, "Unforgettable Fire," *Details*, November 2001.

59. Cathleen Falsani, "Bono Issues Blunt Message for Christians," *Chicago Sun-Times*, December 3, 2002.

60. Cathleen Falsani, "Bono's American Prayer," *Christianity Today*, March 2003.

61. Ibid.

62. "The Heartland of America Tour Day 4: In Church with Bono," WorldVision.org, December 4, 2002.

63. Steve Beard, "Bono Launches AIDS Awareness Tour," *Good News*, January/February 2003.

64. Cathleen Falsani, "Bono's American Prayer," *Christianity Today*, March 2003.

65. Steve Beard, "Bono Launches AIDS Awareness Tour," *Good News*, January/February 2003.

66. Brenda O'Neil, "Bono Launches Blast at Church," *Sunday People* (*The Daily Mirror*), May 5, 2002.

67. Cathleen Falsani, "Pop Band's Lyrics Take on New Weight," *Chicago Sun-Times*, October 12, 2001.

68. Randy L. Rowland, "When God Shows up Unexpectedly," *Worship Leader*, July/August 2001.

69. Chris Heath, "U2 Tour From the Heart," *Rolling Stone*, May 10, 2001.

70. "New Research Shows People Attend Church Service but do not Worship," Evangelical Press News Service (Minneapolis, Minnesota), September 11, 1998, Vol. 47, No. 37, 3-4.